Faulkner and Print Culture
FAULKNER AND YOKNAPATAWPHA
2015

Faulkner and Print Culture

FAULKNER AND YOKNAPATAWPHA, 2015

EDITED BY
JAY WATSON
JAIME HARKER
AND
JAMES G. THOMAS , JR.

UNIVERSITY PRESS OF MISSISSIPPI
JACKSON

www.upress.state.ms.us
The University Press of Mississippi is a member of
the Association of American University Presses.

First printing 2017
∞
Library of Congress Cataloging-in-Publication Data

Names: Faulkner and Yoknapatawpha Conference (42nd : 2015 : University of
Mississippi) | Watson, Jay, editor. | Harker, Jaime, editor. | Thomas,
James G., Jr., editor.
Title: Faulkner and print culture / edited by Jay Watson, Jaime Harker, and
James G. Thomas, Jr.
Description: Jackson : University Press of Mississippi, [2017] | Series:
Faulkner and Yoknapatawpha series | Includes bibliographical references
and index.
Identifiers: LCCN 2016051441 (print) | LCCN 2016051984 (ebook) | ISBN
9781496812308 (hardback) | ISBN 9781496812315 (epub single) | ISBN
9781496812322 (epub institutional) | ISBN 9781496812339 (pdf single) |
ISBN 9781496812346 (pdf institutional)
Subjects: LCSH: Faulkner, William, 1897–1962—Criticism and
interpretation—Congresses. | Literature publishing—United
States—History—20th century—Congresses. | Literature and
society—United States—History—20th century—Congresses. | BISAC:
LITERARY CRITICISM / American / General. | LITERARY COLLECTIONS /
American / General.
Classification: LCC PS3511.A86 Z78321139 2017 (print) | LCC PS3511.A86
(ebook) | DDC 813/.52—dc23
LC record available at https://lccn.loc.gov/2016051441

British Library Cataloging-in-Publication Data available

Contents

Introduction

Jaime Harker and Jay Watson

William Faulkner's first ventures into print culture began far from the world of highbrow publishing with which he is typically associated—the world of New York publishing houses, little magazines, and literary prizes—though his work would come to encompass that world as well. With that in mind, this collection explores Faulkner's multifaceted engagements, as writer and reader, with the US and international print cultures of his era, along with the ways in which these cultures have mediated his relationship with a variety of twentieth- and twenty-first-century audiences. The fourteen essays gathered here address the place of Faulkner and his writings in the creation, design, publishing, marketing, reception, and collecting of books; in the culture of twentieth-century magazines, journals, newspapers, and other periodicals (from pulp to avant-garde); in the history of modern readers and readerships; and in the construction and cultural politics of literary authorship.

In this context, one illuminating way to trace the arc of Faulkner's career is to follow his changing relationship to book production. We use the term *production* here to get at a wide-ranging enterprise of *making* books that includes print publication but is not ultimately limited to it. This allows us to think along with Faulkner over forty years as *he* thinks about the book as a material artifact, an aesthetic object, and an economic commodity. The first books to bear Faulkner's authorial imprint were a pair of handmade efforts from 1921: *Vision in Spring*, a lyric cycle presented to Estelle Oldham Franklin, and *The Marionettes*, an illuminated verse play that Faulkner distributed to friends and fellow members of the drama club, also named the Marionettes, at the University of Mississippi. For these apprentice works, Faulkner served not only as author but as graphic designer and illustrator as well, which makes sense in light of the fact that the young writer's earliest published forays into the arts were in the realm of visual culture: cartoons and illustrations for his high school yearbook and for the university annual, *Ole Miss*.[1] *Vision in Spring* and *The Marionettes* reflect the influence of

William Morris and the late-nineteenth-century Arts and Crafts Movement in the attention devoted to the book as a handmade craft object, and they follow Art Nouveau principles in their use of hand lettering to call attention to orthography, namely, the look of individual characters on the page as an integral element of design, mood, and meaning.[2] For the early Faulkner, then, literary authorship included a sense of the writer not only as originating creative source but as artisan, bookmaker, and publisher as well.

Faulkner produced a number of other handmade books during the 1920s: the 1926 poem cycle *Helen: A Courtship*; the hand-illustrated prose romance *Mayday*, also in 1926; and *The Wishing Tree*, a children's tale presented to young Margaret Brown in 1927 and subsequently to Estelle's daughter Victoria Franklin. Along the way, however, Faulkner was also beginning to make books in other ways, turning first to that lifeline for the unknown, emerging writer: self-publication on vanity presses. With *The Marble Faun* of 1924, book production became a collaborative enterprise for Faulkner, undertaken in partnership with the Four Seas Company of Boston and with his friend Phil Stone, who helped bankroll the project and wrote the introduction to the volume. Two years later, Faulkner experimented with collaborative authorship on the *Sherwood Anderson and Other Famous Creoles* volume, brought out with artist William Spratling on the Pelican Bookstore Press, a vanity imprint based in New Orleans. From this point forward, all of Faulkner's books are best understood not as manifestations of solitary authorial effort but as cooperative ventures, with agents, editors, publishers, marketing departments, typesetters, jacket designers, and the occasional coauthor. As we'll soon see, the particulars of these collaborations had a profound impact—by turns constraining, nurturing, even liberating—on the way Faulkner was able to envision and build "his" books in the years to come.

In 1926 Faulkner moved from avant-garde and vanity publishing to the full tumult of New York publishing. The business was going through a substantial transformation in the 1920s. Once the domain of genteel "gentlemen publishers" such as the Harper brothers and Charles Scribner and Sons, it was invaded by a host of new firms: Harcourt, Brace and Co.; Alfred A. Knopf; Simon and Schuster; and three firms that would have considerable bearing on Faulkner's literary fortunes: Boni & Liveright, Cape and Smith, and Random House. These young guns were associated with the "modern" movement in literature; rejecting squeamish taciturnity regarding sexuality, they sought writers with the power to shock the old guard and its Victorian mores. But it is important not to equate their interest in the modern with more recent understandings of modernism as an aesthetic movement untainted by marketing and commerce. This new generation upended the genteel world of publishing in both aesthetic content and business practice. The new publishers embraced advertising, experimented with new forms of book distribution, and treated books as commodities to be marketed and sold. If they emphasized literary quality, as Alfred A. Knopf and Random House did, they also understood that literary quality was a brand that would help the bottom line. Simon and Schuster, for example, had its first best sellers through crossword puzzle books, a new national craze. Alfred Boni entered publishing through a cheap reprint series, The Little Leather Library, and Boni & Liveright, the house he went on to found with Horace Liveright, created the Modern Library imprint. In 1925 Boni and Liveright sold the Modern Library to one of their employees, Bennett Cerf, who would later become a power at Random House. Older publishers saw these upstarts as crass. That a number of them were Jewish only fed into the rampant anti-Semitism of the inter-war period. All of which is to say that placing William Faulkner within American print culture—interwar, wartime, and Cold War—means navigating a complicated terrain of commercialism, bravado, hyperbole, and innovation that has yet to inform most literary criticism about either Faulkner or modernism. Faulkner's entry into mainstream publishing also brought him into a newly emerging modern American public media and public relations industry, one that would have as much to do with his critical and commercial success as did his experimental prose.

Take the New York publisher for his first two novels, found with some assistance from Sherwood Anderson. John T. Matthews has described Boni & Liveright as committed to "iconoclasm, novelty, and daring": sexual frankness, the critique of small-town and middlebrow values, politically radical writing, and African American literature.[3] Horace Liveright was also famous for making advertising central to his business, offending the "traditionally conservative field of book publishing."[4] Ann Douglas describes Liveright as a "hard-drinking and witty man-about-town" who "had been a stockbroker before going into publishing."[5] He used unconventional ad campaigns to sell books, including publishing "the opinions of America's reigning movie queens on the nature of love."[6] Writers in the Liveright stable in the 1910s and 1920s included Sigmund Freud, Ezra Pound, Eugene O'Neill, D. H. Lawrence, H.D. (Hilda Doolittle), Hart Crane, Anita Loos, Frances Newman, Jean Toomer, John Reed, Max Eastman, Upton Sinclair, Mike Gold, and Jessie Fauset. One can already see a wide range of literary styles in this list. H.D., Pound, and O'Neill had unassailable avant-garde credentials. Loos was most famous for her satiric novel *Gentlemen Prefer Blondes* (1925), written in the not-so-literate style of narrator Lorelei Lee. Reed, Eastman, Sinclair, and Gold were all political radicals who leaned toward straightforward, realistic prose. Fauset is often credited with publishing the first novel of the Harlem Renaissance, though she was dismissed as an old-fashioned, genteel writer by many of the younger set. Rebellion against the white, conservative middle-class status quo defines this modern canon, with a special emphasis on sex, radical left-wing politics, and bohemian disruption.

One can see, then, how Faulkner's early work would have appealed to Boni & Liveright. What Liveright got from Faulkner in 1926–1927 was right in line with the publisher's profile: an early World War I novel, *Soldiers' Pay*, and a satire of sexual mores and the bohemian life among the contemporary New Orleans smart set, *Mosquitoes*. Faulkner later dismissed these novels in light of the Yoknapatawpha County fiction to come, but we should appreciate what a significant leap he had made in moving from vanity presses to a major publishing venue for Anglo and African American modernism in the space of only a year or so.

After helping Faulkner get this reputable, trendsetting publisher, Anderson then helped him lose it. Around the same time he set Faulkner up with Liveright, the elder writer gave Faulkner a transformative bit of advice, to go back to north Mississippi and write about the world he knew there, the material he knew best. To his credit, Faulkner took this advice, moving home in 1926 and working for most of the following year on two projects set in Mississippi, his first Yoknapatawpha writings: the never-completed Snopes narrative *Father Abraham* (1983) and a novel, provisionally titled "Flags in the Dust," which he jauntily sent off to Liveright late in 1927, only to have the publisher reject the manuscript. Faulkner had found his sweet spot as a writer—indeed, his mother lode—but it wasn't Liveright's sweet spot, and the result was a permanent parting of the ways. Part of the problem may have been Boni & Liveright's financial situation. The firm always lived on the edge, spending its profits on lavish parties and stock speculation. The sale of the Modern Library in 1925 had given the company a temporary infusion of capital but hurt its long-term interests. At any rate, Liveright's rejection left Faulkner vulnerable. Eleven publishers later, the chastened young novelist managed to place "Flags in the Dust" with Harcourt, where it was published in abridged form as *Sartoris* in 1929. (The complete text was later published, in 1973, as *Flags in the Dust*.)

Harcourt, Brace and Co. was formed in 1919 by Alfred Harcourt, a former employee of Henry Holt and Company, and his Columbia classmate Donald Brace. The firm published a wide range of American writers, but it first found success as the publisher of novelists Dorothy Canfield and Sinclair Lewis. Canfield's novel *The Brimming Cup*, serialized in 1920, was widely read as a middlebrow rejoinder to Sinclair Lewis's blistering account of middle-class life, *Main Street*, also published in 1920. The debate between these two novels may have divided the literary world, but it united Harcourt into a solvent firm.[7] Harcourt was less known as a modern press than as a publisher of quality fiction across the brow levels. The firm's publication of *Sartoris* suggests that Faulkner's shift to Mississippi material may have been seen as a retreat from the modernism of *Soldiers' Pay* and *Mosquitoes* into genteel nostalgia, as Jeff Karem's account of the novel's revision and early reception tends to corroborate.[8]

At Harcourt, Faulkner began a relationship with editor Harrison Smith that was to last for the next six years. In 1929 Smith formed a partnership with English publisher Jonathan Cape, who wanted to enter the American market; the "alliance," book historian John Tebbel notes, "intrigued the book world . . . because it was the first time in many years that an English publisher had brought his imprint to America."[9] Smith brought his own American contacts with him, including William Faulkner. The relationship produced some of the greatest and most prolific work of Faulkner's career. Cape and Smith published *The Sound and the Fury* (1929), *As I Lay Dying* (1930), *Sanctuary* (1931), *These 13* (1931), and *Light in August* (1932). The firm "was not strong enough to survive the Crash" of 1929, however, and in 1931, Smith resigned from Cape and Smith and formed his own publishing company with Robert Haas, who had previously worked on the Book-of-the-Month Club (BOMC). That change did not affect Smith's relationship with Faulkner, who published *A Green Bough* (1933), *Dr. Martino and Other Stories* (1934), and *Pylon* (1935) with Smith and Haas.

Smith clearly encouraged, and rewarded, Faulkner's penchant for taking risks as a writer; together the two made literary history. But he also brought considerable experience in publishing; as Tebbel notes, "Besides his work at Harcourt, Brace, [Smith] had been with Century Co. for two years, had worked for the *New York Tribune*, spent six months in Russia and the Far East free-lancing magazine articles, and was editor of Foreign Press Service at the time he came to Harcourt, Brace."[10] He was, in other words, not only a discerning editor but a savvy marketer, with deep connections to newspapers and a knack for making his authors news. The media sensation that *Sanctuary* became likely has much to do with Smith's contacts.

The fact that two of Faulkner's collaborations with Smith were short story collections allows us to shift gears for a moment, to reflect on the fascinating ways in which Faulkner's emergence onto the national short story market in the early 1930s changed his understanding of the artistic and financial possibilities of the book and in some dramatic instances went on to change the way he constructed books, including novels. So let's set the stage: by the end of 1929, Faulkner had written six novels and published four of them, but he had yet to publish a single short story in a magazine with a large national readership. To this point he had placed stories only with newspapers—the *Mississippian* in 1919 and the *New Orleans Times-Picayune* in 1925—and, a single time, with a little magazine in New Orleans, the *Double Dealer*. Faulkner understood the economics of publishing in the late 1920s, a time when placing a story in one of the big "slicks" like the *Saturday Evening Post* could earn a writer more than he would make from publishing a novel, and he tried unsuccessfully during this period to sell stories to the magazines.[11] Unlike the little magazines, which paid poorly and stayed afloat through patronage and (to a lesser extent) subscriptions, the slicks were supported mainly through advertisements. But even among the slicks, there were distinctions. *Vanity Fair* and the *New Yorker*, for instance, were targeted to the young, rebellious moderns; Harold Ross's famous tag line from the *New Yorker*, "not for the little old lady from Dubuque," sums up the attitude of these magazines. The *Saturday Evening Post*, however, *was* for the little old lady from Dubuque. It featured the iconic middlebrow paintings of Norman Rockwell, and it was suspicious of the explicitness and experimentation of emerging modernisms. If you had to pick one magazine from the interwar era that represented a middlebrow sensibility, you could do worse than the *Saturday Evening Post*. What does it mean that Faulkner was so fixated on the *Post* when there were other high-paying outlets for his short stories? Does it suggest how he viewed himself as a writer generally, or how he specifically viewed his short stories as opposed to his novels?[12] Did Faulkner's alienation from the "smart set" in New York make him identify with the despised readers in the heartland? Or did Harrison Smith's expertise make him more open to these middlebrow markets?

Whatever this *Post* obsession ultimately means, Faulkner's persistence finally paid off. His novels, despite selling poorly with the general public, eventually managed to create enough interest in him to allow him to crack the short story market in 1930, a full year before the publication of *Sanctuary* would bring him notoriety. That year he published four stories, two in the *Post*. He found the short story to be a lucrative literary asset and a flexible one as well, capable of creating multiple revenue streams. For example, authors often republish stories in book form in collections and mix in previously unpublished material alongside previously published tales, as Faulkner did in both *These 13* and *Dr. Martino*. When they do, they can get even more books out of the bargain. Stories can be optioned for film adaptation, as in the case of "Turnabout," the 1932 *Post* story that was adapted (by Faulkner himself) into the 1933 MGM feature *Today We Live*. Stories could serve as sequels or extensions of novels, helping to generate interest in previously published books, as in the case of "There Was a Queen," the 1933 *Scribner's* story that gestured back toward both *Sartoris* and *Sanctuary*. Stories rejected by magazines could be brought out as limited-edition books for the collector's market, as with "Idyll in the Desert" (Random House, 1931) or "Miss Zilphia Gant" (Book Club of Texas, 1932). Faulkner's short fiction could be developed or expanded into novels, like "Honor" (*American Mercury*, 1930), which directly informed the plot structure of *Pylon*. Finally, novels could themselves be built largely or even entirely out of previously published story material. The emergence, in the late 1930s and early 1940s, of the "anthology novel" as a characteristic Faulkner form reflects this insight: *The Unvanquished* (1938), *The Hamlet* (1940), and *Go Down, Moses* (1942) were constructed this way, and a case could be made for *Knight's Gambit*, the 1949 anthology of crime fiction featuring lawyer-detective Gavin Stevens, as continuing the trend. Faulkner wasn't doing any of this before 1930, the year the magazines abruptly awakened to his short fiction.

What is more, he wasn't publishing anthology novels with Hal Smith at the helm. It wasn't until after his (and Smith's) move to Random House in 1936 (following the bankruptcy of Smith and Haas) that Faulkner began exploring the aesthetic and economic possibilities of this new form.[13] The timing suggests that his new publisher may have played an important role in fostering, or perhaps just tolerating, Faulkner's efforts in the hybrid genre. Random House was a small firm in 1936; the only indication of its meteoric rise in influence in the Cold War Era was the charismatic personality of its founder, Bennett Cerf. Cerf started his career in publishing under Horace Liveright. Like Liveright, he had begun as a stockbroker but turned his outsized personality and love of socializing to publishing; unlike Liveright, he made publishing a highly lucrative career. Taking advantage of one of Liveright's "periodical financial crises, arising from his determination to get a divorce," Cerf bought the Modern Library with his friend Donald Klopfer and turned it into a profitable enterprise that eventually branched out into "luxury editions."[14] Cerf's talent for marketing the modern as a desirable luxury good would lead him to hang onto Faulkner and develop him, over time, into a recognizable and valuable asset.

To get a better sense of the implications of Random's receptive stance toward Faulkner, consider what it would have meant, from the publisher's point of view, for Faulkner to assemble novels like *The*

Unvanquished and *Go Down, Moses* from stories originally published in slicks like the *Post*. The move made perfect sense for Faulkner, of course, but for Random? When not thousands but actually millions of readers already had access to most of the material incorporated into those novels? Yet for over ten years Random accepted this strategy as Faulkner's primary template for creating new books. This points to a remarkably flexible and innovative publisher-author relationship, in which Random opted to look beyond the immediate bottom line while, as Jay Satterfield puts it in these pages, continuing to build the Faulkner brand. In this light, we might recall that, five years before Faulkner moved permanently to the company, it had been Random House that published "Idyll in the Desert" as a stand-alone collectible book, right around the time Faulkner was getting the attention of national magazine editors. (Indeed, Random would express its ongoing interest in Faulkner by bringing out *Sanctuary* as a Modern Library edition in 1932.) Interestingly, the larger firm proved more imaginative and opportunistic than the maverick Smith in developing the short story's multifaceted potential for the business of book production.

The final, postwar phase of Faulkner's career was marked by further adventures in reprinting, repackaging, and repurposing the Faulkner brand. There were many factors behind Faulkner's rise to international prominence during this period. The role of *The Portable Faulkner* in reviving his literary fortunes has been discussed frequently; the story of his second-prize award in an *Ellery Queen* mystery writing competition is recounted by John N. Duvall in this collection; and the larger cultural Cold War literary atmosphere, in which an "American Tolstoy" was deemed essential for anti-Communist propaganda along an ever-widening cultural front, has been dissected by both Lawrence Schwartz and, more recently, Greg Barnhisel, in this collection and elsewhere.[15] The ascendancy of Random House as a firm, however, should not be ignored. During World War II, Random had collected "the brilliant staff of editors, perhaps the most formidable in publishing history, that would make the house highly successful in the postwar years,"[16] and Bennett Cerf was a best-selling humor author, a columnist for the *Saturday Review of Literature*, and a radio celebrity. He acquired other firms—most famously Alfred A. Knopf in 1960—expanded his range of publishing, and eventually went public with Random House stock, repositioning the firm as a corporation. Random House's string of best sellers kept the house financially strong, and its commitment to modern authors, first signaled by its successful lawsuit to publish *Ulysses* in 1933, was rewarded by William Faulkner's 1949 Nobel Prize in Literature.

During the postwar years, Faulkner's resurgence as a novelist, with a half-dozen new titles to his credit, was matched book for book by a series of anthologies and collections including *The Portable Faulkner* (1946), *Knight's Gambit, Collected Stories* (1950), *The Faulkner Reader* (1954), *Big Woods* (1955), and *Three Famous Short Novels* (1958), all of which reprinted material drawn largely from his interwar career. Again he experimented with the boutique publication of short(er) fiction, bringing out a version of the "Notes on a Horsethief" material from *A Fable* with Greenville, Mississippi's Levee Press in 1950. Four of his books from the postwar era were listed as featured or alternate selections for BOMC, which offered an alternative distribution network to rival that of the nation's bookstores and arguably helped Faulkner expand and diversify his audience by targeting middlebrow readers.[17] At the same time—and building on the innovative way BOMC had wedded the publishing strategies of the book industry with marketing and distribution techniques gleaned from the magazine business—the midcentury paperback revolution introduced Faulkner to hundreds of thousands of new readers, as pulp publishers like Avon and the New American Library (NAL) took the novelist's work (especially his genre and formula fiction), tarted it up with racy cover art, and published it on cheap stock in huge runs sold at newsstands, drugstores, department stores, airports, bus and railway stations, and hundreds of thousands of other outlets.[18] In the 1930s, Faulkner had published (or republished) short fiction and novel excerpts in pulp periodicals alongside the work he was placing with the slicks. By the late 1940s, however, the pulping of William Faulkner extended to reprints of full-length novels like *Mosquitoes*, *Sanctuary*, and *The Wild Palms*; as David M. Earle has noted, of all the major American modernist writers, Faulkner was by far the most frequently and comprehensively pulped in this way.[19] These novels ultimately reached millions more readers—and a demonstrably wider spectrum of readers—through pulp editions than through the cloth or paperbound versions brought out by Random House and its subsidiaries, Vintage Books and the Modern Library. Here, then, was a writer ever on the lookout for new ways of making books and getting them into the hands of consumers. Though scholars have tended to present him as a modernist paragon who courted a select readership with an elitist aesthetic of the autonomous art object, he ultimately resists such a one-dimensional categorization.

Gordon Hutner, for example, cites Faulkner repeatedly as a paradigmatic instance of the highbrow author who defined himself (or whose publishers, reviewers, and critics defined him) against the "middle-class modernism" of the twentieth century's middle decades.[20] This may have been true to a degree of Random House, which, as Satterfield shows, promoted Faulkner from the outset as a literary classic. But as the novelist's arrangements with NAL and BOMC demonstrate, Faulkner and his agents took a more ecumenical approach to print culture than Hutner's study would suggest. In her history and ethnography of BOMC, Janice A. Radway credits the company with seeking out titles whose "literary excellence was tempered by the presence of features usually associated with more commercial fiction."[21] This balancing act for Radway epitomizes the middlebrow mission of the BOMC, but it equally characterized Faulkner's agenda during his heyday, the 1930s, when he produced a series of novels subsequently enshrined by critics as pinnacles of high modernism, including *Sanctuary*; *Light in August*; *Pylon*; *Absalom, Absalom!*; and *The Wild Palms*. These works, however, could just as easily be studied (or marketed!) as exercises in popular genre fiction: a gangster novel, a racial thriller, an aviation narrative, a historical romance (moreover, incorporating elements of another in-demand genre, the Civil War novel), a modern romance ("Wild Palms"), and an adventure tale ("Old Man"). At the same time, these were *Faulkner* fictions: strange, disturbing, resistant to readerly effort. As such, they occupied a niche not so far removed from Radway's evocations of middlebrow literature, which "acknowledged the reader's expectations" about genre "but pushed beyond them just enough to surprise the reading self."[22] Such midlist books "both gratified readers' immediate desires and confirmed their sense of themselves as people willing to be expanded and challenged" by their reading.[23] Though Faulkner may have pushed his readers somewhat harder and farther than the middlebrow authors at the heart of Radway's study, one could argue that by flirting with formula but also exceeding it, the financially strapped Faulkner of the Depression years was seeking, albeit with only partial success, to expand the audience for his novels from the citadels of high culture to the reading public identified by Radway as well as the one discussed by Earle. We could think of Faulkner, in other words, as a pioneering figure in the rise of a midlist modernism to complement Hutner's middle-class version.

Moreover, from early on in his career, Faulkner seems to have recognized that being read widely meant being read by women. It might surprise readers of this volume, for instance, that in his quest to place his short fiction in well-paying venues, Faulkner not only bombarded the *Post* and *Scribner's* with submissions but sent no fewer than ten stories to the *Woman's Home Companion* (whose circulation at the time was around four million) during a single eight-month stretch in 1931.[24] As Jaime Harker notes in these pages, the awareness that an extensive female readership wielded a powerful influence in and on the nation's print culture never seems to have left Faulkner, resurfacing powerfully in the 1950s, a decade when the novelist published fiction in *Mademoiselle* and *Harper's Bazaar* and created, in *The Mansion's* Linda Snopes Kohl, the sort of strong, independent female character featured in much midcentury middlebrow fiction by, for, and about women.[25]

Faulkner's engagement with women's magazines points to a larger truth: *book* history can tell only part of the story of the author's imaginative investments in print culture. He published in, and wrote about, a wide variety of other print media: newspapers, slicks, little magazines, pulp periodicals, academic journals. Throughout his career, he was remarkably opportunistic and savvy about the trends and conventions that governed print publication in the United States. As noted above, Faulkner took advantage of the still-robust newspaper culture in interwar Oxford and New Orleans to become a published author. He didn't pursue newspapers as an outlet for fiction after that (although newspaper coverage would figure prominently in his literary notoriety). He only occasionally published in little magazines like *Story* and *Furioso*, periodicals that "refus[ed] to conform to the dictates of mass-market appeal" and were "dedicated to literary experiment."[26] In 1948 he published "A Courtship" in the *Sewanee Review*, a quarterly journal housed at a university and supported by US government dollars, illustrating the evolution of the literary magazine in the developing environment of the cultural Cold War. "The quarterly," argues Edward Chielens, "owes much of its endurance and success to its alliances with some of the agrarians who were also some of the best literary editors of this century—[Allen] Tate, Cleanth Brooks, Robert Penn Warren, John Crowe Ransom."[27] Faulkner's emergence as the great American author—in both New Critical and Agrarian circles—may have influenced the *Sewanee Review's* decision to publish him. But Faulkner seems to have turned to these less remunerative venues only when he failed to place a story with the slicks.

Indeed, once he broke through with the *Post* in 1930, Faulkner consistently sought out the mass-market magazines that so infuriated modernist expatriates. *Scribner's*, *Harper's*, *Collier's*, and the *Atlantic*, for example, figured prominently among his preferred outlets for short fiction in the 1930s and early 1940s. Though all four aspired to the circulation figures and advertising dollars of the *Post*, all had actually reached the height of their literary influence in the nineteenth century, and—for both reasons, no doubt—all were associated with the genteel culture and middlebrow readership that young moderns disdained. While *Scribner's*, for example, is often associated with Ernest Hemingway, having paid him $16,000 to serialize *A Farewell to Arms* in 1929, the magazine had in fact "enraged" the author for what he termed its "'emasculation' of 'the unprintable words'" in his novel.[28] Even publications like H. L. Mencken's *American Mercury*, whose "brand" was youth rebellion, were enmeshed in the consumer culture of the slicks. This might help explain why, despite Mencken's bad reputation in the South for his "Sahara of the Bozarts" essay of 1917, Faulkner published eight short stories in the *American Mercury*, three in 1935 alone. Tracing the hundred-odd stories Faulkner published during his lifetime to their print sources reveals not only Faulkner's prolific efforts in a form he sometimes disparaged but also the astonishing diversity and fecundity of the periodical market in twentieth-century America—one reason why magazine history and culture receive as much attention in these pages as the book business.

We open, however, with a group of six essays that focus on *Sanctuary* as a case study illustrating William Faulkner's multifaceted relationship to the print ecology of his time. *Sanctuary* emerged as the star text at the 2015 conference, Faulkner and Print Culture—and with good reason, since it was the book that first made Faulkner a print culture celebrity (or perhaps villain). For this reason, a close examination of *Sanctuary*'s imaginative and strategic investments in the world of print, and of the novel's impact at various levels of the ambient print culture, sheds instructive light not only on the text itself but on the range and depth of critical insight that scholarship attuned to the material conditions, aesthetic possibilities, and social reach of print is capable of generating. Accordingly, this cluster of essays traces *Sanctuary*'s path from the wellsprings of Faulkner's artistic vision—in which print turns out to play a foundational role—to the novel's reception among reviewers, tastemakers, intellectuals, and other readers of the early 1930s.

Aesthetic and material considerations converge, for example, in Kristin Fujie's "Trashing *Sanctuary*: The Material Origins of Faulkner's Art." Unpersuaded by critical approaches that pit Faulkner the aesthetic modernist against Faulkner the potboiling pulpmeister, Fujie instead nominates *Sanctuary* as an exemplary instance of how Faulkner's fiction poses "the question of art's relationship to physical reality and the material circumstances of its creation," self-consciously "erod[ing] the split between high and low, pure art and pure trash" by taking up precisely that "collapse . . . as a theme or topic" across the Faulkner oeuvre. Drawing on "pre-texts" such as *Flags in the Dust*, *Mosquitoes*, and the unfinished "Elmer" manuscript of 1925 as products of the same imaginative soil out of which the original draft of *Sanctuary* germinated, Fujie also traces how important "post-scripts" like Faulkner's 1932 introduction to the Modern Library edition of *Sanctuary* (an essay, writes Fujie, best approached as a work of fiction in its own right) took what was in truth "a reasonably ambitious, recognizably modernist, and complexly motivated work" and methodically "trashed" it by aligning it directly with mass culture. By thus "connecting [Faulkner's] most commercially popular novel back to the creative matrix of his early work" while simultaneously "recovering, from within that matrix, a preoccupation with art's inescapable materiality," Fujie performs her own critical suturing work across modernism's so-called great divide.

Sanctuary's fraught composition history, which unfolded between the creation of *The Sound and the Fury* and *As I Lay Dying* and then again between the latter novel and *Light in August*, prompts Robert Jackson to call for new ways of bridging another great divide in Faulkner studies: the rift between the so-called major and minor works. Convinced that this opposition is much exaggerated by scholars in ways detrimental to fuller critical understanding of Faulkner's body of writing, Jackson borrows a concept from recording technology to improvise a critical methodology around the metaphor of the B-side. "Balance, Bonus, Bastard: Faulkner's B-sides" taps into the multivalent connotations of this twentieth-century media form—its association with anonymity, obscurity, marginality, and subordination on one hand, and with "innovation, experimentation, and unintended consequences" on the other—to explore Faulkner's "turn to more popular forms, genres, and themes at specific moments in which his work on the more 'experimental' modernist works was coming slowly, not generating substantial income, or both." Posing novels like *Sanctuary*, *Pylon*, and *Intruder in the Dust* as B-sides to, respectively, *The Sound and the Fury*, *Absalom, Absalom!*, and *A Fable* drives home the fact that "Faulkner made decisions about what to write based on very immediate perceived needs and exigencies," that he "was not a writer who set out to write an ambitious modernist masterpiece every time he sat down at his typewriter." Faulkner's career also illustrates a truism in the music industry: that sometimes the "flipside" turns out to be the real hit, as in the cases of *Sanctuary* and *Intruder*, Faulkner's best-selling pre–Nobel Prize novels. Jackson is both modest and provocative in submitting his thought experiment, with its fine-grained attention to texts too often relegated to the periphery of Faulkner criticism, as "a flip side to the venerable, yet questionable, scholarship that shaped the field in earlier generations."

As Mary A. Knighton points out, Faulkner came of age, artistically, within a print culture zeitgeist, encompassing avant-garde movements along with "the rise of modern advertising poster art as well as comics and caricatures in newspapers and little magazines," that "encoded the literary as partners with visual art." In "William Faulkner's Illustrious

Circles: Double-Dealing Caricatures in Style and Taste," Knighton traces the writer's participation in multimedia networks of "parody and homage" from 1919, when a student at the University of Mississippi published a send-up of Faulkner's "Ballade d'une Femme Perdue" (Ballad of a Lost Woman) in the campus newspaper, to 1947, when Faulkner parodied both his earlier parodist and his own prose style in the exuberant "Afternoon of a Cow." Such "exchanges in parody," Knighton argues, "vividly demonstrated his visual/literary ambitions and modernist imagination." They helped him, for example, to negotiate his literary independence from mentor Sherwood Anderson, first in Faulkner's 1926 collaboration with illustrator William Spratling, *Sherwood Anderson and Other Famous Creoles*—itself additionally parodying the recently published volume of caricatures by Miguel Covarrubias, *The Prince of Wales and Other Famous Americans*—and later in the 1933 short story "Artist at Home." Covarrubias repaid Faulkner in kind in 1932, when he teamed with writer Corey Ford to pillory the Mississippian visually and verbally in "Popeye the Pooh," a spoof, obviously, of *Sanctuary*. As we might guess, the publication of that novel marks a turning point within the network of parody circulating around Faulkner; as his "most hyped violation of style and taste," *Sanctuary* laid its author open as never before to print culture notoriety and caricature. As the "circles of affiliation and allegiance" widen to include Faulkner's relationship with celebrated dust jacket artist E. McKnight Kauffer, we see "art and commerce intersect" in lively and illuminating ways.

Knighton's circles of parody, of course, were far from the only period print culture responses to *Sanctuary*. Carl Rollyson examines the newspaper reviewers and reporters who first brought Faulkner and his novel to the attention of US mass culture. In "Faulkner's First Biographers: Early Notices," Rollyson reconstructs the elaborate dance that unfolded in 1931 between Faulkner and print journalists as they collaboratively constructed a literary sensation. Rollyson suggests that Faulkner approached the newspaper interview as a game, an exercise in make-believe that allowed him and the journalist to pursue their own interests. Experienced Faulkner readers will recognize early versions of performative moves that Faulkner went on to perfect with agents, editors, scholars, presidents, and prize committees: the wounded and/or inept aviator, a persona that allowed the young writer "to project himself and his work on a world stage," and the "down-home country boy who had nothing whatsoever to do with the highfalutin literary world." Rollyson also introduces us to readers, like the Illinois coed who reviewed *Sanctuary* for her college newspaper, who demonstrate that Faulkner appealed right away to "a much broader and more understanding audience" than most critics have appreciated, one that "welcome[d] his deviation from the norms established by the mainstream print media." These "early notices" form an important archive documenting Faulkner's evolving stances and strategies as he "come[s] to terms," for the first significant time in his career, "with what it meant to be a public man."

Tim A. Ryan takes up a middlebrow tastemaker who played a prominent role in Faulkner's emergence as a literary icon and enfant terrible in the wake of *Sanctuary*. "Fabbulous Monsters: Faulkner, Alexander Woollcott, and American Literary Culture" reintroduces us to the cultural influence wielded by Woollcott in the 1930s, when he worked across diverse print and broadcast media to champion an "eclectic and expansive . . . conception of modernist culture" defined by "a dynamic interrelationship between highbrow literature, middlebrow writing, and lowbrow mass culture." Woollcott took up *Sanctuary*'s cause on his popular *Early Bookworm* radio program and, repeatedly, in regular columns for the *New Yorker* and *McCall's* magazine. His remarks on the novel, Ryan argues, reveal a sophisticated and prescient critical sensibility stressing "the complex interplay between the novel's grotesque content and its subtle narrative strategies" while "anticipat[ing] twenty-first-century scholarship's concern with Faulkner's subversion of gender and sexual norms and his . . . emphasis upon both queer and perverse sexualities." Later, by launching Viking's Portable series with his 1943 anthology *As You Were*, Woollcott paved the way for Malcolm Cowley's *Portable Faulkner* volume three years later, a work credited with rehabilitating Faulkner's critical reputation. Ironically, Cowley and his fellow New York intellectuals would celebrate quite a different Faulkner from Woollcott's brow-bridging darling, but with the critical turn toward print culture studies exemplified by this volume, Woollcott's Faulkner is once again having his day in the sun. Ryan's essay offers a useful reminder that Woollcott "was no less important to the literary career and fortunes of the Old Man" than more widely recognized figures like Cerf, Warren, and of course, Cowley.

Not to be outdone by Woollcott's fascination with *Sanctuary* was editor and critic Henry Seidel Canby, who held a decidedly more skeptical view of the novel. In "'A Literary Criticism of Neurotic Literature': The *Saturday Review of Literature* and Faulkner's *Sanctuary*," Sarah E. Gardner traces the checkered history of *Sanctuary* in the journal Seidel founded in 1924 to promote a self-consciously middlebrow, genteel cultural agenda. Canby, who figures prominently in Radway's and Hutner's studies of interwar middlebrow aesthetics and cultural politics, saw the literary critic as, in his own words, a "sanitary officer" whose role, according to Gardner, was "to protect the literary tradition from corrosive elements." In the case of *Sanctuary*, Canby practiced what he preached, placing Faulkner at the head of the class in a Depression Era "school of cruelty" and nominating *Sanctuary* as Exhibit A in the period's "literature of horror." Moreover, in 1934 he enlisted psychoanalyst Lawrence S. Kubie to diagnose and elucidate the textual "neuroticism" of *Sanctuary* by working up Freudian case histories of the novel's leading characters. Canby printed responses to Kubie's article by Evelyn Scott and Van Wyck Brooks in the magazine's letters section, and in 1935 he reprinted Ellen Glasgow's "Heroes and Monsters," an essay that once again skewered *Sanctuary* while also coining the phrase "southern gothic" to attack the work of Faulkner, Caldwell, and other contemporaries whom Glasgow viewed as failed realists. As Gardner points out, "that is a lot of attention to a novel that Canby did not particularly enjoy, by an author he did not particularly admire," but by taking *Sanctuary* seriously, the editor hoped to put his readers in a position to make an informed judgment whether literary renderings of the "horrific" could possess aesthetic value or were simply manipulative and unhealthy: "He might not be able to shield his readers from what he deemed the literature of the perverse, but he could certainly arm them with the latest theories in order to help them make sense of a changing literary landscape."

The final eight essays take up other adventures in Faulkner and print culture; these contributions, ordered chronologically, analyze key moments in Faulkner's literary career from the 1930s through the 1950s. In "Building the Brand: Faulkner at Random," Jay Satterfield considers the role of Bennett Cerf, both at the Modern Library and at Random House, in creating Faulkner's literary reputation. Random House becomes a case study in its own right to understand Faulkner's works "as commodities in a marketplace to be bought and sold, and the implications of their being a commodity on reception and perception." In 1936, when Random acquired Smith and Haas, and with it William Faulkner, Cerf was known "as being a bit over the top, and perhaps not as dignified as what one might expect in a literary publisher," but it was that very quality, his willingness to get his hands dirty and market his books, that made him a successful publisher and his authors, including William Faulkner, famous "brands" of literature. Cerf's marketing strategy was to sell books like other commodities but to "hide Random's commercialism behind a shroud of patronage." With a particular focus on the publication of *Absalom, Absalom!* in 1936 and *Intruder in the Dust* in 1948, Satterfield shows how Random invested in Faulkner for fourteen years, creating a literary brand that finally paid off in cultural and financial capital with the announcement of his Nobel Prize in 1950.

From the broad sweep of Satterfield's overview of Random House, we turn to one careful study of a Faulkner short story in the *Saturday Evening Post*, just as the United States was entering World War II and the *Post* was changing its long-standing editorial policy of isolationism to embrace the war effort. In "Gearing Up for War: Faulkner's 'Two Soldiers' and the *Saturday Evening Post*," Jennifer Nolan details the timing that made "Two Soldiers" the only lead story among the nineteen Faulkner ultimately published in the *Post*. The story arrived the same week that the editorial policy of the magazine was changing in response to the bombing of Pearl Harbor. "In a space of less than four months," Nolan explains, "the *Post* entirely reframed its outlook on the war and seemingly expected its audience to do so swiftly and easily as well." Yet Faulkner's story was not simply a mindless celebration of patriotism and war. Instead, Nolan argues, "'Two Soldiers' provides a rare and much-needed expression of Americans' complex and conflicted feelings about having recently entered the war." Nolan's careful reconstruction of a particular cultural moment provides essential context for understanding both "Two Soldiers" and "Faulkner's nuanced responsiveness to the social context of his time and to the magazines where he placed his work."

John N. Duvall considers a dramatically different reading community for Faulkner in "An Error in Canonicity, or A Fuller Story of Faulkner's Return to Print Culture, 1944–1951." Duvall gives context for Faulkner's 1946 second-place finish in a detective story competition in *Ellery Queen's Mystery Magazine* (*EQMM*). The magazine was edited by "Ellery Queen," which "was the pen name of two Russian Jewish cousins from Brooklyn, Frederic Dannay (1905–1982) and Manfred Bennington Lee (1905–1971)." Ellery Queen published their own mysteries and then acted as curators of sorts, editing a detective story magazine that was firmly "pulp" but published detective fiction by literary stalwarts as well as popular novelists. Indeed, Dannay often insisted on the literary importance of the detective story. Duvall carefully excavates the publication of "An Error in Chemistry" and its placement alongside other selections by well-known authors in the magazine, to argue that *EQMM*'s promotion introduced Faulkner's writing to a much broader popular audience. Dannay continued to champion Faulkner's work, reprinting several stories in subsequent issues of his magazine. *EQMM*'s audience of over two hundred thousand readers, Duvall argues, helped demonstrate to the publishing world that Faulkner could be marketed to much larger audiences through pulp reprints. For these reasons, Duvall concludes, Ellery Queen was as important as Malcolm Cowley in reintroducing Faulkner to a postwar reading public.

Erin A. Smith continues this focus on detective fiction in her essay "Hard-Boiled Faulkner? Gender, Art, and Commerce in William Faulkner's *Knight's Gambit*." After detailing the competition between feminized slicks and masculine pulps in interwar crime fiction, Smith analyzes Raymond Chandler's famous manifesto for hard-boiled detective fiction, "The Simple Art of Murder," and its prescriptions for "realistic" (read "good") mystery writing. Smith reads the title novella of Faulkner's collection as a riposte to Chandler in which the Mississippian "rehearses some of Chandler's premises but ultimately undermines the gendered binaries on which they are based." With her careful attention to the cultural politics of a genre with mass appeal, Smith breathes new life into an understudied Faulkner collection.

Greg Barnhisel's essay, "Packaging Faulkner as a Cold War Modernist," moves the conversation to Cold War culture with his analysis of Faulkner's role as a US government-sponsored cultural ambassador. Through "the State Department's books program" and "United States Information Agency [USIA] goodwill tours and documentary films," Faulkner participated in a "broader reframing of experimental modernism as an expression and defense of the free societies of the West." Modernism's transformation from an antisocial rebellion to the apolitical fruit of democratic liberty is apparent in the switch from "gutter Faulkner" to ennobled and individualist Faulkner. Barnhisel shows how Faulkner's Nobel Prize speech became his ticket for all-expenses paid trips around the world to give addresses that linked creativity and freedom. Faulkner's own speeches and books, however, complicated his effectiveness as propagandist; Barnhisel considers the novelist's efforts at cultural diplomacy a measured success at best.

Yung-Hsing Wu narrows this focus to one provocative episode of Cold War reception in her essay "Middlebrow Patriotism, Neighborly Reading." Wu interrogates Faulkner's participation in the People-to-People program, a 1956 initiative by President Eisenhower, sponsored by the USIA, that sought to draft ordinary Americans, including writers, as de facto ambassadors for the American way of life. When Eisenhower asked Faulkner to chair a writers' committee to "create understanding abroad," Wu argues, he unwittingly placed Faulkner in the middle of an aesthetic debate between passionate identification and critical distance as modes of readerly engagement with the literary. Wu's analysis of how targeted writers responded to Faulkner's initial survey letter about the purpose of the program reveals deep skepticism among the writers themselves about literature's suitability as a vehicle for diplomacy. One of those skeptical figures was Faulkner himself, whose leadership of the Writers' Committee did not last long. "Middlebrow Patriotism" provides a snapshot of the fierce internal debates regarding literature, reading, and ideology that were smoothed over for public consumption during the US's cultural Cold War.

The volume's final two essays take up Cold War men's and women's magazines as contexts for Faulkner's work. In "Programmed for Seduction: Faulkner's Fiction and Men's Magazines of the 1950s," Kristi Rowan Humphreys looks at the publication of two Faulkner stories in *The Dude* and *The Gent*, magazines that enmeshed masculinity solidly in consumer culture while simultaneously framing culture, including literary culture, as macho. The juxtaposition of surrounding articles and advertisements with Faulkner's "Carcassonne" and "Divorce in Naples" is startling, because both stories feature sexual ambivalence, and the latter tale depicts one of Faulkner's most explicit same-sex couples. Humphreys details how Faulkner's alliance with men's magazines complicates the construction of Cold War masculinity and Faulkner's own stake in it. Jaime Harker's essay, "*The Wild Palms, The Mansion*, and William Faulkner's Middlebrow Domestic Fiction," turns to the role of women's magazines in Faulkner's literary creations. Through a comparative analysis of the two Faulkner novels and the content of three women's magazines, the *Woman's Home Companion, Harper's Bazaar*, and *Cosmopolitan*, Harker suggests that Faulkner was much more familiar with the popular milieu he sardonically dubbed "the Kotex Age" than he pretended to his male cronies. Women's magazines created complex sites of female subjectivity and political agency in both the interwar and Cold War eras, and Faulkner's familiarity with and transformation of these motifs suggest that women's magazines might be as important as pulp in his print culture genealogy.

Faulkner's midcentury critical rebranding as strictly a highbrow modernist, disdainful of the market and impervious to literary trends or the corruption of commerce, has buried the much more interesting complexity of his ongoing engagements with print culture and its engagements with him. It is our hope that this collection of essays will spur greater critical interest in the intersection of Faulkner's writing career and the unrespectable, experimental, and audacious realities of interwar and Cold War print culture.

NOTES

1. See Randall Wilhelm, "Pictures and Words in Faulkner's Early Graphic Work," in *Fifty Years after Faulkner: Faulkner and Yoknapatawpha, 2012*, ed. Jay Watson and Ann J. Abadie (Jackson: University Press of Mississippi, 2016), 107–21; Carvel Collins, ed., *William Faulkner: Early Prose and Poetry* (Boston: Little, Brown, 1962), 3–38, 65–69,

78–83, 98, 104–6, 120; M. Thomas Inge, "Faulkner Reads the Funny Papers," in *Faulkner and Humor: Faulkner and Yoknapatawpha, 1984*, ed. Doreen Fowler and Ann J. Abadie (Jackson: University Press of Mississippi, 1986), 153–90; and Lothar Hönnighausen, *William Faulkner: The Art of Stylization in His Early Graphic and Literary Work* (Cambridge: Cambridge University Press, 1987), 51–77.

2. See Judith L. Sensibar, introduction to *Vision in Spring*, by William Faulkner, ed. Judith L. Sensibar (Austin: University of Texas Press, 1984), ix–xxvii; Judith L. Sensibar, *The Origins of Faulkner's Art* (Austin: University of Texas Press, 1984), 6–7, 19–28, 103–205; Noel Polk, introduction to *The Marionettes*, by William Faulkner, ed. Noel Polk (Charlottesville: University Press of Virginia, 1977), ix–xxxii; and Hönnighausen, *William Faulkner*, 9–50, 117–53.

3. John T. Matthews, *William Faulkner: Seeing through the South* (New York: Wiley-Blackwell, 2009), 28.

4. Ann Douglas, *Terrible Honesty: Mongrel Manhattan in the 1920s* (New York: Farrar, Straus and Giroux, 1995), 67.

5. Ibid.

6. Ibid.

7. John Tebbel, *The Golden Age between Two Wars, 1920 to 1940*, vol. 3, *A History of Book Publishing in the United States* (New York: R. R. Bowker, 1978), 134.

8. See Jeff Karem, *The Romance of Authenticity: The Culture Politics of Regional and Ethnic Literatures* (Charlottesville: University of Virginia Press, 2004), 20–26.

9. Tebbel, *Golden Age*, 170, 171.

10. Ibid., 570.

11. See James L. W. West III, *American Authors and the Literary Marketplace since 1900* (Philadelphia: University of Pennsylvania Press, 1988), 107.

12. For more on Faulkner's sometimes overdrawn distinctions between his short fiction and his novels, see Jay Watson, "Escapes and Diversions, Whoring and Trash: Two Case Studies in the Aesthetics, Psychology, and Economics of the Twentieth-Century American Short Story," *Flannery O'Connor Review* 8 (2010): 7–8, 10, 12.

13. The best account of Faulkner's turn to the anthology-novel form in the late 1930s remains Michael Grimwood, *Heart in Conflict: Faulkner's Struggles with Vocation* (Athens: University of Georgia Press, 1987), 87–298.

14. Tebbel, *Golden Age*, 166.

15. Lawrence Schwartz, *Creating Faulkner's Reputation: The Politics of Modern Literary Criticism* (Knoxville: University of Tennessee Press, 1988), and Greg Barnhisel, *Cold War Modernists: Art, Literature, and American Cultural Diplomacy* (New York: Columbia University Press, 2015).

16. John Tebbell, *The Great Change, 1940–1980*, vol. 4, *A History of Book Publishing in the United States* (New York: R. R. Bowker, 1981), 182.

17. On the middlebrow aesthetic and cultural politics of the Book-of-the-Month Club, see Janice A. Radway, *A Feeling for Books: The Book-of-the-Month Club, Literary Taste, and Middle-Class Desire* (Chapel Hill: University of North Carolina Press, 1997), esp. 88–124, 154–86, 261–301.

18. See, in particular, Schwartz, *Creating Faulkner's Reputation*, 38–72; David M. Earle, *Re-Covering Modernism: Pulps, Paperbacks, and the Prejudice of Form* (Burlington, VT: Ashgate, 2009), 203; and Kenneth C. Davis, *Two-Bit Culture: The Paperbacking of America* (Boston: Houghton Mifflin, 1984), 48, 50, 113–23. On BOMC's creative business model, drawing on the practices of the book and magazine industries, see Radway, *Feeling for Books*, 152. On the similarly hybridized strategies of pulp publishers like American Mercury Books, Pocket Books, Penguin, and the Armed

Services Editions, see Janice A. Radway, *Reading the Romance: Women, Patriarchy, and Popular Literature* (Chapel Hill: University of North Carolina Press, 1984), 25–28; Paula Rabinowitz, *American Pulp: How Paperbacks Brought Modernism to Main Street* (Princeton, NJ: Princeton University Press, 2014), 113; and Davis, *Two-Bit Culture*, 47–48, 94–95.

19. Earle, *Re-Covering Modernism*, 202. The pulping of full-length Faulkner works began with the Avon Pocket Size Books edition of *Mosquitoes*, published on November 21, 1941, as part of the firm's inaugural list, which consisted of twelve reprint titles (Davis, *Two-Bit Culture*, 48, 50).

20. See Gordon Hutner, *What America Read: Taste, Class, and the Novel, 1920–1960* (Chapel Hill: University of North Carolina Press, 2009), 31, 47, 155, 276–79.

21. Radway, *Feeling for Books*, 73.

22. Ibid., 102.

23. Ibid.

24. See James B. Meriwether, *The Literary Career of William Faulkner: A Bibliographical Study* (Columbia: University of South Carolina Press, 1971), 180. We cite the circulation figure from "Woman's Home Companion," https://en.wikipedia.org/w/index.php?title=Woman%27s_Home_Companion&oldid=706124338 (accessed March 1, 2016).

25. George Hutchinson has recently argued for a similar awareness on Faulkner's part of the emergence and influence of a large national audience of African American readers in the late 1930s and early 1940s. According to Hutchinson, Faulkner's awakening to this demographic (and market) was one important factor behind a newly sensitive approach to African American characterization and the depiction of southern race relations in Faulkner novels of the 1940s like *Go Down, Moses* and *Intruder in the Dust*. See George Hutchinson, "Tracking Faulkner in the Paths of Black Modernism," in *Faulkner and the Black Literatures of the Americas: Faulkner and Yoknapatawpha, 2013*, eds. Jay Watson and James G. Thomas, Jr. (Jackson: University Press of Mississippi, 2016), 66–67.

26. Edward E. Chielens, ed., *American Literary Magazines: The Twentieth Century* (Westport, CT: Greenwood Press, 1992), 355.

27. Ibid., 324.

28. Ibid., 311.

Note on the Conference

The forty-second Faulkner and Yoknapatawpha Conference, sponsored by the University of Mississippi in Oxford, took place Sunday, July 19 through Thursday, July 23, 2015, with more than two hundred of the author's admirers in attendance. Fourteen presentations on the theme Faulkner and Print Culture are collected as essays in this volume. Brief mention is made here of other conference activities.

The program began on Sunday with a reception at the University Museum for the exhibition *Our Faith Affirmed—Works from the Gordon W. Bailey Collection*. The exhibition featured works by twenty-seven artists born between 1900 and 1959. The exhibition underscored the significance of southern vernacular artists whose influence extends far beyond the realm of aesthetics and bears witness to the considerable weight of southern history, to the saga of American politics, and most clearly, to the artists' faith and clarity of vision. Following the reception, Carl Rollyson presented "Faulkner's First Biographers: Early Notices," followed by Candace Waid's lecture, "Beyond Words: Faulkner Defining and Defying Print through Pictures."

Following a buffet supper at Rowan Oak that evening, George "Pat" Patterson, mayor of Oxford, and Morris Stocks, provost of the University of Mississippi, welcomed participants, and Ted Atkinson, president of the William Faulkner Society, introduced winners of the 2015 John W. Hunt Scholarships. These fellowships, awarded to graduate students pursuing research on William Faulkner, are funded by the Faulkner Society and the *Faulkner Journal* in memory of John W. Hunt, Faulkner scholar and emeritus professor of literature at Lehigh University. James G. Thomas, Jr., the Center for the Study of Southern Culture's associate director for publications, presented the 2015 Eudora Welty Awards in Creative Writing. Corey Davis, a student at Clinton Christian Academy, won first place for her story "The Clean-up Crew," and Carly Sneed, a Pontotoc native who attends the Mississippi School for Math and Science in Columbus, won second place for her poem "Atlas." The late Frances Patterson of Tupelo, a longtime member of the Center's advisory committee, established and endowed the awards, which are selected through a competition held in high schools throughout Mississippi. A reading by Greg Perkins, author of *The Announcers: Darkness before Mourning*, rounded out the evening.

Monday's program began with Charles A. Peek and Terrell L. Tebbetts leading the first Teaching Faulkner session, Print Comes Easy, Culture Comes Hard: Faulkner in, on, and about Print, and a panel titled Faulkner's Collaborators followed, with Melanie M. Sherazi, Laura Goldblatt, and Richard Moreland presenting their work. The panel Print Culture and the Discourses of History, Law, and Medicine was next, featuring Christian Howard, Jay Ingrao, and Michael Lahey. The day's program also included "Collecting Faulkner," by Seth Berner; a keynote lecture, "Building the Brand: Faulkner at Random," by Jay Satterfield; and papers on the topic of Faulkner and the Little Magazine, presented by Elizabeth Cornell, Alexander Howard, and Anne MacMaster. Monday's activities ended with a Faulkner salon at Southside Gallery on the Oxford Square.

Tuesday's program included the second Teaching Faulkner session, Choosing the Texts, led by James B. Carothers, Brian McDonald, and Theresa M. Towner. A panel called The Letter and the Image: Print Culture as Medial Interface, included papers by Sarah Gleeson-White, Michael Zeitlin, Taylor Hagood, and Peter Lurie and was followed by a panel titled Faulkner and the Popular Magazine, featuring papers by Kristi Rowan Humphreys, Jennifer Nolan, and Matthew R. Vaughn. Afterward, Stephen Railton, Johannes Burgers, and Theresa M. Towner presented a progress report on the Digital Yoknapatawpha project at the University of Virginia. That afternoon Erin A. Smith presented her lecture, "Hard-Boiled Faulkner?," followed by a panel titled Pulp Faulkner, with John N. Duvall, Robert Jackson, and Kristin Fujie presenting. An afternoon party at the Oxford Depot rounded out the day.

Wednesday's program began with concurrent panels, one titled Sound, Vision, Print and the other called Composition and Revision. Presentations for the former panel included papers by Peter N. Miller, Serena Blount, and Mary A. Knighton. The latter panel included papers by Carolina Alvarado and Christopher Rieger. A panel titled Translation and Tastemaking followed. Zainah Asfoor, Fábio R. Mariano, and Tim A. Ryan presented papers. The morning ended with the panel Print and the "Potboiler": Faulkner's Popular Reception, for which Amy A. Foley and M. Thomas Inge presented papers. W. Kenneth Holditch lectured on "Growing up in Faulkner's Yoknapatawpha Country," at the J. D. Williams Library, followed by Greg Barnhisel's lecture called "Packaging Faulkner as a Cold War Modernist" and a panel named Faulkner and the Middlebrow, which included papers by Jaime Harker, Sarah E. Gardner, and Yung-Hsing Wu. A late afternoon walk through Bailey Woods ended at Rowan Oak, where the annual picnic on the grounds concluded the day's events.

Guided tours of North Mississippi, including Oxford and Lafayette County and the Mississippi Delta, took place on Thursday, and the conference ended with a closing party at Square Books.

The University Museum hosted two featured exhibitions during the conference: *Our Faith Affirmed—Works from the Gordon W. Bailey Collection* and *V.I.P. Portrait Gallery*, a black-and-white photography exhibition by Andrzej Maciejewski. The University Press of Mississippi exhibited Faulkner books published by members of the American Association of University Presses.

The Faulkner and Yoknapatawpha Conference is sponsored by the Department of English and the Center for the Study of Southern Culture and coordinated by the Division of Outreach and Continuing Studies. The conference planners are grateful to all the individuals and organizations that support the Faulkner and Yoknapatawpha Conference annually. In addition to those mentioned above, we wish to thank the William Faulkner Society, Greg Perkins, Square Books, Southside Gallery, the City of Oxford, and the Oxford Convention and Visitors Bureau.

Faulkner and Print Culture
FAULKNER AND YOKNAPATAWPHA
2015

Trashing *Sanctuary*:
The Material Origins of Faulkner's Art

KRISTIN FUJIE

One day I seemed to shut a door between me and all publishers'
addresses and book lists. I said to myself, Now I can write. Now I
can make myself a vase like that which the old Roman kept at his
bedside and wore the rim slowly away with kissing it.
—William Faulkner, from the 1946 introduction to
The Sound and the Fury

He protested that he didn't see me enough and that it was bad,
physically, to live as he was now. He knew that he should find a girl
("a physical spittoon," he phrased it), but although he had tried, he
was unable to. "I simply won't rise," he wrote. "That's strange, isn't
it? After what I know and don't ever seem to stop remembering
very long, all else is just meat.
—From Meta Carpenter Wilde and Orin Borsten,
A Loving Gentleman: The Love Story of
William Faulkner and Meta Carpenter

I'd like to begin by bringing together two Faulkner quotations that
seem to have little to do with one other. The first, taken from a draft of
the author's never-completed introduction to *The Sound and the Fury*
(1929), is clearly about art and artistic purity; the second, excerpted from
Meta Carpenter's recollection of a letter that she had from Faulkner in
1939, is just as plainly about women and sex. But what I will have to
say will hinge upon the not new but still potent idea that for Faulkner,
art, women, and sex are so intimately bound up that to evoke one is
to evoke the others. As Candace Waid and others have demonstrated,
what this means is that Faulkner obsessively genders and eroticizes art.[1]
His depiction of himself as a writer who, like the old Roman and his
vase, takes his book to bed is just one example of how he renders both

3

the artistic object and the creative process in sexual terms. In a manner equally pervasive, if often less explicit, Faulkner's representations of women and sex frequently double as meditations on art even when art is not ostensibly in the picture, so to speak. His expressed need for a woman like a "physical spittoon," for example, might not bring art to mind, but perhaps only because we envision an art like the vase in the story: that is to say, an art that is private, beautifully crafted, and beloved. The spittoon, in contrast, is a public thing, made not for kissing but for refuse, not for love, but for use. And yet, like the vase in Faulkner's story, it too is an object of oral fixation, one that furthermore evokes the author's favorite figure for art—that of the vessel—albeit in a radically different light. As such, the spittoon seems to present both the double and the antithesis, what Quentin Compson might refer to as the "antic" or "obverse reflection," of the vase, and thus of art and artistic creation.[2]

This essay takes the theme of print culture as an occasion to reassess the place of Faulkner's sixth novel, *Sanctuary* (1931), in his oeuvre. More specifically, I want to revisit Noel Polk's provocative suggestion that notwithstanding the author's public disavowal of its trashy origins, *Sanctuary* grew out of the matrix of his very early career, the same matrix that produced his less commercially popular, but personally beloved, *The Sound and the Fury*.[3] In thinking about this topic, I've been drawn to the twin, gendered figures of the vase and the spittoon because they seem to me to conceptualize in deeply Faulknerian terms not just the relationship between *The Sound and the Fury* and *Sanctuary* as Faulkner represented it, but also a broader critical paradigm that seems to underwrite that relationship, what Vincent Allan King has described, riffing off of Andreas Huyssen, as the "myth of the great divide" in Faulkner's work. This myth has left us, King suggests, with two Faulkners: Faulkner the "modernist" and Faulkner the "purveyor of pulp fictions."[4] *Sanctuary* has proven especially rich for critics interested in troubling this divide, its incorporation of elements from hard-boiled detective fiction, melodrama, pornography, and comics suggesting an author who absorbed popular art forms and, to borrow M. Thomas Inge's phrase, "reshaped [them] for his own artistic purposes."[5] As Peter Lurie has argued, the result is a novel that projects a unique modernism, one that blends high and low in ways that underscore "not the dualistic nature of popular and modernist art, but their mutual identity and constitution."[6] In other words, a modernism that challenges the great divide altogether.

In what follows, I will explore further the idea that *Sanctuary* erodes the split between high and low, pure art and pure trash; however, I'll do so by tracing that collapse not through Faulkner's engagement with popular forms, but rather as a theme or trope that plays out within and across his fiction. More specifically, I want to focus on the fictions that might be said to "make up" the novel's contested origins: on the one hand, the stories that Faulkner retroactively crafted *about* those origins in his postpublication introductions and interviews; and, on the other hand, the early novels that I want to suggest gave rise to *Sanctuary* and, in a palimpsestic fashion, underwrite it. I will have some things to say about the original, uncut version of the novel and the endlessly rich source text of "Flags in the Dust" (completed in 1927, published in 1929 as *Sartoris*), but I want to delve even further back, and deeper, to the truly early novels that occupied Faulkner while he was in Paris in 1925, and thus during the same period when he seems to have first conceived of *Sanctuary*: the unfinished novel *Elmer*, published posthumously in 1983, and his second published novel, *Mosquitoes* (1927). These two clusters of fictions—the early novels and the later commentary, what we can think of as "pre-texts" and "post-scripts"—prove richly conversant and surprisingly dissonant, particularly where they converge upon the figure of the artist and the question of art's relationship to physical reality and the material circumstances of its creation. Reading between them will, I hope, add another dimension to our understanding of *Sanctuary* and of Faulkner's engagement with print culture more broadly, one that undermines the distinction between high art and low pulp by connecting his most commercially popular novel back to the creative matrix of his early work and recovering, from within that matrix, a preoccupation with art's inescapable materiality.

Faulkner's introduction to the Modern Library edition of *Sanctuary* is a most curious piece of self-promotion. In it, the author famously denigrates his own novel as a potboiler, a "cheap idea . . . deliberately conceived to make money" and cooked up by "speculat[ing] what a person in Mississippi would believe to be current trends, ch[oosing] what I thought was the right answer and invent[ing] the most horrific tale I could imagine."[7] It was only by rewriting the book, he claimed, that he was able to make of it "something which would not shame *The Sound and the Fury* and *As I Lay Dying* too much" (178). This account of *Sanctuary*'s conception has been largely debunked by critics such as Gerald Langford, who has suggested that the original version of the text exhibits too much art and too many ties to Faulkner's other work, particularly "Flags in the Dust," to support his characterization of it as a cheaply conceived reaction to "current trends."[8] The manuscript archive also suggests that Faulkner's "rewriting"—which mostly consisted of cutting the Horace Benbow material, reordering what remained, and adding Lee Godwin's lynching and Popeye's backstory—functioned to increase, rather than correct, *Sanctuary*'s affinities with popular fiction of the period by making it more focused, linear, fast-paced, and sensational-ist.[9] Working off this evidence, we might pose the following rejoinder to Faulkner's introduction, that *Sanctuary* was not a reformed potboiler but rather a reasonably ambitious, recognizably modernist, and complexly motivated work, one which was subsequently, and carefully, "trashed." That is, it is a work brought into clearer alignment with commercial fiction, first, through the strategic cuts and revisions, and then, through the introduction itself, all of which worked, I want to suggest, to distance *Sanctuary* from Faulkner's previously published novels and the creative sources that produced them.

All this is not to say that we should write off the introduction alto-gether. For if the counternarrative presented by the novel's textual history discredits Faulkner's story as a factual account, it enhances to the same degree that story's interest as a work of fiction. This story takes on even deeper interest when read in light of David M. Earle's suggestion that the divide between modernist and popular art has been largely contrived by authors, publishers, and critics bent on defining modernism in contradis-tinction to pulp magazines and mass paperbacks. Designed for quick sale, consumption, and disposal, this "literary trash," Earle argues, has come to embody precisely the "material, economic, or physical dynamics" that "pure" modernist art and its supporters supposedly transcend.[10] What makes pulp, in this view, is thus not, or not simply, its content, style, or form, but its relationship to a set of material conditions that link a work to the world beyond the author and his own creative imagination.

What's fascinating about the stories Faulkner told about his work is how they incorporate both the high and low ends of the spectrum Earle describes, such that the trashing of one text has an elevating and purify-ing effect on another. Thus, whereas the Modern Library introduction presents *Sanctuary* as conceived out of pecuniary need and current trends, it says of his previous novel, *The Sound and the Fury*, that it was written only for "pleasure," when the author had "stopped thinking of [him]self in publishing terms" (177). Most striking for our purposes here is how Faulkner leverages what Earle calls the "physical dynamics" of the print process by underscoring, in the case of *Sanctuary*, the incur-sion of print's mechanical constraints into the private space of writing. In the introduction, he wryly recounts how he had to "pay for the privi-lege" of revising the novel because the type had already been set (178), or as he put it in subsequent interviews, "the only way to rewrite that book was to break up those plates,"[11] a circumstance which meant that the book was "in a way already in the public domain."[12] Compare these accounts to the "pleasure" of unfettered creativity that accompanied the initial writing of *The Sound and the Fury* from behind the closed door of the author's imagination, a feeling he claimed in his introduction to that novel was "absent" in the writing of *Sanctuary* and which affected him as "that emotion definite and physical and yet nebulous to describe," an "ecstasy" which "the yet unmarred sheet beneath [his] hand held inviolate and unfailing, waiting for release" (297–98). The freighted, sexual imagery in this sentence is fascinating, but what I want to highlight here is how in this account of a creative process divorced from "publishers' addresses and book lists," the act of writing seems to evade not only commodification but the conscripting effects of print altogether. The "nebulous" ecstasy of autoerotic creation resists *de*scription, even as the writing, itself, seems to escape the physical, embodied impact of *in*scription, the "sheet beneath [his] hand" remaining, even in the moment of writing, unmarred. It's as if the ink never hits the page.

What I've been suggesting thus far is that if *The Sound and the Fury* is, by Faulkner's own account, his "vase," then surely he casts *Sanctuary* in the role of the spittoon. What attracts me to this analogy is how it offers not just a way of conceptualizing the split between pure art and pure trash that Faulkner cultivated in his comments on the novels but also a way of collapsing that distinction by creating a textual bridge between the fictions that Faulkner constructed about *Sanctuary*'s origins and the early novelistic fictions out of which I want to suggest the novel actually emerged. I find it striking in this regard that if we look back to Faulkner's early career, we encounter a series of male artist figures who, like the cloistered, vase-making author in Faulkner's account, aspire to the production of pure shapes divorced from their referents in the physical world and the material conditions of their creation. Most immediately relevant to *Sanctuary* is, of course, the irrepressible Horace Benbow, who, a decade before he wanders into Frenchman's Bend toting a book instead of a gun, returns from World War I in "Flags in the Dust" with a Venetian glass-blowing apparatus. Holed up in his sister's garage, he uses it to create an "almost perfect vase" that he keeps, like Faulkner's Roman, near his bed, calling it by his sister's name and apostrophizing it as, "Thou still unravished bride of quietude."[13]

Faulkner's preoccupation with vases, and with the larger possibility of an artistic ideal "unravished" by external forces, however, does not originate with Horace. We can trace it at least as far back as the protagonist of the unfinished novel *Elmer*, which Faulkner started and then abandoned while abroad in 1925. This would-be artist exhibits from his youth a "strange passion for form" that leads him to admire, among other things, the "pure blank serenity" of a folded sheet of paper, "simple glass vases," and "the thin dropping line" of his sister's sexless torso.[14] When Elmer begins sketching "people armless and sweeping upward in two simple lines from a pedestal-like base . . . pure and meaningless as marble" (378), his father expresses concern over the "irreconcilability" of these lines and a "monetary return," but Elmer has no interest in reconciling his art to money, or to anything else in the outside world; the wrapping paper that serves as his sketchpad is, like Faulkner's own self-renewing, "unmarred page," "clean and virgin to [him] no matter how creased and spotted it might be in reality" (377). For reasons we'll address shortly, Elmer never does get around to becoming an artist, but his passion for shapes "pure and meaningless as marble" finds concrete expression in Faulkner's next novel, *Mosquitoes*, through the work of a sculptor named Gordon who prefers marble above all other mediums for its purity. Against his friend's insistence that artists "cannot afford to ignore people that own food and automobiles," Gordon sequesters himself in his studio, where he labors to create "shapes out of chaos more satisfactory than bread to the belly."[15] The piece that comes closest to his ideal is a female torso, "headless, armless, legless" (11), which moves his self-appointed curator to praise it as "pure form untrammeled by any relation to a familiar or utilitarian object" (26).

Against this interpretation, however, both *Elmer* and *Mosquitoes* expose the "impure" origins of these male artists' ideal forms by revealing how they emerge not out of "chaos," but from external sources and circumstances that must be stripped out in order for the pure shape to emerge. In a subtle but telling revelation, the folded sheet of paper that Elmer admires for its "pure blank serenity" turns out to be neither blank nor serene; it is subsequently revealed to be a letter that his sister Jo Addie leaves behind when she runs away from home, delivering her younger brother into grief. The coupling of loss with writing, impurity with inscription, is further reinforced when she sends Elmer a box of crayons in the mail as a kind of compensatory gift for her absence. Elmer's artistic aspirations are thereafter aligned with his desire to recover this lost sister while at the same time denying, as will Gordon, that the slim, virginal shape that he carries in his mind is beholden in any way to external reality and the material world. That Elmer never becomes an artist owes much to this impossible paradox, which seems to doom to failure any art he could possibly create by casting it as a necessary corrosion of his internal ideal, a soiling of the blank page that had seemed indomitably "clean and virgin" in his youth. In a particularly pregnant scene that both anticipates and undercuts Faulkner's account of the ecstasy "inviolate and unfailing, waiting for release" that he experienced in writing *The Sound and the Fury*, Elmer experiences a form of creative impotence as he "finger[s] lasciviously" a new set of paints, feeling that it would be a "shame to violate" the "smooth dull silver tubes . . .

comfortably heavy to the palm," the "fat portentous tubes in which was yet wombed his heart's desire, the world itself" (345). His suspicion that to release the paint, to actually make art, would be to desecrate the integrity of his own desire, finds symbolic confirmation a few pages later, when he recalls an injury he received during the war. Handed a live grenade, Elmer becomes entranced with its "comfortable feel—that heavy solidity that is almost sensuous to the palm, that you release with regret" (381), a sensation that clearly mirrors the autoerotic pleasure he indulges while holding the unopened paints. When the grenade explodes, exposing the "thin scarcely hidden fiery nerves along his spine" (384), it lays bare a crucial link between art and injury in Faulkner's imagination, one which implies that to give concrete expression to the shape in one's mind—in short, to make art—is to do violence to the purity both of the internal ideal and the artist himself.

It is vital to note here how the disaster associated with releasing the potential contained within the paint tube hinges upon the irreducible materiality not only of the paint but of the artist's own body. What Elmer intuits as he fondles the unopened vessels is in this sense not so different from what Joe Christmas of *Light in August* (1932) will learn when he vomits up the flesh-colored paste of his own "ruined, once-cylindrical tube" in the dietitian's closet, which is just how much of human life must be lived in and through a material reality that one does not want but which, being inclusive of the body, can never be fully expelled.[16] This, of course, does not prohibit Faulkner's male artists from trying to use art as a means of purging their "heart's desire" of its ties to the physical world and thus of escaping their own conditions as embodied subjects. Gordon, for his part, acknowledges that his work functions in precisely this way when he describes his marble torso as his "feminine ideal: a virgin with no legs to leave [him], no arms to hold [him], no head to talk to [him]"—that is to say, a body amputated in order to free the artist from all external demands and, even more importantly, his own dependency upon anything outside of himself (26). Though sardonic, this characterization of Gordon's art as a form of butchery is brutally honest, its ugly truth elsewhere confirmed by the narrative's descriptions of his "surgeon"-like gaze (24) and, more opaquely, the gruesome description of his filthy attic studio as a "Bluebeard's closet of blonde hair in severed clots" (9), clots that turn out not to be hair at all, but the wood shavings shed by the sculptor's chisel.

I want to pause for a moment on this remarkable image. I'm not interested in arguing here that Faulkner had the pulps specifically in mind when he set Gordon's marble form above a scattering of wood chips, although I admit to being tickled by this reading. What I do want to

suggest is something less neat and, I hope, more suggestive, which is that
Faulkner's image of a purportedly "pure form" rising "untarnished and
high and clean" above the physical refuse, or waste, of artistic creation
contains a pointed commentary on what high art discards in order to
make its "pure" shapes pure, namely, anything that ties that shape back
to its origins in the physical world and the material circumstances of its
creation. In *Mosquitoes*, these origins and circumstances return in the
form of a slim, flat-chested young woman named Patricia Robyn who
throws Gordon's world in disarray by confronting him with a real-life
twin to his beloved marble dream. It is worth noting here that with her
modern dance moves, flat chest, and long legs "ending in the twin inky
splashes of her slippers" (19), Patricia bears a striking resemblance to
the drawings of an artist named John Held Jr., a wildly popular commercial artist who is explicitly referenced as such in *Mosquitoes* for his
caricatures of American youth in the 1920s, caricatures that the youth
themselves have in turn taken as models for imitation (230). That Gordon's ideal finds its double in precisely such a caricature of a caricature
from a popular magazine suggests that his pure shape springs from more
common sources that he'd like to admit.

What I want to emphasize here, however, is that Patricia challenges
the purity of Gordon's art less through her ties to money and popular culture than through her simple existence as a body made not of marble but
of flesh, hair, and most importantly, blood. This blood makes a dramatic
return in a strikingly lurid, almost pulpish, episode in which Patricia runs
off into a Louisiana swamp with a yacht steward named David. There,
she is ravished not by the steward but by the novel's mosquitoes, which
in a striking precursor to Temple Drake's rape and "nymphomania" with
Red, torture her into a sexually charged spectacle of agony, driving her
moaning, writhing, and bleeding onto the ground and then into the "hot
ooze, mud, and slime" of the swamp's "thick black water" (179, 188). I
want to evoke again here the idea with which I started, which is that
Faulkner's meditations on women and sex often double as meditations
on art. If, as I've suggested, *Mosquitoes* both stages that doubling and
unmasks its underlying logic by tracing Gordon's feminine ideal back to
its origins in the female body, then by immersing that body in the grossly
material world, its "ooze, mud, and slime," it effectively collapses the
distinction between purity and impurity, marble and mud, art and filth.

In doing so, *Mosquitoes* lays the foundation for some of the most
freighted depictions of female sexuality in Faulkner's mature work, but
along with "Elmer," it also supplies us with the tools for deconstructing
them. Take, for example, the deeply abject images of the female body
that we encounter in *The Sound and the Fury* and *Light in August*, in

which the thick black water of the swamps seems to re-materialize in the "liquid putrefaction," "deathcolored, and foul," that lies concealed beneath the "outward suavity" or "suavely shaped urn" of the female form.[17] These anxiety-ridden descriptions, which come to us via Mr. Compson and Joe Christmas, are both clearly about menstruation, but what the early novels enable us to see is how menstruation's most unsettling truth might be as much about art as women. For as captured so palpably in the image of a vase-like vessel leaking "periodical filth"—a phrase that assumes distinctly pulpish connotations when paired with Faulkner's bizarre description of "writing trash" for the popular magazines as writing for the "Kotex Age"—it seems that no art, whether conceived for profit or for pleasure, for the periodicals or for posterity, is ever pure because no art transcends its physical origins or material circumstances.[18] *All vases are also spittoons.*

This truth lies at the heart of Faulkner's early work leading up to and including his self-described "vase," *The Sound and the Fury*. I want to suggest in closing that it also lies at the heart of *Sanctuary*, but that in order to see it, we have to read between the lines not only of Faulkner's commentary but of the published text itself. Eric J. Sundquist observes that when Faulkner revised *Sanctuary*, he made good use of the "hard-boiled style" that "takes the aesthetics of observation to their limit and intentionally obliterates the inner life of its characters."[19] The result is what Gene M. Moore describes as a "stark flatness" or "depthlessness" that heightens the novel's horror precisely by concealing its origins.[20] As Nicole Molinoux suggests, however, the published version of the novel also reveals "a cunning workmanship" akin to what Horace admires in Ruby's "neatly-darned veil"; that is to say, the cover-up job was artfully done, but the stitches still show.[21] If we extend this parallel to include Temple Drake's body, torn and then "fixed up" by the men around her (149), we come one step closer to appreciating the degree to which the novel is not so much "depthless" as emptied out, its "hard-boiled" surface having been achieved only by making deep cuts to the manuscript and then suturing it closed. One example will have to suffice here, but it is also the most telling of Faulkner's many excisions. Readers of the published version of *Sanctuary* will undoubtedly recall Horace's feeling, during the walk from the spring to Goodwin's house, that Popeye "smells like that black stuff that ran out of Bovary's mouth when they raised her head" (7). In the original version of the novel, this observation appears not once but twice, the second time as part of a waking dream that Horace has, in which his dead mother's body becomes a disastrous fusion not only of his vase-like sister and his spittoon-like wife but also of Ruby Lamar and Popeye. This sickening collapse of all the boundaries that give shape and meaning to Horace's world culminates in the moment when, seeing that Belle's "rich full mouth" is about to yawn open upon his mother's face, he "trie[s] to scream at her, to clap his hand to her mouth" but finds that it is "too late": "He saw her mouth open; a thick, black liquid welled in a bursting bubble that splayed out upon her fading chin and the sun was shining on his face and he was thinking He smells black. He smells like that black stuff that ran out of Bovary's mouth when they raised her head."[22]

Severed from Horace's dream about his mother, the female orifice spewing "black stuff" loses a crucial dimension of its horror. For while the reference to Bovary's "macabre disgorgement" survived uncut, that reference is, itself, part of Horace's, and Faulkner's, attempt to contain the novel's blackness by linking it to the poisonous taint of popular culture.[23] Thus associated with Flaubert's "avid consumer of pulp,"[24] Popeye's "black" smell joins his tight black suits, face like "stamped tin" (4), and "dead, dark pallor" (5) that appears, even in sunshine, as if "seen by electric light" (4)—all of which mark him as other by casting him as urban, modern, and suspiciously mass-produced. Whereas this blackness becomes symbolically linked to the "monstrous and portentous" "shadow" (121) that Horace imagines Popeye—whom he compares to a "modernist lampshade" (7)—to cast over the "otherwise familiar and everyday" scene of Frenchman's Bend (121), the "thick black liquid" that erupts from the maternal body in the excised nightmare evokes a more ancient, stubbornly material blackness that threatens Horace from within the final sanctuary, so to speak, of his carefully structured existence. *This* blackness points back to an underworld centered not in Memphis but rather in the precariously domesticated space of the vacant Benbow family home. More specifically, its presence is felt in Horace's memories of the "black earth," now hidden beneath concrete, that used to show between the "red brick tediously and unevenly laid and worn in rich, random maroon mosaic" and the "blackish substance half earth, half water" that flooded the streets in the days before they were paved and in which, we are told, he and his sister "paddled and splashed with . . . muddy bottoms" (122). Though clearly bound up with his childhood, this blackness draws upon sources deeper than Horace, in the dark waters that Faulkner first plumbed in his early writings and which rise up, periodically, to reclaim the female body not just in modernist tours de force like *The Sound and the Fury* and *As I Lay Dying* but also in more "popular" works such as *Sanctuary* and the "Old Man" sections of *If I Forget Thee, Jerusalem* (1939). By trashing Horace's nightmare during the revisions, Faulkner buried this shared origin, but like the black earth upon which the artist's mosaic has been tediously laid, it continues to haunt the novel, most notably in the recurring image of the *stain*, including Temple's bloodied knickers and the corncob that appears to have been dipped in "dark brownish paint" (283), of course, but also the two stains that compel Horace to leave his wife, thus setting the novel in motion: Belle's handkerchief soiled with "surplus paint" from her mouth (15) and the "trailing moisture" of the shrimp that makes him muse, "Here lies Horace Benbow in a fading series of small stinking spots on a Mississippi sidewalk" (17), an image that I can't help but read in light of our conference theme, Faulkner and Print Culture, and Faulkner's professed ambition to leave behind no mark, "no refuse save the printed book."[25] Mutually inscribed with the physical traces of the body and of art—of blood, paint, and ink—*Sanctuary's* unsettling stains point back to the matrix of Faulkner's early career and to the truth of art's inescapable materiality that lies at the heart of his aesthetic vision.

NOTES

The first epigraph is found in William Faulkner, "Introduction to *The Sound and the Fury*, 1946," reprinted in *William Faulkner: Essays, Speeches & Public Letters*, ed. James B. Meriwether (New York: Modern Library, 2004), 299–300. Subsequent references are to this edition and appear parenthetically in the text.

The second epigraph is found in Meta Carpenter Wilde and Orin Borsten, *A Loving Gentleman: The Love Story of William Faulkner and Meta Carpenter* (New York: Simon and Schuster, 1976), 244.

1. See Candace Waid, "The Signifying Eye: Faulkner's Artists and the Engendering of Art," in *Faulkner and the Artist: Faulkner and Yoknapatawpha, 1993*, ed. Donald M. Kartiganer and Ann J. Abadie (Jackson: University Press of Mississippi, 1996), 208–47; Susan V. Donaldson, "Cracked Urns: Faulkner, Gender, and Art in the South," in *Faulkner and the Artist: Faulkner and Yoknapatawpha, 1993*, ed. Donald M. Kartiganer and Ann J. Abadie (Jackson: University Press of Mississippi, 1996), 51–81; Deborah Clarke, *Robbing the Mother: Women in Faulkner* (Jackson: University Press of Mississippi, 1994); and Diane Roberts, *Faulkner and Southern Womanhood* (Athens: University of Georgia Press, 1994).

2. William Faulkner, *The Sound and the Fury*, rev. ed. (1929; repr., New York: Vintage International, 1990), 170, 86. Subsequent references to this edition appear parenthetically in the text.

3. Noel Polk, "The Space between *Sanctuary*," in *Intertextuality in Faulkner*, ed. Michel Gresset and Noel Polk (Jackson: University Press of Mississippi, 1985), 18.

4. Vincent Allan King, "Faulkner's Brazen Yoke: Pop Art, Modernism, and the Myth of the Great Divide," in *A Companion to William Faulkner*, ed. Richard Moreland (Malden, MA: Blackwell, 2007), 303.

5. M. Thomas Inge, "Popular-Culture Criticism," in *A Companion to Faulkner Studies*, ed. Charles A. Peek and Robert W. Hamblin (Westport, CT: Greenwood Press, 2004), 272.

6. Peter Lurie, *Vision's Immanence: Faulkner, Film, and the Popular Imagination* (Baltimore: Johns Hopkins University Press, 2004), 30.

7. William Faulkner, "Introduction to the Modern Library Edition of *Sanctuary*," in *William Faulkner: Essays, Speeches, and Public Letters*, ed. James B. Meriwether (New York: Modern Library, 2004), 176–77. Subsequent references are to this edition and appear parenthetically in the text.

8. Gerald Langford, introduction to *Faulkner's Revision of* Sanctuary: *A Collation of the Unrevised Galleys and the Published Book* (Austin: University of Texas Press, 1972), 3–33.

9. See Michael Millgate, *The Achievement of William Faulkner* (London: Constable, 1966), 115; Walter Wenska, "'There's a Man with a Gun Over There': Faulkner's Hijackings of Masculine Popular Culture," *Faulkner Journal* 15, nos. 1–2 (1999–2000): 35–60; and Eric J. Sundquist, *Faulkner: The House Divided* (Baltimore: Johns Hopkins University Press, 1983), 44–62.

10. David M. Earle, *Re-Covering Modernism: Pulps, Paperbacks, and the Prejudice of Form* (Burlington, VT: Ashgate, 2009), 7.

11. James B. Meriwether and Michael Millgate, eds., *Lion in the Garden: Interviews with William Faulkner, 1926–1962* (New York: Random House, 1968), 123.

12. Joseph Blotner and Frederick L. Gwynn, eds., *Faulkner in the University* (Charlottesville: University Press of Virginia, 1995), 91.

13. William Faulkner, *Flags in the Dust*, rev. ed. (1929, as *Sartoris*; 1973, as *Flags in the Dust*; repr., New York: Vintage International, 2012), 175, 176.

14. William Faulkner, *Elmer, Mississippi Quarterly* 36, no. 3 (1983): 350, 377, 354. Subsequent references are to this edition and appear parenthetically in the text.

15. William Faulkner, *Mosquitoes* (1927; repr., New York: Liveright, 1997), 50, 47. Subsequent references are to the 1997 reprint and appear parenthetically in the text.

16. William Faulkner, *Light in August*, rev. ed. (1932; repr., New York: Vintage International, 1990), 121. Subsequent references are to this edition and appear parenthetically in the text.

17. See Faulkner, *Sound and the Fury*, 128, and Faulkner, *Light in August*, 189.

18. Joseph Blotner, ed., *Selected Letters of William Faulkner* (New York: Random House, 1977), 96. Cited in Anne Goodwin Jones, "'The Kotex Age': Women, Popular Culture, and *The Wild Palms*," in *Faulkner and Popular Culture: Faulkner and Yoknapatawpha, 1988*, ed. Doreen Fowler and Ann J. Abadie (Jackson: University Press of Mississippi, 1990), 146.

19. Sundquist, *Faulkner*, 46.

20. Gene M. Moore, "The Narrative Surface of *Sanctuary*," in *Etudes Faulkneriennes*, vol. 1, *Sanctuary*, ed. Michel Gresset (Rennes, France: Presses Universitaires de Rennes, 1996), 25.

21. Nicole Molinoux, "*Sanctuary* Revisited," in *Etudes Faulkneriennes*, vol. 1, *Sanctuary*, ed. Michel Gresset (Rennes, France: Presses Universitaires de Rennes, 1996), 14.

22. William Faulkner, *Sanctuary: The Original Text*, ed. Noel Polk (New York: Random House, 1981), 60.

23. André Bleikasten, "'Cet Affreux Gout D'encre': Emma Bovary's Ghost in *Sanctuary*," *William Faulkner: Materials, Studies, Criticism* 5 (May 1983): 2.

24. Andreas Huyssen, *After the Great Divide: Modernism, Mass Culture, Postmodernism* (Bloomington: Indiana University Press, 1986), 46.

25. Blotner, ed., *Selected Letters of William Faulkner*, 285.

Balance, Bonus, Bastard:
William Faulkner's B-sides

ROBERT JACKSON

*The problem for the reader is to determine how far, if at all, to
allow the knowledge of one Faulkner text to shape the reading of
another. . . . If it is wrong to ignore the many reflexive connections
among Faulkner's works, and if it is equally wrong to deny that
there is, in several senses, a "design" within the Faulkner canon, it
must nevertheless be argued that the connections among Faulkner's
texts are problematical rather than absolute, that there are several
different kinds of connections, that it is useful to discriminate
among them, and that, above all, Faulkner's "design" was dynamic.
Reading a Faulkner short story, then, is one thing, reading
"Faulkner's short stories" is another, and "reading Faulkner" is still
another. The art of reading Faulkner's short stories requires the
reader to focus, as Faulkner did, on the immediate text, and to read
among and between the texts for a sense of the developing design.*
    —James B. Carothers, William Faulkner's Short Stories

    *"You know," I said, "you have children all around now. You
won't be proud of all of them, just the same they're around."*
    *"Yes," Faulkner said, "I was surprised to learn how many people
like the stuff."*
    —Ralph Ellison, letter to Albert Murray, April 9, 1953

Thirty years after James B. Carothers drew attention to the complexity
of Faulkner's contexts with himself, his insights bear repeating, albeit
in a quite different spirit. The vast accumulation of scholarship in several areas of Faulkner studies, and in literary and cultural studies more
generally, has ensured that the sort of informed contextual reading practice Carothers advocated in 1985 cannot be constituted by any narrow
intertextual process but demands a knowledge of several subfields, from

print culture history and textual studies to contemporary theoretical traditions as diverse as critical race theory, media theory, postcolonial theory, and feminist and queer theory.[1] This is a tall order, of course, yet it remains one of the great challenges within the field—indeed, it might well be considered the comprehensive charge to the field as a whole. And as the 2015 publication of *The New Cambridge Companion to William Faulkner* demonstrates, recent criticism in emergent areas reveals how Faulkner's remarkable body of work has continued to absorb and reward innovative methodological approaches and queries. In this collection, new media, biopolitical, ecocritical, postcolonial, and several other important new analyses of Faulkner's work (most of which tend to focus on the "major" novels published between 1929 and 1942) utilize Faulkner (and perhaps the reverse is simultaneously true: Faulkner utilizes them) to impressive ends.

Amid these productive readings, Jaime Harker, in "Queer Faulkner: Whores, Queers, and the Transgressive South," echoes Carothers's call for the kind of holistic and inclusive attention that "reading Faulkner" requires. Of the *Companion*'s thirteen essayists, Harker seems most attuned to the limiting effects of the process of selection and marginalization that contributes to the canonization of a writer like Faulkner, and she alone, viewing the field from a vigorous contemporary movement in queer theory, makes this process a central concern of her discussion. She sums up a decades-long postwar tradition of Faulkner scholarship by noting that "Faulkner was read by Cold War critics as upholding the ideals of individualistic masculine virtues like honor, courage, truthfulness, and a willingness to fight for one's beliefs, while such readings tacitly approved the 'universal' truths of female sexuality and subordination." Citing recent scholarship that has aggressively revised such ideologically motivated consensus-era readings, she adds, "But Faulkner as Southern patriarch obsessed with creating dynastic families and enforcing genteel sexual mores always required a breathtaking level of disavowal." Prescriptively, Harker intuits the great critical possibilities in Faulkner's alternative Signet canon of pulp writings, which include *Sanctuary* (1931), *Pylon* (1935), and *The Wild Palms* (1939), among others. "Framing Faulkner's genders and sexualities within this larger pulp tradition," she writes, "might help us reassess the split between 'major' and 'minor' novels that still bedevils Faulkner criticism. A more thorough acknowledgement of how Faulkner absorbed and embraced the pulp tradition, even in novels that are seen as his most experimental and modernist, comes by taking the Signet canon seriously."[2]

The ultimate point of Harker's work (and that of several scholars she cites as contributing to this recent revision, including John N. Duvall and

Minrose C. Gwin) is hardly to out Cold War Faulkner studies for their willful blindness.[3] This work serves instead as a complementary, even collaborative contribution to an ongoing tradition of inquiry that builds on earlier work despite the latter's problematically overdetermined disavowal. And calling for attention to less frequently studied works represents a comparable sort of complementary productivity, suggesting that the insights of queer theory might be understood as a kind of a flip side to the venerable, yet questionable, scholarship that shaped the field in earlier generations. I will return briefly to queer theory and its generative potential below. In any case, however, I think Harker's work provides a good start to developing a prospectus for a more integrated account of Faulkner's entire body of work, and I'd like to focus here on a related and underappreciated aspect of his career: his turn to more popular forms, genres, and themes at specific moments in which his work on the more experimental modernist works was coming slowly, not generating substantial income, or both. This is a pattern that has been apprehended more clearly and acknowledged more openly in the context of the short stories (not surprisingly, the area of Carothers's principal focus) and screen writings, the two areas of Faulkner's career that he explicitly (and perhaps somewhat disingenuously, considering the amount of effort he put into them) dismissed as a waste of time and talent.[4] But even beyond these areas, I think it's important to recognize the frequency with which Faulkner made decisions about what to write based on very immediate perceived needs and exigencies. It bears stating in the most straightforward terms: Faulkner was not a writer who set out to write an ambitious modernist masterpiece every time he sat down at his typewriter. Our inclination to rank his works, with many of the novels from *The Sound and the Fury* (1929) to *Go Down, Moses* (1942) coming in for the bulk of attention and acclaim, is thus a rather anachronistic way of avoiding questions about how Faulkner himself devoted his time and understood his own purposes as a writer for the *longue durée*.

Consider some of the major novelistic examples of what we might call Faulkner's popular turn. Foremost among these is *Sanctuary*. Faulkner conceived this novel, he famously stated, as "a cheap idea, because it was deliberately conceived to make money" in the aftermath of the editorial disagreements and disappointing public receptions connected to *Sartoris* (1929) and *The Sound and the Fury*.[5] After submitting a completed draft of *Sanctuary* to his publisher, Faulkner "set out deliberately to write a tour-de-force," as he said of the quickly written *As I Lay Dying*.[6] Receiving the galley proofs for *Sanctuary* after the 1930 publication of *As I Lay Dying*, he rewrote much of it at his own personal expense and with considerable anguish as to its mixed lineage as both an experimental

novel among his recent masterworks and a "potboiler" in the vein of contemporary crime and exploitation fiction.[7] He even seemed to ridicule
his own cross purposes in the closing line of his 1932 introduction to the
Modern Library edition of *Sanctuary*, recalling that he had been "trying
to make out of it something which would not shame *The Sound and the
Fury* and *As I Lay Dying* too much."[8] Indeed, the 1932 introduction as a
whole constitutes an expression of remarkable ambivalence, as Faulkner
openly fretted about *Sanctuary*'s status alongside the other novels he
wrote during the same period.

    Pylon is another key exhibit here. When asked at the University of Vir-
ginia in 1957 whether he considered *Pylon* a "serious novel," Faulkner
didn't directly answer the question, but he did say this: "I wrote that
book because I'd gotten in trouble with . . . *Absalom, Absalom!*, and I
had to get away from it for a while, so I thought a good way to get away
from it was to write another book, so I wrote *Pylon*."[9] His choice of words
here brings to mind the scandal of an unplanned pregnancy, as if his
encounter with the material of *Absalom, Absalom!* (1936) had knocked
Faulkner up and necessitated a nine-month vacation of sorts, during
which *Pylon* was quietly and rather unceremoniously birthed—and only
reluctantly recognized as a legitimate heir. And *Intruder in the Dust*
(1948) and *Requiem for a Nun* (1951), discussed in more detail below,
were both produced during the decade in which Faulkner labored on
A Fable (1954), a novel he believed would be his greatest achievement
despite its tortured, oft-interrupted gestation.

    These are well-known elements in Faulkner's career, as are the pro-
lific short story writing in the early and mid-1930s and the occasional
screenwriting assignments between 1932 and 1955, but I suggest we
should think more carefully about the relationships these and other of
Faulkner's works have with one another, both in the history of their composition and, perhaps just as importantly, in the development of important strains of criticism and categorization of his entire canon. This is not
a new observation, of course. At least since Malcolm Cowley arranged
the contents of *The Portable Faulkner* (1946), it has been evident that
Faulkner's works bear crucial relations to each other.[10] But I don't know
if we've really given enough consideration to how the works interact with
one another on these many levels of composition, textuality, reception,
and canonization, how they maintain various tensions with one another
and thus might be read across one another, as it were. John T. Matthews
comes close to this awareness when he calls attention to "Faulkner's
habitual frugality in the use of his creative work." He notes the fact that
"Faulkner's short stories tend to orbit his novels," and he argues, most
broadly, that "the stories play a kind of double game, reflecting on the

very market conditions of modern culture under which they appear—
especially the mass production and consumption of cultural goods, and
the commoditization of human relations."[11] These remarks come amid a
discussion of the economic constraints in Faulkner's publishing efforts,
which Matthews sees, correctly, I believe, as important stimuli to new
kinds of creativity.

Matthews's metaphor from astrophysics is bolstered by Faulkner's
comparable description of Yoknapatawpha as "a cosmos of my own."[12]
I would like to suggest another metaphor, which is also, and importantly, a product of "the very market conditions of modern culture" and
which might help us theorize the relations between texts like *A Fable*
and *Intruder in the Dust*, the latter of which was written in about three
months in the winter of 1948 when Faulkner found himself at a creative
and financial nadir. This metaphor comes from mass culture, by way of
the modernist-era music industry, and for those of us who can remember
what records on vinyl were like, it ought to provide a mild gradient of
nostalgia: the B-side.

Before I propose that we view Faulkner's works within a kind of
A-side/B-side dynamic, we should ask whether "B-side" has a generally accepted definition. The *Oxford English Dictionary* defines a B-side
as "(the music recorded on) the supporting or less important side of a
single-playing gramophone record."[13] The *OED*'s authority comes into
question immediately, however, in the incorrect dating of the earliest
known use of the term to 1962. In fact, early Victor jazz records, including the Original Dixieland Jass Band's 1917 recordings, employed an "a"
and "b" split, and the trade journal *Variety* was already classifying songs
as "a-sides" and "b-sides" in the 1930s for promotional purposes by radio
broadcasters.[14] Music historian Richard Osborne emphasizes the intertwined forces of consumer demand and corporate marketing strategy in
deriving this split in the United States in the 1930s, as record companies
settled on recognizable, shared methods of assigning both generic identity and social and economic value to the two sides of a record. "On the
one hand," he writes, record companies "began to use each side of a disc
to highlight an artist's separate styles (usually a fast song coupled with a
slow song), aiming to appeal to different sectors of the market. On the
other hand, they concentrated their promotion on what they now classed
as the 'a-side' of the record" (146).

But the B-side's manufactured subservience, or what Osborne calls
its "obscurity," has also produced a long tradition of innovation, experimentation, and unintended consequences. Citing Elvis Presley's singles
for Sun Records in the mid-1950s, for example, Osborne argues that
"the coupling of songs of different tempos and styles brought forth some

of the most perfectly balanced records" (148). It may be to the point of
Faulkner's work as well that the early Presley records were "symbols for
the miscegenation of rock 'n' roll" and combined, as Osborne notes, "a
countrified blues song with a blues-drenched country tune" (148). "Balance" has an implicitly racial connotation here, suggesting an impulse to
reconcile the hard facts of Jim Crow hierarchies with fundamentally fluid
aesthetic forms. Just so, elsewhere, Osborne writes, "American rhythm
and blues acts would balance their most commercial music with their
most raucous" (148). This pattern is made most explicit in white musicians' covers of black musicians' songs (a frequent occurrence among
rock groups seeking to credit acoustic or electric blues as influences) as
B-sides, and in the "split-single" featuring altogether different groups—
one white, one black—for A-side and B-side singles.

Just as suggestive is the B-side's eventual association with aesthetic—and perhaps other kinds of—purity. "In an industry that can be
obsessed with authenticity," Osborne writes, "the b-side could provide
a safe haven. This is revealed most clearly when the b-side and a-side
traded places: the reversibility of the vinyl format allowed the flipside
to become the hit. Unplanned and unexpected, the chart b-side could
escape the taints of cynicism and commodification" (152). Among the
most famous instances of this widespread phenomenon is Bill Haley's
seminal cover of "Rock Around the Clock," first issued as the B-side to
"Thirteen Women (and Only One Man in Town)" (1954). The Beatles
frequently complicated the A-side/B-side dichotomy with such releases
as "I Am the Walrus," which originally served as the B-side to "Hello,
Goodbye" (1967) but gained enormous popularity in its own right. "We
never consciously write B-sides to records," John Lennon remarked in
1964. "Quite a few of our B-sides could have been A-sides" (quoted in
Osborne, 149). Perhaps a reflection of the prolific collaboration between
Paul McCartney and John Lennon and the synthesis of these two musicians' styles, the Beatles invented what they called the "double A-side"
in 1965, declaring both "Day Tripper" and "We Can Work It Out" to be
A-sides in an attempt to promote them simultaneously and equally.

Like Osborne, who celebrates the latent potential in the "inherently subterranean" nature of the B-side (152), media historian George
Plasketes is drawn to the intriguing implications of the B-side as cultural
artifact:

> The "B-side" endures as a flip-side phenomenon, a cultural catchphrase and
> sub-icon of an icon of the 45 r.p.m. record era. "B's" multiple meanings and
> modifiers range from backside, balance, and bonus to bastard and low budget
> (a common designation for the B-side's secondary sibling in film). True to its

artifact origins in vinyl as a complementary companion to its more prominent, popular and parental-side single, the B-side is both orphan and outsider, inherently unsung, unassuming, and sometimes unusual. As "the under side," it is an under dog, under the radar and underappreciated, though not underground nor subculture. The B-side is situated in a cultural crevice that straddles or lies somewhere between the mainstream and the underground; the blacks and blind spots; the backsides, borders and in betweens.[15]

The B-side's character is relatively anonymous and occasionally obscure; easily or unintentionally overlooked, unnoticed, or sometimes dismissed, a designated fringe dweller, designed and destined for tags such as cult classic or critical favorite, a curiosity or collectible. In short, the B-side embodies the peripheries, those underappreciated artists, productions, genres, rituals, artifacts, and events that are situated on the flip side, slightly outside, buried beneath, a turn over from the A-side plane.

To imagine Faulkner's works as B-sides, then, is to suggest that they function in some of the ways Osborne and Plasketes identify here. Certain works (and discrete genres) present themselves as more obvious and immediate cases than others: the short stories, screen writings, certain essays and public letters, and such novels as *Sanctuary* and *Pylon*. Yet the comparison is inexact and breaks down when envisioned as a facile transposition of one form for another. All the same, if we envision *Intruder in the Dust* as *A Fable*'s B-side, we are presented with new ways of thinking about both works. *Intruder* serves as a kind of counterweight to the longer and more difficult novel, balancing Faulkner's high-modernist pretensions with a more pragmatic recourse to popular forms like the detective novel and, in its MGM adaptation, the Hollywood movie. *Intruder*'s "low budget" might be calculated not so much in financial terms as in terms of time and cultural status, since Faulkner wrote *Intruder* so quickly and with a minimum of anxiety and viewed the novel as a brief diversion from his more meaningful commitment to *A Fable*. (Financially, *Intruder* was recognized as a "major property" by both publisher Bennett Cerf and MGM director Clarence Brown, who worked quickly to purchase its film rights for $50,000 and secured a production budget of nearly $1 million, whereas Cerf and others quickly perceived *A Fable* to have no cinematic potential.) If *A Fable* suffers from being overdetermined, from being what Philip M. Weinstein diplomatically calls "Faulkner's most premeditated novel," *Intruder* feels, in its streamlined and generic form, somewhat underdetermined.[16] And terms like *orphan, outsider,* and even *bastard* apply in interesting ways as well, not just in the canonization of *Intruder* (or noncanonization, since the novel is almost never grouped among Faulkner's best works) but in its very narrative, with the marginal figures of Chick Mallison, Aleck Sander, and Miss Habersham circumventing the official powers of lawyer Gavin Stevens, the police, and other prominent Jeffersonians who seem more fundamentally complicit with an unjust legal system than bent on rectifying a wrong by seeking out the truth; and also, of course, in the person of Lucas Beauchamp himself, he of the mixed racial and familial lineage, the fringe figure who becomes a subject of cult fascination (potentially to the point of his lynching) by the whites of Yoknapatawpha.

Likewise, we might also pursue a reading of A Fable in light of its relations with Intruder, asking a series of important questions. Why, for example, did Faulkner decide to write such an ambitious work at that point in his career? (He began it in the early 1940s, not long after completing Go Down, Moses.) And how do the novel's origins in a Hollywood story meeting with director Henry Hathaway and producer William Bacher complicate its A-side status? Indeed, the novel's associations with Hollywood go farther: Faulkner's lengthy composition, both aided and complicated by his use of elaborate outlines on the walls of his Rowan Oak study, suggests that A Fable may have more B-side connotations than its epic pretensions suggest, since such a method of outlining was commonly associated with the plot-driven mechanics and multiple-collaborator teamwork of the Hollywood studio system. We might also inquire about the novel's ranging far beyond the realm of Yoknapatawpha to the World War I trenches of France even as Intruder, ostensibly a minor novel, revisits some of the most central landscapes and people from Faulkner's major earlier work and advances the Yoknapatawpha chronicle into the postwar era in crucial ways. These insights and queries apply as well to Requiem, another key postwar Yoknapatawpha narrative. Most broadly, we might link the three novels' common vocabulary of extralegal protest, imprisonment, and quarantine and ask why race represents such a central, vexed concern in Intruder and Requiem but features in far more muted ways in A Fable, which was published during the same year that saw the landmark US Supreme Court decision in the case of Brown v. Board of Education. In terms of the reception of these works, questions arise about Faulkner's characterization of A Fable's origin as being a novel of ideas rather than of people or situations (as both Intruder and Requiem had been) and about the novel's widely perceived failures, which led even so sympathetic a Faulknerian as Cleanth Brooks to write, "One is tempted to say that A Fable was flawed at its very inception." Brooks's Yale colleague Harold Bloom—not surprisingly a single-minded partisan of "major-period" Faulkner—dismissed it as "a book of badness simply astonishing for Faulkner," even as many French critics shared the view that *A Fable* represented Faulkner's greatest work.[17] Finally, we might question the novel's postwar historical and cultural connections, many of which are evident in comparable guises in *Intruder* (and *Requiem*), and which Catherine Gunther Kodat has cited in her examination of the novel's articulation of what she calls "the peculiarly American-inflected triumph of consumerist mass culture and the concomitant 'decline of modernism' in the aftermath of the Second World War."[18] From Gavin Stevens's ideologically suspect lectures on southern white paternalism in *Intruder* to Faulkner's recycling of his Nobel Prize acceptance speech in *A Fable*, these works speak to early postwar history with strikingly similar modes of rhetoric and pedagogical import, suggesting the bonus connotation of the B-side even as it becomes more difficult, upon closer examination, to discern which of the novels better deserves B-side identification.

Short of a detailed reading, I'd like to suggest the applicability of this approach to other of Faulkner's works displaying the tension and familial dissonance of A-side and B-side. Imagine, for example, a reading of Faulkner's canon under the title "Faulkner's Bastards"—or perhaps more lyrically, repurposing a line from *Pylon*, "Who's your old man?"— that looks at Faulkner's novels "high" and "low," his short stories, his public statements and private correspondence.[19] Such a reading would unite a work like *Pylon*, with its central questions about paternity, with *Absalom, Absalom!*, whose unfinished manuscript Faulkner temporarily abandoned in order to write *Pylon* quickly in late 1934 (just as he would abandon *A Fable* to write *Intruder* in early 1948). In doing so, it might reveal this temporary abandonment as a necessary part of the process of writing *Absalom*, as Faulkner ventured into a separate but obviously deeply connected creative space to deal with some of the father-son complexities—and with the problem of legitimacy—that would mark *Absalom* so profoundly. Of course, Faulkner himself routinely imagined his own works as his children, some of which he liked to claim as his own more than others, and all of which generated complicated, varied feelings of protectiveness, defensiveness, and disavowal. He recalled his response to the rejection of *Flags in the Dust* by Horace Liveright in parental terms: "I was shocked: my first emotion was blind protest, then I became objective for an instant, like a parent who is told that its child is a thief or an idiot or a leper; for a dreadful moment I contemplated it with consternation and despair, then like the parent I hid my own eyes in the fury of denial."[20] He characterized the origins of *The Sound and the Fury* in similar terms: "So I, who never had a sister and was fated to lose my daughter in infancy, set out to make myself a beautiful and tragic little girl."[21] Closely linking this novel, his "most magnificent failure," with his creation of Caddy Compson, he likened his exceptionally intense feelings for it to how "the parent feels toward the unfortunate child, maybe."[22] Faulkner's bastards offer insight into the variegated market conditions under which he produced such a wide range of writings and in specific cases reveal the ambivalent pressures, both constricting and liberating, that contributed to the composition and publication histories of individual works. Thus, "the two separate Quentins" at the outset of *Absalom*, in describing Thomas Sutpen's children *"which should have been the jewels of his pride and the shield and comfort of his old age, only—(Only they destroyed him or something or he destroyed them or something. And died)*," reflect as well something of Faulkner's uneven, often restive paternal feelings toward the writings he produced and cast into the world like so many irrepressible descendants.[23]

I have quoted from the *OED* to reveal the challenges in defining the B-side; more constructive and authoritative on the subjects of popular, pulp, and punk culture, perhaps, is the online Urban Dictionary, the crowd-sourced compendium of slang and colloquial English. Here we learn that "in most urban street circles, B-side has come to be known as the more 'real' or 'true-to-the-streets' recordings of an artist. Ones that are less 'main-stream' and less endulging [sic] of censors critics and airplay."[24] This certainly squares with an important strain of Faulkner criticism, as represented by the work of Carothers and other readers of the short fiction and by Joseph R. Urgo, James G. Watson, Theresa Towner, Noel Polk, and other critics who have argued in various ways on behalf of Faulkner's B-sides.[25]

Another Urban Dictionary entry defines the B-side as an "unpopular person" with the sample sentence, "What are all these B-sides doing here?"[26] This is a provocative question indeed, particularly as we consider questions of canonization and Faulkner's familial dissonance with contemporaries and heirs, whether on the right (the southern Agrarians and New Critics), the left (the French existentialists, the New York intellectuals), of the Third World or Global South, or in such emergent traditions as—here I borrow the professional Faulknerians' terms—"the black literatures of the Americas," represented not just by the canonical figure of Toni Morrison, but also by the likes of W. E. B. Du Bois, Jean Toomer, Claude McKay, Ralph Ellison, James Baldwin, Ernest J. Gaines, Marie Vieux-Chauvet, Edwidge Danticat, Edward P. Jones, and Natasha Trethewey.[27] Recounting the scene of his brief 1953 conversation with Faulkner on the occasion of the National Book Award ceremony, during which the younger writer congratulated Faulkner on his many "children" and added, "You won't be proud of all of them, just the same they're around," Ellison concluded with a sly question to his friend Albert Murray, a question suggesting Faulkner's intimate ties to African American culture: "You thinks he's been hanging around with Mose?"[28] It is tempting to imagine Faulkner's hands perspiring and his mind straining for small talk during such dreaded public events, especially one such as this, when a young writer of color, meeting him for the first time, refers to his sprawling brood of offspring. It is tempting to cast him with severe social anxiety disorder and a provincial stubbornness that grated on the manners of an increasingly, and startlingly, diverse community of world letters, and to envision him more placidly in his private library of classics, poetry, and nineteenth-century European and American fiction. But with the B-side in mind, perhaps we should balance this image of a reactionary and reclusive Faulkner with that of Cash Bundren, the pragmatic artisan who recovers from a broken leg and other inconveniences of travel and overcomes his grief for departed family members by spinning records on the graphophone brought into the family by his new stepmother. "It's a comfortable thing, music is," he says.[29] Unlike his brother Darl, who prices himself out of the market of ordinary human relationships, Cash embraces his place within a robust, collaborative, entirely messy community of contemporary culture: "And everytime a new record would come from the mail order and us setting in the house in the winter, listening to it, I would think what a shame Darl couldn't be to enjoy it too. But it is better so for him. This world is not his world; this life his life."[30] Cash's mail-order records give us another model of Faulknerian popularity—a restorative, even generative one.

Most in the spirit of the Urban Dictionary's effort to give voice to the underground in all its diversity, finally, are several highly suggestive entries connecting the B-side to non-normative sexuality. Some of the more restrained sample usages include the following constructions: "Hey, look at [the] B Side of that lady, isn't it tempting;) [sic]." And "Wendy loves nothing more than to be flipped over and played on the b-side!"[31] There are others as well, I promise you. This important connotation reminds us that to talk about Faulkner's B-sides is, eventually and necessarily, to talk about queer Faulkner. Hence the productive quality of Jaime Harker's comments on the pulp tradition and the arbitrary, ideologically driven "split between 'major' and 'minor' novels" in this context. If we want to develop integrated interpretations of Faulkner's entire career, we should consider the B-side an integral piece within it, highly useful in getting at the challenge of understanding Faulkner's whole body of work. For as the Urban Dictionary reminds us with its own contemporary pulp style, every body has a B-side.

NOTES

My thanks to John Duvall and Kristin Fujie, my fellow panelists at the 2015 Faulkner and Yoknapatawpha Conference, for fellowship and valuable feedback on earlier versions of this work, and to numerous other F&YC organizers and attendees, notably Leigh Anne Duck, Sarah Gardner, Sarah Gleeson-White, Jaime Harker, Peter Lurie, Rick Moreland, Taylor Hagood, Jay Watson, and Mike Zeitlin, for helping me make my work better, and for other kindnesses large and small.

The first epigraph is found in James B. Carothers, *William Faulkner's Short Stories* (Ann Arbor, MI: UMI Research Press, 1985), 4.

The second epigraph is found in Ralph Ellison and Albert Murray, *Trading Twelves: The Selected Letters of Ralph Ellison and Albert Murray*, ed. Albert Murray and John F. Callahan (New York: Modern Library, 2000), 45.

1. As a model of this kind of "intertextual" reading, Carothers (146) cites John T. Irwin, *Doubling and Incest/Repetition and Revenge: A Speculative Reading of Faulkner* (Baltimore: Johns Hopkins University Press, 1975).

2. Jaime Harker, "Queer Faulkner: Whores, Queers, and the Transgressive South," in *The New Cambridge Companion to William Faulkner*, ed. John T. Mathews (New York: Cambridge University Press, 2015), 108, 115.

3. See John N. Duvall, *Faulkner's Marginal Couple: Invisible, Outlaw, and Unspeakable Communities* (Austin: University of Texas Press, 1990); and Minrose C. Gwin, *The Feminine and Faulkner: Reading (Beyond) Sexual Difference* (Knoxville: University of Tennessee Press, 1990).

4. See Carothers, *William Faulkner's Short Stories*; Hans H. Skei, *Reading Faulkner's Best Short Stories* (Columbia: University of South Carolina Press, 1999); Bruce Kawin, *Faulkner and Film* (New York: Frederick Ungar, 1977); and Peter Lurie and Ann J. Abadie, eds., *Faulkner and Film: Faulkner and Yoknapatawpha, 2010* (Jackson: University Press of Mississippi, 2014).

5. William Faulkner, *Essays, Speeches, and Public Letters*, ed. James B. Meriwether (New York: Modern Library, 2004), 176.

6. Joseph Blotner, *Faulkner: A Biography* (Jackson: University Press of Mississippi, 2005), 248.

7. Ibid., 293.

8. Faulkner, *Essays*, 178.

9. Stephen Railton, "The English Club," *Faulkner at Virginia*, University of Virginia, http://faulkner.lib.virginia.edu/display/wfaudio02_2#wfaudio02_2.19 (accessed January 25, 2016).

10. On Cowley's selection of materials for *The Portable Faulkner* and the politics of canonization therein, see Joseph R. Urgo, *Faulkner's Apocrypha: "A Fable," Snopes, and the Spirit of Human Rebellion* (Jackson: University Press of Mississippi, 1989).

11. John T. Matthews, *William Faulkner: Seeing through the South* (Malden, MA: Wiley-Blackwell, 2009), 7–8.

12. James B. Meriwether and Michael Millgate, eds., *Lion in the Garden: Interviews with William Faulkner, 1926–1962* (New York: Random House, 1968), 255.

13. "B," *OED Online*, http://www.oed.com (accessed May 12, 2016).

14. Richard Osborne, *Vinyl: A History of the Analogue Record* (Burlington, VT: Ashgate, 2012), 145. Hereafter cited parenthetically.

15. George Plasketes, *B-Sides, Undercurrents and Overtones: Peripheries to Popular in Music, 1960 to the Present* (Burlington, VT: Ashgate, 2009), 6.

16. Philip M. Weinstein, introduction to *The Cambridge Companion to William Faulkner*, ed. Philip M. Weinstein (New York: Cambridge University Press, 1995), xix.

17. Cleanth Brooks, *William Faulkner: Toward Yoknapatawpha and Beyond* (New Haven, CT: Yale University Press, 1978), 235; Harold Bloom, *Novels and Novelists* (New York: Chelsea House, 2009), 315.

18. Catherine Gunther Kodat, "Writing a Fable for America," in *Faulkner and America: Faulkner and Yoknapatawpha, 1998*, ed. Joseph P. Urgo and Ann J. Abadie (Jackson: University Press of Mississippi, 2001), 85.

19. William Faulkner, *Pylon*, in *Novels 1930–1935*, ed. Joseph Blotner and Noel Polk (New York: Library of America, 1985), 787.

20. Quoted in Blotner, *Faulkner*, 206.

21. Ibid., 212.

22. Stephen Railton, "McAleer's Literature Class," *Faulkner at Virginia*, University of Virginia, http://faulkner.lib.virginia.edu/display/wfaudio05_1#wfaudio05_1.15 (accessed January 25, 2016).

23. William Faulkner, *Absalom, Absalom!*, in *Novels 1936–1940* (New York: Library of America, 1990), 6–7.

24. "B-side," *Urban Dictionary*, http://www.urbandictionary.com/define.php?term=B-side (accessed December 8, 2015).

25. See Urgo, *Faulkner's Apocrypha*; Theresa M. Towner, *Faulkner on the Color Line: The Later Novels* (Jackson: University Press of Mississippi, 2007); Noel Polk, *Faulkner's "Requiem for a Nun": A Critical Study* (Bloomington: Indiana University Press, 1981); Michel Gresset and Patrick Samway, eds., *A Gathering of Evidence: Essays on William Faulkner's "Intruder in the Dust"* (Philadelphia: Saint Joseph's University Press, 2004).

26. "B-side," *Urban Dictionary*.

27. See Jay Watson and James G. Thomas, Jr., eds., *Faulkner and the Black Literatures of the Americas: Faulkner and Yoknapatawpha, 2013* (Jackson: University Press of Mississippi, 2016).

28. Ellison and Murray, 45.

29. William Faulkner, *As I Lay Dying*, in *Novels 1930–1935* (New York: Library of America, 1985), 159.

30. Ibid., 177–78.

31. "B-side," *Urban Dictionary*.

William Faulkner's Illustrious Circles: Double-Dealing Caricatures in Style and Taste

MARY A. KNIGHTON

Experimenting with French Symbolism in the August 1919 *New Republic*, William Faulkner's first published poem, "L'Apres-midi d'un Faun" (Afternoon of a Faun), found its doppelgänger in parody. Fellow students in the *Mississippian* burlesqued Faulkner and his poems. They mocked his "Ballade d'une Femme Perdue" (Ballad of a Lost Woman) with their "Ballad d'une Vache Perdue" (Ballad of a Lost Cow), snickering at the florid style and pretensions of "Count No 'Count" Faulkner. Seventeen years later at a private dinner party in Hollywood, Faulkner would adopt a hokey pseudonym, Ernest V. Trueblood, and read to dinner guests his "L'Après-midi d'une Vache" (Afternoon of a Cow), one-upping his early parodists with self-parody on a bovine theme. Maurice Coindreau, a French dinner guest, admired this comic sketch. It saw print in Coindreau's 1943 French translation, appeared in English in 1947, and finally was respectably collected in *Parodies: An Anthology from Chaucer to Beerbohm*, edited by Dwight Macdonald in 1960.[1] Faulkner must have relished this delayed retort, particularly from the vantage point of literary success—and particularly since cows were already on his mind in the late 1930s, which was when he developed the scene that would become Ike's love affair with the cow in *The Hamlet*.[2] They were on the mind of Bennett Cerf of Random House, too, when he inadvertently parodied Faulkner's success and *The Hamlet* in a memo to his sales representative in March 1940: "A cow will sell THE HAMLET as a corncob sold SANCTUARY."[3] Throughout his career, William Faulkner and his work participated in lively exchanges in textual parody and visual caricature with those in his "illustrious circles," artists and writers defining art at the limits of taste and commerce.

Exploring Faulkner's circles of acquaintances from the 1920s into the 1940s reveals diverse wellsprings for his literary and visual imagination.

Tracing circles rather than following only direct lines of influence may risk excessive sweep, but this method also affords a more inclusive and global look at how Faulkner's work and reputation circulated, encompassing indirect as well as direct exchanges over time and geographical distance. The strikingly small New York publishing and artistic coteries of the interwar period steadily pulled Faulkner into overlapping orbits with the likes of Anita Loos, William Spratling, Miguel Covarrubias, the Algonquin tastemakers, Bil Baird, and E. McKnight Kauffer.[4] Faulkner found his voice in "the age of satire"—F. Scott Fitzgerald's apt characterization of the 1920s—from his very start as a professional writer. He experimented in these currents, and his exchanges in parody and caricature vividly demonstrated his visual/literary ambitions and modernist imagination. In spotlighting the artistic and commercial exchanges that converged around Faulkner's most hyped violation of style and taste, *Sanctuary* (1931), I argue that Faulkner's literary aesthetic adapts the mixed visual and literary features of the era's print culture.[5] Although publishers early on discouraged his attention to conventional illustration and dust jacket art, displacing Faulkner's visual energies onto the printed text in his books instead, that hardly means Faulkner paid no heed to the bookmaking process or the ways in which lines of art and text so often shared their profits and their wit in caricature.

Double-Dealing in Images and Words

Early on, Faulkner aspired to be an artist and a poet. Panthea Reid Broughton, M. Thomas Inge, and other scholars have long taken seriously Faulkner's early experiments in comics, drawing, and poetry, whether recognized as apprenticeship or as part and parcel of his modernist innovations.[6] Arguably, Faulkner's "sketches" (many collected in *New Orleans Sketches* [1958]) facilitated his transition away from drawings and poetry to short stories and novels.[7] The sketch as a literary genre shares techniques with the fluid modes of visual caricature and textual parody, particularly in their emphasis on decisive detail, concise imitation, quick consumption, and unfinished ephemera. Faulkner's sketches served as studies for short stories that were perpetually reworked into the quilt pieces that stitched together his major novels.

Words combine with images in what can only be called Faulkner's bookmaking: the spectrum ranges from stylized drawings and comics for university publications to making the children's book *The Wishing Tree* (1927) and creating and illustrating his own hand-made and hand-lettered books, *The Marionettes* (1920) and *Mayday* (1926). Pictograms inserted rebus-fashion in his texts, such as the coffin in *As I Lay Dying*, and bizarre punctuation, italics, and even colored typographical passages used to indicate different narrative voices in *The Sound and the Fury* are now justifiable hallmarks of Faulkner's experimental modernism. No less do they index his attention to the material shape of words on the page that epitomizes his literary/visual aesthetic.[8]

Bennett Cerf liked to say Faulkner was easy to deal with, never meddling in business matters concerning his books' production, but that was not entirely true early in his career.[9] In a letter to Horace Liveright on October 16, 1927, regarding *Flags in the Dust*, Faulkner makes suggestions for the printer, asking that his punctuation not be constantly "corrected." He concludes with a postscript: "I also have an idea for a jacket. I will paint it and send it up for your approval soon."[10] Despite Faulkner's evident desire to create his own cover art and participate in the making of this book in visual as well as textual ways, Liveright's rejection of his manuscript apparently nipped his enthusiasm in the bud. As Cerf makes clear in his praise of Faulkner, cover art is the publisher's advertising business, well beyond the author's purview.[11] As time went on, Faulkner's desire to illustrate his own dust jackets, together with his eye for caricature and care for bookmaking and illustration overall, was displaced onto sculpting typography and text for visually and psychologically arresting narrative ends. How vindicating for him, then, as he became truly a celebrated figure after the publication of his scandalous *Sanctuary*, that several of his dust jackets would be designed by E. McKnight Kauffer, the artist who produced one of the most famous graphic designs ever, for James Joyce's banned *Ulysses*.[12] An unexpurgated *Ulysses* finally appeared in the United States in 1934 after challenges to obscenity law by Faulkner's publisher, Random House. Those legal challenges were already ongoing when Faulkner's own notorious *Sanctuary* caught Bennett Cerf's attention and convinced him that a scandalous Faulkner would best fit in his stable of modern authors.[13]

Critics Judith Sensibar and Lothar Hönnighausen have noted Faulkner's admiration and almost slavish imitation of T. S. Eliot and Aubrey Beardsley in his early poems and visual and textual juvenilia, respectively.[14] Just as important, though, is how a broader zeitgeist— Decadent Aestheticism, Imagism/Vorticism, and the rise of modern advertising's poster art as well as comics and caricatures in newspapers and little magazines—encoded the literary as partners with visual art over and beyond Faulkner's youthful taste. Such double vision served parodic ends in the *Double Dealer* in New Orleans, a magazine that prided itself on proving satirist H. L. Mencken wrong for condemning southern letters as a "Sahara of the Bozart" in 1917. Its October 1921 Beardsleyesque cover, for instance, might just as well be serving up Mencken's head in spirited riposte and homage to Mencken's satire of southern letters as riffing on Beardsley's *Salome* illustrations for Oscar Wilde's.[15] In 1926 Faulkner would himself collaborate in a double-dealing send-up of his circle of New Orleans artists and *Smart Set* fashion and later correspond directly with Mencken at the *American Mercury*.[16]

Also in Faulkner's circles (first in New Orleans, later in New York and Hollywood) was Anita Loos, whose 1925 spoof, *Gentlemen Prefer Blondes*, caused Mencken to say, "I'd publish this in the *American Mercury*, but I don't dare to affront my readers. Do you realize, young woman, that you're the first American writer ever to poke fun at sex?"[17] The blockbuster success of her book was inseparable from Ralph Barton's caricatures that illustrated its serialization first in *Harper's Bazaar* and then for Boni & Liveright's book edition. Inspired by her close friend "Henry" Mencken, Loos's novel uses the gold-digging Lorelei Lee's illiterate and naïve observations to take men down a peg, as well as to satirize literary, intellectual, and high society figures: "I think that practically every married girl ought to have a career if she is wealthy enough to have the home life carried on by the servants. . . . For if Henry and I spent all of our time together neither of our ideas would be so bright. And it is bright ideas that keep the home fires burning, and prevent a divorce from taking all the bloom off Romance."[18] Faulkner wrote directly to Loos in 1926 after reading Spratling's copy of *Blondes*, conspiratorially praising it and saying he envied her character Dorothy. He likened Loos's novel to the infamous Spectra hoax, in which poets Witter Bynner and Arthur Davison Ficke took pseudonyms (Emanuel Morgan and Anne Knish, respectively) and claimed to be founders of a new poetry movement called Spectra.[19] Besides publishing in major venues like the *New Republic*, Spectra issued a poetry volume complete with manifesto and several drawings done in colored inks. Parodying the era's numerous literary and artistic manifestoes, Spectric aesthetics urged poets to write by methods not unlike those of futurist painting, sensitive to the seen and unseen specters of light around objects, inspired by prisms and the spectrum of colors.[20] Although Bynner had expected to be exposed right away, the hoax took on a life of its own when little magazines and major poets touted the new movement. Harriet Monroe devoted a special issue of *Others* in January 1917 to Spectricism. As Suzanne W. Churchill notes, "The school acquired acolytes around the country, and the *Wisconsin Literary Magazine* even published a parody of the parody, introducing the Ultra-Violet school. The Spectric school earned critical acclaim from respected critics and poets; E. L. Masters praised its practitioners for getting 'to the core of things.'"[21]

In referencing the hoax in his letter to Loos, Faulkner congratulates her for fooling a public more apt to be entertained by "that moron of a cornflower" Lorelei than to grasp the wit of Dorothy. Generally accepted to be the voice of Loos herself, Dorothy gets filtered through both Barton's flapper-girl illustrations and Lorelei's ungrammatical, malaprop-spouting diary, allowing the author to speak through both sides of her mouth. Faulkner's letter to Loos dismisses mentor Sherwood Anderson for not discerning Loos's wit and technique as accurately as he himself has. Faulkner was in good company: Edith Wharton called *Blondes* "the great American novel (at last!)," while James Joyce, despite his failing eyesight, read Loos's book cover to cover.[22]

Private Jokes and Public Venues

Although Faulkner had learned from Sherwood Anderson to turn to native materials for art and credited him for this debt by dedicating *Sartoris* (1929) to him, Faulkner began to resist their mentor-apprentice relationship as Anderson depicted it in his 1925 sketch, "A Meeting South."[23] Set in New Orleans, the story is narrated by a paternalistic Anderson, who shepherds the young aspiring poet "David" to Aunt Sally's, a house of ill repute run by a fellow midwesterner. Throughout, Anderson ruminates on regional identity and southern local culture. But the past is never past in print culture, it appears, for when Anderson republished the sketch in 1933 (in *Death in the Woods and Other Stories*), Faulkner updated the terms of their relationship via parody. In "Artist at Home" (1933), a handsome if comical young poet cuckolds a "fattish, mild, nondescript man of forty" who serves as mentor to younger writers.[24] The older writer, already successful in New York, now shares a new home with his wife in rural Virginia. Faulkner reverses Anderson's superior lines of influence over him as protégé by having his story's poet displace the husband from his marital perch (a rather literal play on cuckoldry as stemming from the cuckoo bird usurping other birds' nests). Faulkner's poet is depicted too as necessarily wandering, his only real home in the literary marketplace. In fact, in 1929 Anderson had moved with his wife Elizabeth Prall to the rural Ripshin Farm in Virginia, designed by William Spratling. Prall would leave Anderson at Ripshin and soon divorce him before heading for Mexico to join the *Double Dealer*'s Natalie Scott and Spratling. Faulkner's parody, part of a 1933 print culture exchange with Anderson's republished sketch of him as a young artist in New Orleans, stings with details from reality, sharpening the fictional lines of caricature.

Faulkner had first resisted Anderson by gently parodying him in New Orleans in 1926: "One trouble with us American artists is that we take our art and ourselves too seriously."[25] Faulkner's language mimics Anderson's preachy idealism but also echoes Virginia Woolf's mocking words in her "American Fiction" essay in New York's *Saturday Review of Literature* the year before, doubling the salt already thrown at Anderson's wounded ego:

> Mr. Anderson is forever repeating over and over like a patient hypnotizing himself, 'I am the American man' and 'Behold in me the American man striving to become an artist, to become conscious of himself, filled with wonder concerning himself and others, trying to have a good time and not fake a good time. I am not English, Italian, Jew, German, Frenchman, Russian. What am I?' Yes, we may be excused for repeating, what am I?"[26]

Faulkner parrots the British Woolf in gently mocking Anderson's concern with regional authenticity, reframing him as an "American" writer who is at risk of losing himself among too many "creole" masks. After all, Sherwood Anderson and Other Famous Creoles (1926) marked Faulkner's break from Anderson with William Spratling, the artist, architect, designer, and silversmith, who exerted the greatest formative impact on Faulkner's evolving visual/textual fusion in form. First living together in New Orleans, then traveling in Europe to see architecture for Spratling's work and do celebrity literati scouting at Shakespeare & Company in Paris, the two "Bills" ate, drank, wrote, sketched, and schemed together. In their parody, Spratling and Faulkner nod to Mencken but explicitly dedicate their parody to another parody, Miguel Covarrubias's The Prince of Wales and Other Famous Americans (1925).[27] The Mexican artist was lifelong friends with Spratling, particularly after Spratling settled in Taxco and became close with muralist and political dissident Diego Rivera, working with the US ambassador to Mexico, Dwight Morrow, and Covarrubias to gain for Rivera a major commission for a mural in New York City.[28] As the two Bills's homage makes clear, Covarrubias was not simply a cartoonist; simultaneously, he acted as arbiter of high society taste and illustrator for fine limited-edition literary works, including those from Harlem then in vogue (Melville's Typee, Stowe's Uncle Tom's Cabin, W. C. Handy's Blues: An Anthology, John Huston's Frankie and Johnny, Langston Hughes's The Weary Blues, Zora Neale Hurston's Mules and Men, to name a few). His caricatures not only had a great impact on fellow studio artist Al Hirschfeld, but their prominence in slicks like Vanity Fair also pronounced sly judgments on high society, political, and intellectual figures such as Mae West, Clark Gable, Mussolini, and of course, the Prince of Wales.[29] Between 1931 and 1934, Covarrubias's caricatures were paired with Corey Ford's parodic dialogues to produce Vanity Fair's "Impossible Interviews" series, where, for instance, John D. Rockefeller "impossibly" meets Joseph Stalin and Jean Harlow lies on Freud's couch.

With their New Orleans parody, Faulkner and Spratling do not simply borrow Covarrubias's title but also don his reputation as arbiter of style and taste. Before long, Covarrubias pays Faulkner back in the same parodic coin, collaborating with Ford ("John Riddell") on "Popeye the Pooh" for the aptly titled *In the Worst Possible Taste* (1932).[30] Covarrubias renders Faulkner as the corncob pipe–smoking hillbilly author of *Sanctuary*, while Ford parodies *Sanctuary* by way of three British authors, including A. A. Milne, suddenly transported to bootlegger Lee Goodwin's Mississippi farm (see Figure 1). Clearly, Faulkner had "made" it. Coming full circle since his visual/textual collaborative parody of Anderson with Spratling, Faulkner skewers, and is now skewered on, famous artists' pens throughout the 1930s after *Sanctuary*. His notorious fate as "the corncob man" is sealed.

Privately, too, Faulkner continually faced artists' burlesqued versions of himself and his work. Joseph Blotner tells us, for instance, of the puppeteers Bil and Cora Baird in New York, who invited Faulkner to a dinner party in 1938 that included Corey Ford and Faulkner's close friend and confidant Eric James Devine. At each of their places at the table were cards depicting Faulkner novels in bawdy caricatures (see Figure 2). Blotner confirmed with Bil Baird that Faulkner enjoyed this exchange so much that he took the drawings home with him. Baird even created a wine label especially for the party, "Applesome Absalom."[31] Baird, mentor to Jim Henson of the Muppets as well as the artist behind the puppet sequence in *The Sound of Music*, was one of America's, and the world's, most famous puppeteers. Like his good friend Covarrubias, Baird occasionally acted as dust jacket artist and illustrator, lending his caricatures to Devine's book on yachting, for instance.[32] At the Bairds' dinner party attended by Faulkner, shared devotion to art and bookmaking sit at the same table with parody and caricature.

Bloomsbury Circles in New York

After *Sanctuary* was published in early 1931, Faulkner's cultural capital, if not his actual fortunes, turned, and he became a celebrity. He wrote giddy letters home from New York about the famous people he was drinking with or soon to meet in Hollywood: Dashiell Hammett, Lillian

Fig. 1. Miguel Covarrubias caricature of William Faulkner as "Popeye the Pooh." Ink wash and white, 35.6 x 28 cm. Permission of Maria Elena Rico y Covarrubias, the estate of Miguel Covarrubias. Reproduced by the Harry Ransom Center, University of Texas, Austin, from the Nickolas Muray Collection of Mexican Art.

Fig. 2. Bil Baird caricature of *Sanctuary* for place setting at a party hosted by Baird and attended by Faulkner. Courtesy of the Baird Estate. Small Special Collections, University of Virginia Library

Hellman, Carl Van Vechten, Tallulah Bankhead, Anita Loos, Dorothy Parker.[33] Meanwhile, across the pond, whoever was left of the Bloomsbury Group gathered around Virginia Woolf at the dining table, reported Rebecca West, discussing Faulkner's *Sanctuary* in such "terribly subtle" terms that a servant, eavesdropping, was eager to get his hands on the "saucy" material.[34]

Soon after *Sanctuary*, Faulkner's English publisher became Chatto & Windus, the firm that would take over Virginia and Leonard Woolf's Hogarth Press by 1946 and that became a necessary stop for Faulkner whenever he visited London. Bridging Bloomsbury and New York via Faulkner's circles was not only Woolf spoofing Anderson or Wyndham Lewis making hay with *Sanctuary* in "The Moralist with a Corncob," but also an American expatriate in Great Britain, E. (Edward) McKnight Kauffer. Ted, as he was called, was an intimate of the Bloomsbury coterie and exhibited with the Omega Workshop of Roger Fry, who wrote introductions for catalogues of Kauffer's exhibitions and praised his poster art. Kauffer had made his fame already by the 1920s in England, first as a Vorticist member of Wyndham Lewis's London and X Groups, then as a poster artist who designed advertising's first cubist poster. Kauffer even redesigned Vanessa Bell's wolf's-head colophon for the Hogarth Press run by his friends, Leonard and Virginia Woolf. In 1926 he did the title sequence for Hitchcock's silent film *The Lodger*, and he not only was involved with experimental film while in London but was greatly influenced by Man Ray, who shared his studio in London at one point. Today, Kauffer is best remembered as a modernist poster artist, particularly for

Frank Pick's London Underground transport, as a major illustrator and book jacket artist on a par with New Directions's Alan Lustig, and as a mentor to designer Paul Rand.[35]

Kauffer did numerous covers for the Modern Library, including Faulkner's *Sanctuary*, *Light in August*, *Requiem for a Nun*, and *Intruder in the Dust*. His name was synonymous with the craft of bookmaking, as he had worked closely with all the quality letterpresses and small presses in London—Hogarth, Curwen, Nonesuch, Cassell, Faber—and in the United States for the limited edition lines at Alfred Knopf's Borzoi Books and for the Bollingen Series, where he succeeded George Salter's brother, Stefan Salter. Kauffer worked most often with lithographs, by watercolor stenciling, and in gouache and ink. Roger Fry praised Kauffer's art for its "Cubisto-cabbalistic forms" and defined the role of book illustrations in the context of Kauffer's work: "It seems to me that real illustration in the sense of reinforcing the author's verbal expression by an identical graphic expression is quite impossible. But it may be possible to embroider the author's ideas or rather to execute variations on the author's theme which will not pretend to be one with the text, but rather, as it were, a running commentary, like marginal notes written by a reader."[36] Kauffer's art covered and, in Fry's sense, annotated works Faulkner surely held in his own hands: Burton's *Anatomy of Melancholy*, Hudson's *Green Mansions*, D. H. Lawrence's *Women in Love*, Cervantes's *Don Quixote*, Melville's *Benito Cereno*, Joyce's *Ulysses*.

Although the dust jacket had since the 1920s proclaimed itself the domain of advertising, Kauffer insisted in Omega Workshop fashion that graphic design did not have to sever the labor of making art for a living from aesthetic value. Kauffer openly criticized New York advertising art as always "hitting below the belt," using sex and money too explicitly to sell a product.[37] His disdain especially targeted crass commercialism, which, we might say, had no little in common with Faulkner's introduction added to the Modern Library's *Sanctuary* in 1932 (and rather scandalously excised after Faulkner's death).[38] On dust jacket flaps, publishers tried to spin Faulkner's "cheap idea" into the spun gold of his masterworks, but Faulkner's infamous introduction all but proclaims *Sanctuary* a potboiling hoax on his readers—"maybe 10,000 of them will buy it." Partially, of course, Faulkner voices during the Great Depression his frustration at the limited commercial success of *The Sound and the Fury* and *As I Lay Dying*; certainly, Faulkner's substantial revisions to *Sanctuary* appear to belie his claims.[39] And yet the introduction unequivocally shows us that Faulkner's eye took in a popular readership and not only the rarefied literary one that esteemed his earlier novels. Faulkner repurposed for titillating narrative ends the real-life gangster story of Popeye Pumphrey and the relatively new cartoon character Pop-eye.[40] Just as *Sanctuary's* scandalous subject matter got the attention of both Virginia Woolf's dinner guests and Rebecca West's servant, it surely fooled many readers expecting explicit scenes of murder, lynching, corn-cob rape, or brothel sex.

Be it deliberately or artlessly, Faulkner's introduction staged a pro-vocative and ambiguous debate about "cheap ideas" and the advertising role of authors, publishers, prefatory materials, and dust jackets even before the paperback revolution gained its foothold. Dust jackets and their artists acted as a historical transition between the book as artwork and paperback books' emphasis on the art of selling books by their cov-ers. Paperbacks may well have kept Faulkner in print in the 1940s, as Schwartz, Earle, and Jaillant persuasively argue, but Faulkner himself often enough conflated "cheap ideas" and "cheap books."[41] High, mid-dlebrow, and low culture prejudices surely informed his attitude, but Faulkner's concerns too for the material culture and quality of books cannot be easily dismissed.[42] In implying a relationship of tension between the market economy and the cultural and material productions of literary authors, Faulkner successfully powered decades' worth of critical commentary on his introduction to *Sanctuary* that to this day often overtakes discussion of the novel itself.

In 1940, the same year that Kauffer returned for good to the United States, he did the Modern Library cover art for *Sanctuary*, where his signature and the date stand out. He saw dust jackets as mini-posters, meant to be aesthetically pleasing but also to "move" the viewer to action, be it to take the Underground to the Natural History Museum or to purchase Eno's Fruit Salts. The symbolic and nonrepresentational aspects of Kauffer's cover art may be characterized best as modernist abstraction or surreal figuration. Aldous Huxley, in his introduction to Kauffer's 1937 MOMA poster art exhibition in New York, suggests that Kauffer's artwork reimagines objects and a book's contents as if through a dream.[43] With his book jackets, Kauffer interprets and, in Roger Fry's key phrase, "embroiders" the book's content, inscribing "a reader's" "marginal notes" and "running commentary" in visual form.

The simplicity of Kauffer's dust jackets for Faulkner derive from the graphic artist's sophistication and experience in design. A single cover or series of illustrations would often evolve through numerous studies, or sketches. In Figure 3, for instance, we can see Kauffer's study for the cover of *Sanctuary* (see Figure 3). Sketched in graphite, the figure crossed out gets reworked to highlight beady eyes, a scrawny Adam's-apple neck, a beat-up hat, cigarette smoke. He is a humble but perhaps also viciously ignorant bumpkin. He is not yet either Popeye or Lee

Fig. 3. Rough study for 1940 Modern Library dust jacket for *Sanctuary* by E. McKnight Kauffer. Copyright © Simon Rendall. Permission of the Cooper Hewitt, Smithsonian Design Museum / Art Resource, NY

Goodwin, certainly not Horace Benbow. In the upper frame, a window looks out over a town with a courthouse. One can almost see Faulkner's aquiline nose in the face crossed out and imagine that is his pipe resting on the handkerchief in the window. This sketch leads to the final cover (see Figure 4).

While the final Kauffer jacket appears to be as representational as the study, reading it in tandem with the book's content soon alters that impression. Kauffer limits himself to three colors to simplify the cover's task: a muddy skin color, the wood's brown, and the shirt's blue.[44]

Fig. 4. Modern Library dust jacket of *Sanctuary* by E. McKnight Kauffer (1940). Copyright © Simon Rendall. Courtesy of Penguin Random House LLC

The study's stereotypical hillbilly has become specifically Popeye with a dandy's veritable Marcel wave in his hair. His face lacks a chin and dangles a cigarette from his lips while smoke wreathes his face. Except for the blue eyes and missing hat, Popeye's face could have come from the opening pages: "His skin had a dead, dark pallor. His nose was faintly aquiline, and he had no chin at all. His face just went away" (4).

Of course, Faulkner's literary composition of Popeye, unlike the cartoon namesake, defies easy visual representation, despite the repetition of such memorable details as his girlish small hands, the hat drawn low, his oily brilliantined hair and tight black suit, his whinny. If Faulkner condenses "evil" in Popeye's abstract and impossible figuration, Kauffer draws less Faulkner's Popeye than Kauffer's Popeye, the dust jacket artist's marginal dream notes on the author's book.

Note how the intersecting planks of wood form a "V" behind which Popeye peers out with a concentrated gaze that indexes the unseen object in his pop-eyed line of sight. The prominent knothole in the wood reminds us of his role as voyeur, watching Red and Temple Drake in Miss Reba's brothel. The wood not only forms a roughly hewn bed frame tilted, but in doing so also suggests sexuality. The wood parodies Popeye's impotence even as its V alludes to female sexuality, both a delta of Venus and, specifically, a violated "temple." The lettering in the title mimics a typographic structure hastily built of the same wood, tinged with the blue of Popeye's shirt. It skitters off the page to the right, slanted and decentered, like Temple Drake herself running running running for a sanctuary that does not exist.[45] With this cover, Kauffer shows us the few simple materials out of which Faulkner's complex book is built, its visual and symbolic power to suspend whole worlds made of nothing more than words. Such a cover is appropriate for a writer who liked to describe himself as a carpenter as much as a writer.

For an author who also made his own books and hand lettered and illustrated them, a writer who so loved the word *dust*, how could Faulkner not care for the art of the dust jacket, especially Kauffer's? How farfetched is it to imagine their circles having overlapped at some point between New Orleans, New York, London, and Mexico? Consider that both Kauffer and Faulkner's longtime friend Stark Young had worked together as early as 1925 on a play and as late as the 1940s to produce artwork under the auspices of the WPA; or, recall that Kauffer did covers for *Fortune* magazine and posters for the Container Corporation of America, as did Covarrubias, and both did caricatures of Carl Van Vechten as part of the circle of illustrators for his books.[46] Kauffer, like Covarrubias and Faulkner, knew Carl Van Vechten, who took all their photos and guided them around Harlem.

While Faulkner frequently stayed at the Algonquin when he was in New York and drank with the "vicious circle" that included Dorothy Parker, Kauffer spent his time at Frances Steloff's Gotham Book Mart, where fine limited and handpress editions of books were sold.[47] Ultimately, Kauffer was a prize for the Modern Library brand and for Bennett Cerf, who had desired from the day he acquired Modern Library in 1925 to emulate the quality of fine British presses such as Francis Meynell's Nonesuch. Cerf immediately sought Meynell in London to learn about quality books, and when Meynell visited Cerf in New York in 1929, Cerf was eager to show him off. Meynell praised Kauffer's extensive work for Nonesuch without stint.[48] Correspondence in the Random House archives makes clear that when Modern Library became the US distributor for Nonesuch in 1927, Cerf was as keen to include "Ted" Kauffer's illustrations for *Benito Cereno* as to market the Nonesuch brand itself.[49] And, of course, after 1940 Faulkner could very easily have met Kauffer in the Random House offices where both submitted their work. In at least one letter, close friend and editor Saxe Commins urges Faulkner to take notice of the fine work Kauffer did on his covers.[50]

One letter, however, sets some of these questions to rest, even while raising new ones. On Random House stationery, administrative assistant Mary Barber typed up a letter dictated to her or scribbled out for her. She addressed it to E. McKnight Kauffer and dated it June 29, 1951. The signature is in William Faulkner's inimitable hand.

> Dear Mr. Kauffer:
> I was genuinely surprised and pleased when Mr. Robert Haas gave me the original drawing for the jacket of my new book, with your gracious inscription. I am taking it home with me and will hang it in a niche of its own in my workroom. It's a gift that I shall treasure.
> Thank you very much.
> Sincerely,
> William Faulkner[51]

The deferential, respectful tone of this letter suggests that Faulkner knew Kauffer's stature even if he had not met him personally. And while it is possible that Mary Barber composed the letter, at the very least Faulkner signed and approved it. With this gesture, Faulkner's and Kauffer's social circles, and their professional ones, converge.

The original cover art for Faulkner's "new book" that Kauffer presents to Faulkner is for *Requiem for a Nun* (see Figure 5). This first edition cover features as many as five colors (black, brown, blue, yellow, and white, where some colors may result from overlap) and represents in its central image Alexander Holston's giant fifteen-pound lock from the novel's long opening prologue. The lock is affixed to the roughly hewn wooden log door of the jail. In drawing the reader's focus to the cool blue metal of the lock, sited between the brightly visible wood freshly augured and the shadowy dark metal plate attached to the wood that wraps around the book's spine, Kauffer takes as his subject not only a

$3.00

REQUIEM

FOR A NUN

BY

WILLIAM FAULKNER

A RANDOM HOUSE BOOK

REQUIEM
for a NUN

by WILLIAM FAULKNER

The new novel by the 1950 winner of the Nobel Prize for literature is one of the most notable achievements of William Faulkner's distinguished career. In form a startling departure from his previous nineteen books, it marks yet another advance in his powers as a story-teller and chronicler of his people and his time. *Requiem for a Nun* reaffirms William Faulkner's almost undisputed position as the most renowned novelist in the world today.

Jacket design by M. McKnight Kauffer

RANDOM HOUSE, INC.
Publishers of The American College Dictionary *and* The Modern Library

Fig. 5. First edition Modern Library dust jacket of *Requiem for a Nun* by E. McKnight Kauffer (1951). Copyright © Simon Rendall. Courtesy of Penguin Random House LLC

representational object that appears in Faulkner's book but, more importantly, the symbolic power of that object. The lock functions first of all as advertising lure to the new reader, suggesting that the book contains secrets and something valuable that will be disclosed. It connotes as well a diary, whose secrets of confession are locked to voyeuristic eyes, thus bringing the keyhole and lock in dialogue with *Sanctuary*'s cover's emphasis on knotholes for peeping. For the reader who knows *Sanctuary* and expects its sequel in this book, the lock wraps a chastity belt around *Requiem*'s Temple/temple and its nun.

Faulkner's "monster lock" in Kauffer's hands is as mobile and elusive as the actual lock to which it refers in Faulkner's sleight-of-hand prose.

After all, the characteristic of this lock in Faulkner's opening section is precisely that it is not a lock at all: it fails to keep people in or out of the mailbags or jail doors to which it is affixed and itself gets stolen and needs to be accounted and paid for. As a symbol, only in absence can the lock stand for civilization and law and order, just as its theft and the inability to compensate its worth will require that a courthouse be built to adjudicate such matters, leading to a name and a proper founding for the town. The whole world of Faulkner's Jefferson, as we are first told in the dust jacket image and then in the opening section of the novel, will be built upon the foundation of this missing lock. Moreover, we learn that the lock breaks the law, since to attach it is to violate and even to presume the violability of the very morality and ethics it is supposed to uphold and protect. It is upon this paradox that Faulkner's novel-play opens, a paradox that Kauffer's cover art rehearses in simultaneously locking and unlocking the book for potential readers.

Why would Kauffer contact Faulkner and give him the original cover art for this novel? We can only speculate. As we have seen, Cerf had wooed Nonesuch and Kauffer and Commins had praised Kauffer's cover art, so perhaps Faulkner and Kauffer had actually met at some point. Perhaps he just liked Faulkner's work. But then again, perhaps the gift had something to do with the quality of Random House's postwar bookmaking and some desire to appeal to the author directly, as his real client. For on the first printing of the first edition dust jacket of *Requiem for a Nun*, there was an error: Kauffer's name was listed as "M." rather than "E." McKnight Kauffer. Such a typo of its celebrated cover artist's name by Random House on a first edition surely rankled; it inadvertently caricatures the dust jacket artist as something less than a real artist with a name that matters enough to reproduce correctly. Kauffer did not see dust jacket work as a lesser art. He saw it as bookmaking, all serious art and craft; he was careful to sign and sometimes even date his art, as he had on the *Sanctuary* cover for Modern Library in 1940.[52] He believed in the integrity of his production and in the artist's right to proper compensation and acknowledgement for his creation. Together, the lock that embraces Faulkner's *Requiem for a Nun* and the letter from Faulkner thanking Kauffer for his original work mark an exchange between artists, subverting the chain of mass production that isolates artists from the material conditions of their artistic labor.

Art and commerce intersect in relays of parody and homage that create intimate circles as well as those exaggerated for public performance. Such exchanges structure the circuits in which Faulkner and his work moved among artists and writers. The crossed artistic spheres of Kauffer and Faulkner raise questions about high modernist commercial alliances

in advertising and art but also about advertising's self-conscious cooptation of high art and literature for its own elevation. In ways all too predictable now, advertising's cooptation of modernist art has increasingly
functioned as parody of art's pretensions rather than tribute to its prestige. And yet, in redrawing the frames of literary criticism to encompass
the production and material culture of print, as this volume and much
recent scholarship in modernist literary studies do, critics engage, and
may even undermine, such cooptation. By probing how books get made
and sold at every level, critics draw themselves into circles of affiliation and allegiance with diverse artists and individuals involved in bookmaking. Even when distorted under the bell jar of celebrity, politics, or
ambition, Faulkner's illustrious circles speak doubly: to the business of
making a living in the public eye as much as to the need to form sup-
portive artistic coteries and networks.

NOTES

Research for this article was possible thanks to the generosity of the Lillian Gary
Taylor Fellowship in American Literature at the Albert and Shirley Small Special
Collections at the University of Virginia and the support of the Virginia Foundation for
the Humanities in the summer of 2015. Special thanks to emerita professor Carolyn
Porter at the University of California, Berkeley; Chris Rieger of the Center for Faulkner
Studies at Southeast Missouri State University; Brandon Westerheim of the New York
Public Library; George Riser, Hoke Perkins, Molly Schwartzburg, and Steve Railton at
the University of Virginia; Andrew Gardner and Caitlin Condell, assistant curators at
the Cooper Hewitt, Smithsonian Design Museum; Simon Rendall of the E. McKnight
Kauffer estate; Grace Schulman; Graham Tremlow; Maria Elena Rico y Covarrubias
of the Covarrubias estate; Mavis H. Baird of the Baird estate; Edith Blanchard at the
Charles H. MacNider Art Museum; and Reid Echols and Chelsea Weathers at the Harry
Ransom Center, University of Texas, Austin.

    1. Joseph Blotner, *Faulkner: A Biography*, vol. 1 (New York: Random House, 1974),
262–71. The "Count" was what the parodist in the *Mississippian* called Faulkner and what
Ben Wasson would adapt in the title of his reminiscences of Faulkner, *Count No 'Count:
Flashbacks to Faulkner* (Jackson: University Press of Mississippi, 1983). "Afternoon of a
Cow" also appears in Joseph Blotner, ed., *Uncollected Stories of William Faulkner* (New
York: Random House, 1979), 424–34, accompanied by an endnote on its fascinating oral
and publication history. According to Blotner's note, Maurice Coindreau heard the story
at the 1937 dinner, received the manuscript from Faulkner the next day as a gift, and went
on to publish it in French in Algiers in 1943 since publications by Americans were banned
in German-occupied France. It appeared in English first in *Furioso* 2 (Summer 1947):
5, 8–10, 13, 16–17. Dean Faulkner Wells, ed., *The Best of Bad Faulkner* (San Diego:
Harcourt Brace Jovanovich, 1991), collects Faulkner's "Afternoon of a Cow" as well as
such posthumously penned parodies of his style as Peter DeVries's "Requiem for a Noun,
or Intruder in the Dusk" and winners from the annual Faux Faulkner contest sponsored
(initially) by American Airlines and by Wells, Faulkner's niece.

2. Blotner notes that "in February 1939, working on part 2, Chapter One, of 'The Long Summer,' Book Three of *The Hamlet*, Faulkner apparently thought back to this story and appropriated elements of it for the mock chivalric romantic treatment of Ike Snopes's love for Jack Houston's cow" (Blotner, ed., *Uncollected Stories*, 702–3).

3. Bennett Cerf quoted in Lise Jaillant, *Modernism, Middlebrow and the Literary Canon* (London: Pickering & Chatto, 2014), 131.

4. We might understand this methodology in the language of Édouard Glissant, who suggests that scholars would do well to consider "mutual influence or confluence" and "abolish the arrow-like trajectory of influence" if they wish to better weigh "the equivalencies of relation." See Édouard Glissant, *Poetics of Relation*, trans. Betsy Wing (Ann Arbor: University of Michigan Press, 2006), 31, and Annette Trefzer, introduction to *Global Faulkner: Faulkner and Yoknapatawpha, 2006*, ed. Annette Trefzer and Ann J. Abadie (Jackson: University Press of Mississippi, 2009), ix.

5. William Faulkner, *Sanctuary* (New York: Modern Library, 1932). Hereafter cited parenthetically.

6. Panthea Reid Broughton, "The Cubist Novel: Toward Defining the Genre," in *"A Cosmos of My Own": Faulkner and Yoknapatawpha, 1980*, ed. Evans Harrington and Ann J. Abadie (Jackson: University of Mississippi Press, 1981), 36–58; Carvel Collins, introduction to *William Faulkner: New Orleans Sketches*, ed. Carvel Collins (New Brunswick, NJ: Rutgers University Press, 1958), xi–xxxiv; M. Thomas Inge, "Faulkner Reads the Funny Papers," in *Faulkner and Humor: Faulkner and Yoknapatawpha, 1984*, ed. Doreen Fowler and Ann J. Abadie (Jackson: University Press of Mississippi, 1986), 153–90; Candace Waid, *The Signifying Eye: Seeing Faulkner's Art* (Athens: University of Georgia Press, 2013).

7. Carvel Collins, ed., *William Faulkner: New Orleans Sketches* (New Brunswick, NJ: Rutgers University Press, 1958).

8. See Joseph Blotner, ed., *Selected Letters of William Faulkner* (New York: Vintage, 1978), 44, 71.

9. As Cerf explained in an interview in 1967, "What I loved about William Faulkner—it was true till the day of his death—was his firm belief that the author wrote the book and the publisher published it, unlike many authors who come in and tell you what jacket they want and what color binding, what advertising campaign, and where you should advertise. They pester the hell out of you from beginning to end. Faulkner would come in and give me a manuscript and I'd say, 'Bill, don't you want to talk about how the book should come out and how we should advertise it?' And Bill would say, 'Bennett, that's your job. If I didn't think you did it well, I'd go somewhere else.'" Robin Hawkins, interview with Bennett Cerf (1967, 1968), transcripts session 7, page 327, Columbia University Libraries Oral History Research Office, http://www.columbia.edu/cu/lweb/digital/collections/nny /cerfb/index.html (accessed February 24, 2016).

10. Blotner, ed., *Selected Letters of William Faulkner*, 38.

11. This has been the case ever since the modern dust jacket became popular and essential from the 1920s on as a selling tool and not just for protection of the physical book.

12. For the Joyce cover designed by Kauffer in 1946, which finds echoes in his jacket for Faulkner's *Light in August* (New York: Modern Library, 1955), and for an excellent brief biography of Kauffer and examples of his poster art mentioned elsewhere in this essay, see Steven Heller, "E. McKnight Kauffer: A Biography" (1992), AIGA, http://www .aiga.org/medalist-emcknightkauffer (accessed January 27, 2016). John Updike considered Kauffer's *Ulysses* cover the most "legible" of its modern American dust jackets. See John Updike, "Deceptively Conceptual," *New Yorker*, October 17, 2005, http://www.newyorker .com/magazine/2005/10/17/deceptively-conceptual (accessed April 2, 2015).

13. See Jay Satterfield's essay in this volume for more on Bennett Cerf's irrepressible character and legacy in publishing.

14. Judith Sensibar, *The Origins of Faulkner's Art* (Austin: University of Texas Press, 1984); Lothar Hönnighausen, *William Faulkner: The Art of Stylization in His Early Graphic and Literary Work* (Cambridge: Cambridge University Press, 1987).

15. This mock-*Salome* cover was drawn by Olive Leonhardt, an artist who would spend time in Mexico with fellow *Double Dealer* contributor Natalie Scott and who knew Spratling. It can be seen on the Encyclopedia of Louisiana online site, http://www.knowla.org/image/442/&view=summary (accessed February 24, 2016). I thank Gay Leonhardt for insights into her grandmother's New Orleans and Mexico circles. For colorful stories of the Pelican Bookshop and *Double Dealer* crowd that Faulkner moved in, including New York editors, writers, and publishers who made periodic forays to New Orleans, see Shelby Foote, "Bohemians and Shenanigans in the 1920s French Quarter: An Excerpt from *Dixie Bohemia*," *Southern Cultures* 19, no. 2 (Summer 2013): 32–51; John Shelton Reed, *Dixie Bohemia: A French Quarter Circle in the 1920s* (Baton Rouge: Louisiana State University Press, 2012); and W. Kenneth Holditch, "William Spratling, William Faulkner, and Other Famous Creoles," *Mississippi Quarterly* 51, no. 3 (Summer 1998): 423–31.

16. See Blotner, ed., *Selected Letters of William Faulkner*, 32, 49.

17. Quoted in Regina Barreca, introduction to *Gentlemen Prefer Blondes* and *But Gentlemen Marry Brunettes*, by Anita Loos (New York: Penguin Classics, 1998), xii.

18. Anita Loos, *Gentlemen Prefer Blondes* and *But Gentlemen Marry Brunettes* (New York: Penguin Classics, 1998), 127.

19. Blotner, ed., *Selected Letters of William Faulkner*, 32.

20. See William Jay Smith, *The Spectra Hoax* (Middletown, CT: Wesleyan University Press, 1961), esp. "Anne Knish's" Preface, 77–79.

21. Suzanne W. Churchill, "The Lying Game: *Others* and the Great Spectra Hoax of 1917," *American Periodicals: A Journal of History, Criticism, and Bibliography* 15, no. 1 (2005): 23–41.

22. Cited by Barreca, introduction, xi. In a letter to Harriet Shaw Weaver, Joyce famously wrote that he had been "reclining on a sofa and reading *Gentlemen Prefer Blondes* for three whole days." James Joyce, *Letters of James Joyce*, vol. 1, ed. Stuart Gilbert (New York: Viking, 1957), 246.

23. Sherwood Anderson, "A Meeting South," *Dial* 78 (April 1925): 269–79.

24. William Faulkner, "Artist at Home," *Collected Stories of William Faulkner* (New York: Random House, 1950), 627. The story was originally composed around 1931, according to Blotner's biography, and first published in *Story*, August 1933, 27–41.

25. William Spratling and William Faulkner, *Sherwood Anderson and Other Famous Creoles* (New Orleans: Pelican Bookshop, 1926), n.p.

26. Virginia Woolf, "American Fiction," *Saturday Review of Literature*, August 1, 1925, 1–3.

27. Spratling and Faulkner, *Sherwood Anderson*, n.p. See the caricature of the architect Nathaniel C. Curtis, who appears as a face in profile on a coin from which a watering can dangles, with the caption "Irrigator of the Sahara of the Bozart."

28. Adriana Williams, *Covarrubias* (Austin: University of Texas Press, 1994); Susan Danly, "The Morrows in Mexico: A Pictorial Essay," *Hopscotch: A Cultural Review* 2, no. 4 (2001): 86–107.

29. Unlike little literary magazines like the *Double Dealer*, the "slicks" included magazines like *Vanity Fair*, the *New Yorker*, *Esquire*, and *Vogue*. See David M. Earle, *Re-Covering Modernism: Pulps, Paperbacks, and the Prejudice of Form* (Burlington, VT:

Ashgate, 2009). Earle's first chapter is a particularly rich treatment of Mencken's divided artistic and commercial energies between literary and pulp magazines.

30. This parody first appeared in *Vanity Fair* but without Covarrubias's sketch. Faulkner's letter to Ben Wasson assures him, "I liked Corey's takeoff fine. I enjoyed it a lot. I want to write him, but I have been and am busy as I can be getting this thing typed. Explain to him and tell him how much we both liked it. When I get caught up, I think I will write some John Riddell in the style of Faulkner." Blotner, ed., *Selected Letters of William Faulkner*, 61.

31. Blotner, *Faulkner: A Biography*, 973–74.

32. Eric Devine, *Down the Hatch* (New York: Sheridan House, 1945). This is a book of "gay yachting yarns," sailing stories, illustrated by Alden McWilliams with jacket design by Bil Baird.

33. Faulkner wrote to Estelle in November 1931 from New York:

> I have created quite a sensation. I have had luncheons in my honor by magazine editors every day for a week now, besides evening parties, or people who want to see what I look like. In fact, I have learned with astonishment that I am now the most important figure in American letters. That is, I have the best future. Even Sinclair Lewis and Dreiser make engagements to see me, and Mencken is coming all the way up from Baltimore to see me on Wednesday. (Blotner, ed. *Selected Letters of William Faulkner*, 53)

34. As cited in Helen Southworth, *The Intersecting Realities and Fictions of Virginia Woolf and Colette* (Columbus: Ohio State University Press, 2004), 135.

35. Nate Evuarherhe, "Borrowed Aesthetics: E. McKnight Kauffer, Book Jacket Design and the Avant-Garde," *Art in Print* 5, no. 2 (July–August 2015), https://artinprint .org/article/borrowed-aesthetics-e-mcknight-kauffer-book-jacket-design-and-the-avant -garde (accessed February 24, 1016). For insights into Kauffer's aesthetics by a woman who knew him personally and an expert on his artistic techniques, respectively, see Grace Schulman, "Marianne Moore and E. McKnight Kauffer: Two Characteristic Americans," *Twentieth Century Literature* 30, nos. 2–3 (1984): 175–80, and Graham Twemlow, "E. McKnight Kauffer—The Stencilled Book Illustrations," *Parenthesis* 16 (February 2009): 32–34.

36. Roger Fry, "The Author and the Artist," *Burlington Magazine*, July 1926, quoted in Helen Southworth, "Bloomsbury and the Book Arts," in *The Cambridge Companion to the Bloomsbury Group*, ed. Victoria Rosner (Cambridge: Cambridge University Press, 2014), 155–56. In a wonderful description of the exchanges between the visual and the written word, Fry also writes that book illustration is "a battle ground, a no-man's land raked by alternate fires from the artist and the writer, claimed by both, sometimes nearly conquered by one, but only to be half recaptured by the other." Quoted in Southworth, *Intersecting Realities*, 155.

37. E. McKnight Kauffer, "Advertising Art Now: An Address Given at the Art Directors Club of New York," *A-D Magazine* 2, no. 8 (December–January, 1941–1942): 1–16.

38. See Jaillant's chapter on the divisive role the introduction has played in the advertising and critical reception of *Sanctuary*: "'If It's Like Any Introduction You Ever Read, I'll Eat the Jacket': Faulkner's *Sanctuary*, the Modern Library and the Literary Canon," in *Modernism*, 123–44. Jaillant also notes that withdrawing authorial introductions in this fashion is a rare event, suggesting that we must pay as much attention to that act as to what Faulkner meant to say and do with the introduction itself. I'm grateful to Jay Satterfield for steering me to Jaillant's book.

39. Noel Polk, *Sanctuary: The Original Text* (New York: Random House, 1981). See also Polk, "The Space between *Sanctuary*," in *William Faulkner's Sanctuary: Modern Critical Interpretations*, ed. Harold Bloom (New York: Chelsea House, 1988), 103–20.

40. James G. Watson, *William Faulkner: Self-Representation and Performance* (Austin: University of Texas Press, 2000), 85–86.

41. Lawrence H. Schwartz, *Creating Faulkner's Reputation: The Politics of Modern Literary Criticism* (Knoxville: University of Tennessee Press, 1988); Earle, *Re-Covering Modernism*; Jaillant, *Modernism*. Despite being indebted to pulps for survival in print, Faulkner's letters reveal him more than once making fun of the lurid covers and cheap paper of paperbacks on display at his local store, marking the difference between him as a "book author" and those who wrote paperbacks and journalism: "The magazine store here carries nothing that has not either a woman in her underclothes or someone shooting someone else with a pistol on the cover; that includes newspapers, too." Faulkner to Mr. Chase of Harcourt Brace Jovanovich, April 13, 1929, in Blotner, ed., *Selected Letters of William Faulkner*, 43.

42. Jaillant notes that "scholars of the middlebrow . . . [argue] with Jaime Harker that 'modernism' is a critical construction that cannot account for the entire range of writing and authorship in the interwar period" (*Modernism*, 149), and Jaillant herself insists that the "blurring of cultural categories [high, middle, low] typical of the interwar period is also a feature of our present time" (143). See Jaime Harker, *America the Middlebrow: Women's Novels, Progressivism, and Middlebrow Authorship between the Wars* (Amherst: University of Massachusetts Press, 2007).

43. Mark Haworth-Booth, *E. McKnight Kauffer: A Designer and His Public* (London: V&A Publications, 2005), 99.

44. Cover illustrators also had to limit their colors for cost reasons on the publisher's side.

45. From the time that Temple Drake experiences the car crash until she leaves in the car with Popeye for Memphis, few commas slow her frantic pace: "Still running her bones turned to water and she fell flat on her face, still running." Faulkner, *Sanctuary*, 44.

46. At different times and for different editions, both Kauffer and Covarrubias suggested drawings for Van Vechten's cover and illustrations to *Nigger Heaven*, for instance, although Aaron Douglas produced the artwork for the novel's first edition in 1926.

47. Frances Steloff, "In Touch with Genius," *Journal of Modern Literature* 4, no. 4 (April 1975): 749–887, esp. 824–26 on Kauffer.

48. See Jay Satterfield, *The World's Best Books: Taste, Culture, and the Modern Library* (Amherst: University of Massachusetts Press, 2002). For more on Kauffer's relationship with Nonesuch, which began in 1919 when Meynell purchased Kauffer's famous Vorticist/Cubist poster, "Flight," for the *Daily Herald*, see Francis Meynell's autobiography, *My Lives* (London: Bodley Head, 1971), esp. 167–69.

49. Francis Meynell to Bennett Cerf, January 18, 1927, Random House Archives, Rare Book and Manuscript Library, Columbia University, New York. Meynell approves of Cerf's choice of Kauffer's illustrated *Benito Cereno* as a "good starter" for their new arrangement with Modern Library/Random House as Nonesuch's exclusive US distributor.

50. Regarding the dust jacket for *Intruder in the Dust*, see Saxe Commins to William Faulkner, September 3, 1948, Erskine Papers, William Faulkner Correspondence, Albert and Shirley Small Special Collections Library, University of Virginia. Commins writes, "I particularly like the jacket, done by MacKnight Kauffer [sic], and I hope you approve of the copy I wrote."

51. After contacting assistant curator Caitlin Condell and working closely with curatorial assistant Andrew Gardner, I learned of this previous sketch for *Sanctuary's* cover and this uncatalogued letter in the E. McKnight Kauffer archives of the Cooper Hewitt,

Smithsonian Design Museum in New York. This same letter is also in the Albert and Shirley Small Special Collections at the University of Virginia as a carbon copy without Faulkner's signature.

52. The only thing to have changed between the 1932 *Sanctuary* edition and the 1940 edition was Kauffer's dust jacket and possibly the correction of some misspellings that were gradually, and quietly, inserted into new printings of the book throughout the 1930s. It is worth noting here that, had Kauffer not dated his cover design for *Sanctuary*, we would have had a hard time establishing a date for the 1940 edition.

Faulkner's First Biographers: Early Notices

CARL ROLLYSON

"The mysterious man from Mississippi cat-footed off the coastwise steamer Mallory at dawn today and ducked into a taxi."[1] The *New York World-Telegram* profile, "William Faulkner, 'Literary Hope' from Mississippi Likens Himself in City to a 'Houn' Dawg under a Wagon,'" published in 1931, presented an enigma, a man who said he had one friend in the North, one man he liked. What did the press and the first major profiles make of this startling writer? How did those early notices shape our vision of an artist biographers are still trying to comprehend? And how did Faulkner comport himself in the literary marketplace? Did what he said to a newspaper reporter reflect a ploy, a persona? He had seen enough of the world to decide how to calculate his words in the newspaper-driven media of the day, with local papers picking up stories about writers and what they said.

The dog under a wagon quip—what we might call a sound bite now—ran in regional newspapers, such as the *Iola Register* (November 5) in Kansas. Faulkner actually used the term "spring wagon," which I had to look up: "an important vehicle in the late horse-drawn era. Built with two removable seats, its practicality made it popular both in rural areas and in cities and towns where, with a single seat, it served as a business wagon. Many spring-wagons had fringed, canopy tops."[2] I guess that in 1931 most people still knew what a spring wagon was. At any rate, employing the term was certainly a good way to cultivate the image of a down-home country boy who had nothing whatsoever to do with the highfalutin literary world. If he cat-footed his way through New York, he was shunning the very publicity that a newspaper profile provided but still exciting readers with the idea that the stealthy author had been exposed—if only briefly. Early on, whether he intended to do so or not, Faulkner was following the Cary Grant rule of stardom: always play the role of the pursued, not the pursuer. So he appears in Anthony Buttitta's memory of the fall of 1931, after *Sanctuary* became a sensation: "Publishers who had turned him down on previous books were flashing contracts in his face. It made Bill dizzy. He fled south."[3]

In the column My New York, James Aswell often reprinted little bits of widely distributed but erroneous information, such as this item from the *New Castle News* (August 8, 1931) in Pennsylvania: "On the wall of the publishers, Jonathan Cape and Harrison Smith, in 46th Street, there is a famed manuscript page from 'The Sound and the Fury,' By William Faulkner, who laboriously PRINTED every word because he was to [sic] poor to employ a typist."[4] Faulkner's poverty and aversion to urban life were staples in the columns written about him.

In the November 4, 1931, issue of the *New Castle News*, Aswell related another anecdote that left me puzzled for a few minutes:

> The story told by William Faulkner, latest literary lion of the cognoscenti, about the guy touring a nut house and being convinced that one of the inmates was sane. "Sure I'm sane. Getting out tomorrow in fact. . . . Relatives wanted my money but they've repented and got me free. . . . A job? I'm a certified public accountant and have training as a civil engineer. Then I had a year of newspaper work. But"—with a grin—"if the worst comes to worst, I can always be a teapot!"

A teapot? After exercising my masterful command of Google, I lighted upon that elderly countrywoman often depicted wearing a peasant costume, Mother Goose:

> *I'm a little teapot*
> *Short and stout*
> *Here is my handle*
> *Here is my spout.*
> *When I get all steamed up*
> *Hear me shout*
> *"Tip me over*
> *and pour me out!"*

It is a delightful contrast, the "latest literary lion" alluding not to James Joyce—who was often linked with Faulkner in the press—but to a children's nursery rhyme. This Faulkner was not modern at all, but rather a throwback to the nineteenth century. Others might tout his avant-garde bona fides, but Faulkner quite carefully shunned a modernist pedigree.

What happens to hound dogs under wagons? Are they run over? Certainly they are vulnerable, as Faulkner might well have felt he was amidst the onrush of New York City. Hal Smith was his one northern friend. Two years earlier, on February 15, 1929, William Harcourt had written to Faulkner, "A couple of us have read it [*The Sound and the Fury*] with mingled admiration and doubts as to whether its unusual qualities could find a profitable market. Hal Smith dropped in this morning and explained to us that you brought it in for his personal opinion and not with the idea of regularly submitting it to Harcourt, Brace and Company." Harcourt said he was returning the manuscript to Smith and that Faulkner would hear from Smith directly. Three days later, Faulkner replied to Harcourt: "About the Sound & Fury ms. That is all right. I did not believe that anyone would publish it; I had no definite plan to submit it to anyone. I told Hal about it once and he dared me to bring it to him. . . . I am sorry it did not go over with you all, but I will not say I did not expect the result."[5] So Faulkner stood alone, seeming not at all troubled that he had only one friend. His manners were impeccable and impregnable. If he felt any disappointment, Alfred Harcourt would be the last to know about it. Faulkner was no longer "a vestal in the field of professional lit," addressing himself to "you folks in the publishing business," as he put it to Horace Liveright in 1927.[6]

In 1931 Faulkner, a neophyte no more, appeared regularly in the New York papers, often referred by way of Arnold Bennett's salute. Part of a review of *Soldiers' Pay* that appeared in the *London Evening Standard* on June 26, 1930, read, "Faulkner is the coming man. He has inexhaustible invention, powerful imagination, a wondrous gift of characterization, a finished skill in dialogue, and he writes, generally, like an angel. None of the arrived American stars can surpass him in style when he is at his best."[7] Bennett's encomium often got reduced to "writes like an angel." Bennett, a highly regarded novelist and respected book reviewer, could not have given Faulkner a better calling card.

By temperament—which can also mean by design—Faulkner withheld himself, like the dog that you could coax out from under that wagon "just a little bit, but not too far," Faulkner told Evelyn Seeley, the *New York World-Telegram* staff writer. It is often the case with writers that they withdraw from public attention after achieving fame. But in Faulkner's case, the withdrawal began when he first appeared in the public media. To Seeley, he added his hometown druggist (Mac Reed) to the southern-northern axis of his literary life. Faulkner said he could not stand literary groups or bear consorting with other writers. "Faulkner in Seclusion, Writing Movie Script," the *Memphis Press-Scimitar* reported on December 1, 1931. "The reason I'm going to New York," Estelle Faulkner told Marshall Smith, the *Press-Scimitar* reporter, "is to keep people away from him." Faulkner was then working on the twenty-eighth floor of an apartment building, where he "could forget the noise, and see the sun and sky."[8]

Literary life meant city life and was just so much "noise" to William Faulkner. And the noise got louder once he had published the notorious *Sanctuary*. "William Faulkner Rakes up Human Garbage to Fashion a Powerful Magnum Opus," ran the headline in the *Brooklyn Daily Eagle* on April 1, 1931. The reviewer sold the book in the first paragraph, announcing that the author had "assembled the gloomiest elements of social decay to be found in the South, but with a masterful restraint has whipped them into one of the most powerful heartrending novels of the past ten years."[9] A March 15 column in the same paper had labeled the novel "melodramatic" and "gruesome," and then added, "but maybe you like things like that."[10] A May 31 story in the *Daily Eagle* about a cruise to France reported that a "hard boiled newspaperman . . . shuddering and feeling degraded" threw *Sanctuary* into the sea. The novel received twice as many reviews as any of Faulkner's previous books and raised the ante of his literary career,[11] catapulting him into his first sojourn in Hollywood and into a reading public larger and more diversified than his earlier poetry and fiction had attracted.

I've chosen the year 1931 to measure the parameters of Faulkner's early biography as reported in newspapers. I'm interested in him as "news" in a time when writers still made the front pages of the dailies, as Faulkner did in the *Brooklyn Daily Eagle* on December 14, appearing as the first item in a column titled Odd and Interesting: "William Faulkner is the newest literary light for whose first editions collectors are scrambling." Faulkner regularly appeared in the *Eagle*'s book gossip columns as the master of "frank decadence" (July 22) and as a recluse who rarely ventured among the literati. In the *New York Times* (February 15, 1931), John Chamberlain called him "Dostoyefsky's Shadow in the Deep South."

Fragments of Faulkner biography filtered through the press: "William Faulkner, who wrote *Sanctuary*, had a great-grand pappy who wrote fiction about the glorious old south. One such effort was *The White Rose of Memphis*, which some authors rewrite at stated intervals even yet," the *Illinois Daily Illini* reported on August 7. On May 31, the same newspaper carried a review of *Sanctuary* by E. David Levitin: "Another novel by the only American who received the distinction of being denounced by J. B. Priestley in the latter's recent lecture here! *Sanctuary* is a typical Faulkner book, possibly somewhat more filthy than usual, a little crazier, but all in all a good deal like his other creations, wild, passionate, beautiful, but slimy, gory, overly realistic."[12]

I confess I was looking for reviews and articles that specifically linked Faulkner's books to his personality, and Levitin did not disappoint: "Created out of the personality of Faulkner, perhaps, they may justify

Priestley's assertion that Faulkner is in need of medical attention. Personally, I cannot see that this objection, even if true, is anything against his work. Do we object to Dostoieveski on the ground that the morals of a dementia praecox are detrimental to our youth?"

In fact, the *Illinois Daily Illini* had published a review of *Sanctuary* written by a female undergraduate, Mary Morris, on March 15:

> Do you recall how often you have begun to read a book which so fascinated you that you plunged through the intricacies of its plot to an unknown but magnetic ending? And when late at night you closed the last cover as you breathed a sigh of relief that the heroine was saved from a perilous attack? I have done just that. But, this time, when I finished *Sanctuary*, it was different. I didn't have a feeling of relief because the heroine had not been saved. I didn't have a feeling of assurance. Rather, I closed the last cover slowly as I realized that the book contained more than the mere words of black print on white pages, that the book contained a potent drug for the imagination—that the book would never be finished by reading the final word but would require a tallying of events before finding out just exactly what had occurred. *Sanctuary* is different. I read bits of it aloud to my roommate and we were both caught in the whirlwind of its spell and swept along. I couldn't cease reading—she couldn't cease listening. My throat became dry; my eyes blurred; before I knew it, I had read SO many pages aloud.[13]

We might as well be in that dormitory room with Quentin and Shreve!

This coed's response to *Sanctuary* suggests that Faulkner attracted a much broader and more understanding audience of readers than the professional reviewers of his work had the capacity to imagine. Like Shreve in *Absalom, Absalom!*, she is caught up in the story and wants to share it. She is familiar with conventional popular stories and is aware of how far Faulkner departs from women's domestic fiction. She does not call Faulkner gruesome, sordid, or crazy. Instead she welcomes his deviation from the norms established by the mainstream print media. She has no concern with the morality of the novel over which critics fretted. What captures her, instead, is the work's compelling style. Her reading of the novel may be outside the range of most early responses to the text and to Faulkner, but it is just as likely that he was beginning to attract readers whose experience of the fiction was not represented in the public prints. At the same time, she shows why the novel became a best seller—not simply because it was sensationalistic in its treatment of sex and crime but because it was gripping in a way the readers of popular fiction demanded. If reviewers recoiled from certain scenes in *Sanctuary*, they might have been having the kind of visceral reaction that this coed valued for its own sake.

Sanctuary put Faulkner under much greater scrutiny, and when pressed by a *New York Herald Tribune* interviewer, his first reaction was truculence. "Mr. Faulkner hates interviews, hates being asked questions," read a piece headlined "Slavery Better for the Negro, Says Faulkner."[14] Millgate and Meriwether suggest that an offended Faulkner assumed "a tone of deadpan, hostile irony" as a defense against "invasions of his privacy."[15] As the narrator of *Absalom, Absalom!* might say, Millgate's and Meriwether's observation may be "true enough," but this is also the Faulkner who wrote *Flags in the Dust*, in which the Negro characters—as they would have been called then—are presented with a somewhat paternalistic air not entirely out of keeping with the Faulkner who told the *Herald Tribune* that he pictured "a kind of 'benevolent autocracy' as the ideal condition for the Negroes."[16]

Although Meriwether and Millgate seem to be right—that long before the publication of *Sanctuary*, Faulkner had "developed various defenses against invasions of his privacy," and that these defenses remained remarkably consistent throughout his career—his comment about slavery reflects, it seems to me, a writer who had not yet fully come to terms with what it meant to be a public man.[17] Or to put it another way, he had not reached the moment when he believed that what he said made a difference or mattered a damn.

Certainly, Faulkner did not mind repeating tales about his World War I exploits, going "into action in France," crashing a plane, and in one account "hanging upside down in his plane with both legs broken."[18] These comments all appear in interviews conducted in 1931, long after the war was over and after, one might suppose, Faulkner had any need to aggrandize his modest and very brief military adventure. Meriwether and Millgate suggest that these "errors," as they delicately phrase it, are "presumably" the result of a "certain amount of enjoyment" on Faulkner's part and served as a measure of "how well privacy had been preserved."[19] But other motivations may well have been at work, including Faulkner's need, right from the beginning of his writing career, to project himself and his work on a world stage—even as he shaped his own person into a comic, almost Chaplinesque figure, as if to bridle his braggadocio.[20] Here is his *Bookman* interview rendition of his biography, one that reads like so many title cards in a silent film scenario: "Quit school and went to work in grandfather's bank. Learned the medicinal value of liquor. Grandfather thought it was the janitor. Hard on janitor. War came. Liked British uniform. Got commission R.F.C. pilot. Crashed. Cost British government 2000 pounds. Quit. Cost British government $84.30. King said, 'Well done.' Returned to Mississippi."[21] Interviewer Marshall Smith, Faulkner's straight man, immediately follows up with the blunt statement, "The war hurt Faulkner. It took him time to recover."[22]

The "hurt Faulkner" first showed up, as James G. Watson observes, in those 1918 snapshots of the returning war-weary veteran. "Like the letters that preceded them, these snapshots give information whose value, as Susan Sontag has said of photographs, 'is of the same order as fiction.'"[23] And it took Faulkner over a decade to finally drop this Chaplinesque pose as he geared up to function in the post-*Sanctuary* world of publicity—soon to be complicated by his sojourns in Hollywood.

Faulkner's disparaging comments about Hollywood and about the press (note that in his joke, the man in the asylum spent a year as a journalist) mask his own fascination with the age of mechanical reproduction, as Walter Benjamin termed it. Watson calls attention to the "Faulknerian mode of self-making . . . and his recurrent metaphors for himself extended from one medium to another." Watson notes, for example, Faulkner's description of his "tanned face and sun-faded hair as looking like 'a kodak negative.'"[24] One of Faulkner's favorite photographers, J. R. Cofield, remembered that "cameras always did fascinate him. I never took a shot that he was not at my elbow taking in the complete picture."[25] This attitude reminds me of another one of my subjects, Marilyn Monroe, who never passed up the chance to learn something from a photographer. This reciprocal process—the give-and-take of self-projection, using a medium as a means of self-expression—defines Faulkner as well. While working in Hollywood he could not resist replaying his war stories for Meta Carpenter, even as he worked on war stories for Howard Hawks.

And yet the Faulkner persona in 1931, and for the rest of his life, hinged on his disaffection with fame, although the evidence of his early letters suggests an acute awareness of fame—even if he presents that obsession as comedy. "Oh, yes. I have already stopped traffic in the streets," he writes from Yale to his parents. "Fame, in fact, has lighted early upon my furrowed brow."[26] Fame, in fact, takes him unawares as he is lectured by a traffic cop for failing to heed a stop sign, escaping one car that almost ran over his feet, while another brushes the "skirts of my coat, while a trolley nearly clips his hat brim."[27] As James G. Watson observes, the sense of timing in this letter is cinematic, making me wonder about that cat-footing Faulkner who is supposedly dodging attention. Isn't nimbleness itself a sign of his media-savvy sensibility?

Although Faulkner often treated the press as his nemesis, journalists did their part in fashioning the effigy the writer made of himself, and Faulkner put them in his stories—for example "Evangeline," one of the important precursors of *Absalom, Absalom!* Indeed, Joseph Blotner speculates that Faulkner's encounter with Marshall J. Smith, the Memphis journalist cited earlier in this essay, may have inspired the writing of "Evangeline."[28] Smith approached what he called "a new luminary in the South, in the very darkest part of the South," looking for "an author whose interest was in idiocy, rape, suicide and a lost gentility,' and was surprised to see Faulkner "squatting on the floor beside a cracked churn siphoning scummy homebrew out through a piece of hose into second-hand ginger ale bottles."[29] Of course, Faulkner was not putting on a show by doing something he would not ordinarily do, but he was nonetheless using what he had, so to speak, to put up a barrier—and also to seem ordinary, not Smith's notion of a half-crazed author. Smith realized as much even as he put himself at the author's service. It may be a mistake to conclude, as Joseph Blotner does, that Smith was naive and took Faulkner's statements—such as the one about writing *As I Lay Dying* to the hum of a power plant dynamo—"literally."[30] It is in the nature of much profile writing that the price of access to the subject is just this kind of collaboration in make-believe. The journalist and his subject are creating a story together, serving their mutual interests. The interview can be a form of play—although Faulkner often did not want to play, or he gamed the interviewer, as seems to have been the case with his remarks about slavery in the *New York Herald Tribune*. Some journalists were fools, others not.

When Louis Cochran submitted his 1931 interview with Faulkner to Phil Stone at Faulkner's suggestion, Stone provided the kind of correctives that show he and Faulkner had anticipated the media attention *Sanctuary* stimulated. In other words, Stone wanted to correct the impression that Faulkner was taken unawares by sudden fame: "He and I have always been sure that the present furor would arrive in time."[31] Stone, I realize, cannot always be trusted, given his resentments, but other sources confirm his comments to Cochran about Faulkner's interest in aesthetics of self-presentation, no matter how much Faulkner complained about the literary crowd in New York, where "everybody talks about what they are going to write, and no one writes anything."[32]

An interview is a performance, one that allowed Faulkner considerable flexibility in shaping a persona. He could not control this persona as carefully as he could, say, in his letters, but interviews nevertheless gave him ample room to maneuver, to present contradictory impressions as the occasion and the mood suited him. It is the performing self I proposed to explore when I decided to write a biography of Faulkner. I suspected that this aspect of his life had been understudied and that my own experience in Hollywood equipped me to see how early on William Faulkner began to act as William Faulkner. As it turns out, my take on Faulkner is not quite so original as I supposed. Catching up on the Faulkner scholarship produced over the last several decades while I was away working on other biographies, I discovered that James G. Watson and Peter Lurie, among others, had prepared the way for precisely the kind of narrative biography I wanted to write.[33] But what I have lost in originality, I have gained from the depth and suggestiveness of their analyses. Now it is time to turn their insights into the story of a writer whose life and work are still growing in its fascination and importance. What a new biography can do is situate Faulkner even more centrally in a culture he thoroughly absorbed, no matter how often he claimed to retreat and remove himself from the public's gaze.

NOTES

1. "William Faulkner, 'Literary Hope' from Mississippi Likens Himself in City to a 'Houn' Dawg under a Wagon,'" *New York World-Telegram*, November 14, 1931, clipping file, Special Collections, University of Virginia Library, Charlottesville.

2. "Spring Wagon/Democrat Wagon," Hansen Wheel & Wagon Shop, http://www .hansenwheel.com/custom-showcase/custom-vehicle-showcase/spring-wagon-democrat -wagon (accessed January 25, 2016).

3. Anthony Buttitta, "A Memoir of Faulkner in the Early Days of Fame," *San Francisco Chronicle*, July 15, 1962, 20, repr. in *Conversations with William Faulkner*, ed. M. Thomas Inge (Jackson: University Press of Mississippi, 1999), 15–17.

4. I accessed these regional newspapers through http://www.newspaperarchive.com.

5. Harcourt's letter to Faulkner is in the Albert and Shirley Small Special Collections Library, University of Virginia, Charlottesville. Joseph Blotner includes Faulkner's reply in *Selected Letters of William Faulkner*, ed. Joseph Blotner (New York: Random House, 1977), 42–43.

6. Blotner, ed., *Selected Letters of William Faulkner*, 34.

7. Arnold Bennett, review of *Soldiers' Pay* by William Faulkner (1930), repr. in *William Faulkner: The Critical Heritage*, ed. John Bassett (London: Routledge & Kegan Paul, 1975), 61–62.

8. Marshall Smith, "Faulkner in Seclusion, Writing Movie Script," *Memphis Press-Scimitar*, December 1, 1931, clipping file, Albert and Shirley Small Special Collections Library, University of Virginia, Charlottesville. The clipping does not contain a page reference.

9. Unless otherwise noted, all newspaper citations have been accessed from http://www .freenewspaperarchives.us/free-north-east-newspaper-collections.

10. "The Week of a New Yorker," *Brooklyn Daily Eagle*, March 16, 1931, 21.

11. M. Thomas Inge, ed. *William Faulkner: The Contemporary Reviews* (Cambridge: Cambridge University Press, 1995), xiii.

12. E. David Levitin, review of *Sanctuary*, by William Faulkner, *Illinois Daily Illini*, May 31, 1931, Illinois Digital Newspaper Collections, http://idnc.library.illinois.edu (accessed May 17, 2016).

13. Mary Morris, review of *Sanctuary*, by William Faulkner, *Illinois Daily Illini*, March 15, 1931, Illinois Digital Newspaper Collections, http://idnc.library.illinois.edu (accessed May 17, 2016).

14. This November 14, 1931, interview is included in James B. Meriwether and Michael Millgate, eds., *Lion in the Garden: Interviews with William Faulkner 1926–1962* (New York: Random House, 1968), 19–22.

15. Ibid., ix.

16. Ibid., 20; Frederick Karl, *William Faulkner: American Writer* (New York: Ballantine Books, 1990), 462: "The lies, deceptions, tall tales, and exaggerations are evident; leading us to believe the interview about Negroes and slavery in the *Herald Tribune*—while devastating when coming from a white Mississippian—was simply talk." But Karl can't leave it at that: "However, one cannot avoid the view that what comes from the mouth of someone drinking deeply is often what sits in that person's subconscious. We must conclude that while Faulkner's public statements about race would continue to create outrage, they would not at all coincide with the way he presents race fictionally." Note that Karl seems to assume that Faulkner was drinking.

17. Meriwether and Millgate, *Lion in the Garden*, 13.

18. Ibid., 17, 23–24.

19. Ibid., 10–11.

20. James G. Watson, *William Faulkner: Self-Presentation and Performance* (Austin: University of Texas Press, 2013), Kindle edition, analyzes "a passage of pure performance" in one of Faulkner's 1918 letters from Yale to home, noting that it is like "Charlie Chaplin's cinematic confrontations with outraged policemen. The moment is as carefully paced as a scene in a silent film" (n.p.).

21. Meriwether and Milgate, *Lion in the Garden*, 13.

22. Ibid.

23. Watson, *William Faulkner*, n.p.

24. Quoted in ibid.

25. Ibid.

26. Ibid.

27. Ibid.

28. Joseph Blotner, *Faulkner: A Biography*, vol. 1 (New York: Random House, 1974), 696.

29. Meriwether and Millgate, *Lion in the Garden*, 9.

30. Joseph Blotner, *Faulkner: A Biography*, rev. ed. (1974; repr., New York: Random House, 1984), 279.

31. Phil Stone to Louis Cochran, December 28, 1931, in *William Faulkner of Oxford*, ed. James W. Webb and A. Wigfall Green (Baton Rouge: Louisiana State University Press, 1965), 226.

32. William Faulkner quoted in Louis Cochran, "A Front Steps Interview," in *William Faulkner of Oxford*, ed. James W. Webb and A. Wigfall Green (Baton Rouge: Louisiana State University Press, 1965), 104.

33. Thanks are due to Jay Watson, no relation to James G. Watson, for first alerting me to the importance of the latter's work.

Fabbulous Monsters: Faulkner, Alexander Woollcott, and American Literary Culture

TIM A. RYAN

Few modernist American authors were ostensibly as different as William Faulkner and Alexander Woollcott. One quietly produced complex and experimental novels in his Mississippi hometown, while the other was an aggressively middlebrow New York critic, broadcaster, essayist, and professional ham who supposedly wrote little of lasting value yet established himself as one of the leading literary celebrities and cultural arbiters of his era. Woollcott's status, popularity, and influence—apparently dependent upon his fame and outsized personality—dissolved abruptly after his death in 1943. Few remember him today except, perhaps, as the model for the irascible Sheridan Whiteside in George S. Kaufman and Moss Hart's 1939 play *The Man Who Came to Dinner*.[1] Faulkner's reputation, in contrast, rose dramatically in the years immediately following Woollcott's demise, and he stands today, of course, as one of the twentieth century's most revered authors. As far as history is concerned, then, one was a serious craftsman who produced great art for the ages, while the other was a trivial celebrity whose frothy and popular writings were entirely ephemeral.

The meager historical record suggests that the two authors barely knew each other. During frequent visits to New York, Faulkner habitually chose to stay at the Algonquin Hotel—where Woollcott presided over the famous Round Table—but he preferred the company of Dorothy Parker to that of the domineering critic.[2] According to Ben Wasson, in fact, the relationship between Faulkner and Woollcott did not go beyond a single, very brief meeting in the latter's apartment in the fall of 1931. Woollcott—in a tattered red dressing gown, his naked stomach bulging over unbuttoned pajamas—greeted the author with customary whimsy, addressing him as "Master Faulkner" and inquiring as to the whereabouts of his corncob. Faulkner promptly exited without a word, later allegedly explaining to Wasson, "I'd prefer to keep company with Frankenstein's monster."[3]

There is a curious echo of this characterization in Woollcott's biography. At the age of ten, upon being asked to write about what he wanted to do when he grew up, Woollcott—rejecting conventional childhood ambitions—grandly declared, "I would rather be a Fabbulous [sic] Monster."[4] To some, the adult Woollcott *was* just as fabulous as he was monstrous. The comedian Harpo Marx provides a memorable account of his first confrontation with the "supercilious" and "hoity-toity" critic.[5] "He looked like something that had gotten loose from Macy's Thanksgiving Day Parade," Harpo recalled, adding that Woollcott "couldn't help needling [people] any more than a wasp could help stinging."[6] Unlike Faulkner, however, Harpo recognized that there was much more to Woollcott than the cartoonish and acerbic public persona, and the comedian became one of the critic's closest and most devoted lifelong friends.

Although Faulkner's biographers and scholars—like the author before them—barely acknowledge Woollcott's existence, "Old Vitriol and Violets"[7] was no less important to the literary career and fortunes of the Old Man than such esteemed editors, publishers, and critics as Malcolm Cowley, Bennett Cerf, and Robert Penn Warren. On two particular occasions, in fact, Woollcott played a crucial role in expanding Faulkner's readership and burnishing his literary reputation: first, through his glowing reviews and ongoing coverage of *Sanctuary* in various media in the early 1930s, and second by his creation of the Viking Portable series of literary anthologies in the mid-1940s.

Woollcott's involvement with Faulkner also demonstrates that the critic contributed rather more to American literature than a few sharp insults, witty quips, and sentimental anecdotes. Although he once famously demanded of a friend, "I ask only to be entertained by some of your grosser reminiscences,"[8] Woollcott's commentaries about *Sanctuary* reveal an astute and prescient appreciation of the book's achievements, not just a gleeful reveling in its sensationalistic content. Furthermore, some of Woollcott's subsequent writings clearly suggest Faulkner's influence.

That a writer and broadcaster primarily renowned for treacly radio monologues, spiky put-downs, and arch bon mots was also inclined both to evangelize and channel the great Mississippi author says much for Woollcott's eclectic and expansive—or, as he once put it, "incorrigibly miscellaneous"[9]—conception of modernist culture. In Woollcott's canon, the Algonquin Round Table mattered as much as the Bloomsbury Group, Ogden Nash as much as T. S. Eliot, magazine illustrator Neysa McMein as much as Marcel Duchamp, and Irving Berlin as much as

Arnold Schoenberg. Woollcott's values resound in the prospectus for the *New Yorker* magazine written by his friend Harold Ross: "It will not be what is commonly called radical or highbrow. It will be what is commonly called sophisticated, in that it will assume a reasonable degree of enlightenment on the part of its reader."[10] The breadth of Woollcott's vision is implicit in the activities of another close friend, journalist and editor Herbert Bayard Swope, who "covered the Versailles Peace Conference in striped trousers and a cutaway coat, [then] returned home and promptly reported the Dempsey-Carpentier prizefight, quoting no less an intellectual than George Bernard Shaw on the outcome of the match."[11] In Woollcott's world, in short, one "could speak highly of William Faulkner in one breath and of *Goodbye, Mr. Chips* in the next."[12] Although one critic complained that Woollcott "seems to get most excited and most persuasive over the trivial and the second rate," another noted that the works he reviewed on radio and collected in his anthologies were often "hard books and some of them were harsh books."[13] Joan Shelley Rubin argues that "while it is indisputable that mass culture overrode Victorian strictures in the early twentieth century, and equally true that the avant-garde exhibited new vitality, there remained a middle ground between the 'popular' and the 'high,' with paths leading to both"—and she identifies Woollcott as a prominent citizen of this fluid middle ground.[14]

Such a capacious and inclusive conception of modernist culture evaporated almost immediately after Woollcott's death and the end of World War II. Lawrence Schwartz contends that the New Critics and New York intellectuals who dominated American letters throughout the Cold War redeemed Faulkner by casting him as an avatar of Anglo-American high modernism and apolitical literary universality.[15] Where Woollcott had argued for a dynamic interrelationship between highbrow literature, middlebrow writing, and lowbrow mass culture—and for a pantheon consisting of expressions from all three—postwar academics sought to isolate great literature from the baneful contamination of popular culture.

The wheel has turned full circle, however, and our twenty-first-century William Faulkner bears at least as much resemblance to Woollcott's "Master Faulkner" as to the eminent experimenter and moralist sage celebrated by scholars in the years immediately after World War II. Woollcott's campaign in the early 1930s on behalf of a novel that gleefully dismantles conventional categories of literary value and boldly subverts heteronormativity reverberates throughout Faulkner scholarship of the present day. Woollcott understood—as we now understand—that great literature could encompass both art and trash, heart and glands,

Tyrrhenian vase and physical spittoon, second place in an *Ellery Queen Mystery Magazine* competition and the Nobel Prize.[16] We, too, are fascinated by the ways in which Faulkner's work bridges the "great divide" between avant-garde literature and the broader "media ecology" of his day,[17] as well as by the author's interrogations of sexual and patriarchal politics. Yet we still do not seem to have moved beyond the outdated and limiting assumption that Faulkner and Woollcott belonged to separate and irreconcilable literary spheres.

The most Woollcott seems to warrant in any Faulkner biography— and the majority simply do not mention him at all—is Joseph Blotner's brief aside about the gushing 1931 radio review that, according to legend, caused *Sanctuary* to outsell Faulkner's two preceding books in just three weeks.[18] This legend has subsequently faded into obscurity: surveys of Faulkner's critical reputation neglect Woollcott no less than biographers since Blotner, and he does not even rate a mention in such collections as *Faulkner and Humor* (1986) and *Faulkner and Popular Culture* (1990).[19] By the same token, the small body of critical writing on Woollcott barely acknowledges Faulkner, implying that there simply were not any substantial or meaningful intersections between the Mississippi modernist and New York wit.[20]

Quiet as it is now kept, nobody during the 1930s doubted that Woollcott was responsible for making *Sanctuary* a best seller and Faulkner a household name. As Samuel Hopkins Adams avers, "He got people to reading books who had never read before" and assumed "the solemn duty of salvaging from oblivion masterpieces unrecognized by hoi-polloi."[21] In his 1940 study of the relationship between radio and literature, Paul Lazarsfeld confirms that Woollcott was instrumental in popularizing four particular books published in the late 1920s and early 1930s: *Sanctuary*, *The Maltese Falcon* (1930), Paul Alverdes's *The Whistler's Room* (1929)— which had gone out of print, but for which Woollcott whipped up such enthusiasm that the publisher had to set up new type and reissue it—and James Hilton's *Lost Horizon* (1933), which "had been on the shelves for two years, in little demand, when Woollcott 'went quietly mad' about it, causing it to become a steady favorite for years."[22] As Harpo Marx put it, Woollcott was "the most conspicuous persuader in America. . . . When Woollcott enthused, everybody else, by God, had to enthuse too."[23] Blotner mentions—if only in a footnote—how Woollcott informed listeners of his *Early Bookworm* radio show[24] that *Sanctuary* was an "extraordinary" work of "grandeur," while also warning, "There are plenty of intelligent and sensible people whom the book would make really ill. For compared with 'Sanctuary,' the later Emile Zola's most earnest quests into the squalor of life seem like merry sunlit pages out of 'Little Women.'"[25]

If the erasure of this significant and influential review from the historical record were not already sufficiently problematic, nobody has ever acknowledged that Woollcott's boosting of Faulkner's career went well beyond a single radio spot.[26] The critic also endorsed *Sanctuary* in print as part of his regular Reading and Writing column in *McCall's* magazine in July 1931. This repetition is reminiscent of Woollcott's Second Thoughts on First Nights column in the Sunday *New York Herald* in the 1920s, which provided an opportunity for the critic to reconsider and revise "his spontaneous judgments and the frequently effusive quality of his nightly reviews" of new plays.[27] His second public assessment of *Sanctuary* observes that

> all those who care for sweet and sentimental books should be warned what a terrific experience awaits them within its covers. But I would not have you think it gross. Indeed, its great power derives from all the art of implication and understatement. Faulkner has a knack for filling his pages with a nameless dread so that his reader feels like an uneasy wayfarer who has found lodging for the night in some sinister house, where . . . the darkness is alive with evil and mischance but dimly comprehended.[28]

Unlike other early reviews of *Sanctuary*—which either laud it as a masterpiece of (or despite its) outrageous brutality, or which lament its extremes and its failure to match *The Sound and the Fury* and *As I Lay Dying*[29]—Woollcott's second account emphasizes the complex interplay between the novel's grotesque content and its subtle narrative strategies. If virtually everybody overlooked this characteristic of *Sanctuary* at the time, scholars now habitually discuss what Florence Dore calls its "vexing . . . structural duality: its hyperbolic indecency, on the one hand, and its unspoken quality on the other."[30] In *McCall's*, Woollcott describes *Sanctuary* as "a masterly canvas," an expression of "the rapt aloofness of the artist," a book "without anger and without blame," and the triumphant culmination of the artistry of "Faulkner, the new poet and prophet"—yet he simultaneously characterizes it as "a tale of evil unspeakable" with "moonshiners, rum-runners, half-wits and worse, all dancing a monstrous and profoundly hopeless jig," and he even suggests it is likely that "the late Colonel Faulkner [sic] turned in his grave" when it was published.[31] Woollcott recognized *Sanctuary*, in other words, as what critics now call "an unpredictable mash-up of elitist literary experimentation and pulp sensationalism,"[32] a novel that exemplifies Rubin's "middle ground between the 'popular' and the 'high,'" with "paths leading to both" the Memphis underworld and the Luxembourg Gardens, a Prufrockian intellectual and his bourgeois sister, a privileged debutante and a fading streetwalker, Tchaikovsky and the blues, Popeye the Sailor Man and Horace the lyric poet, and a pulp-fiction gangster who simultaneously reminds people of both *Madame Bovary* and a modernist lampstand.[33]

Woollcott's intense enthusiasm for *Sanctuary*—with its unblinking treatment of congenital impotence, homoerotic tensions, and gender slippage—is also striking given his own sexual situation. Woollcott sometimes claimed to have been rendered physically incapable of erotic activity by a case of mumps he suffered at the age of twenty-two. Before the 1970s, biographers were inclined to deny the possibility or cast a veil over the subject, but later accounts suggest that Woollcott's condition—whether a consequence of viral disease or hormonal imbalance—may have provided a convenient cover story for his repressed homosexuality.[34] Howard Teichmann cautiously concludes that Woollcott "probably had little active sex life" and that his inclinations "may have ranged from heterosexual to bisexual to homosexual, but the taboos of his time were so strong they frightened off his freedom of sexual expression."[35] While occasionally acknowledging his erotic incapacity, Woollcott felt obliged to conform to sexual norms by enacting "a lifelong series of fabled and fake romances" with numerous—and mostly married—women.[36] In an age of rigid gender codes and binaries, furthermore, Woollcott seems to have been what we would now call transgendered: he allegedly confessed to Anita Loos that he had "always wanted to be a girl," and—while an undergraduate at Hamilton College—he often appeared at parties in women's clothes and had calling cards printed that read "Alexandra Woollcott."[37]

It was this critic who went out of his way to recommend to bourgeois readers across the nation a complex literary work rife with suggestions of homosexuality and impotence as well as a devastating critique of patriarchal heteronormativity. In this "book about impotent men"—as Robert Dale Parker has it[38]—Popeye will "never be a man, properly speaking" because of inherited syphilis,[39] and the hapless—and perhaps equally impotent—Horace Benbow flees his wife, flirts with a series of inaccessible or attached women (his sister Narcissa, his stepdaughter Little Belle, former streetwalker Ruby Goodwin), and briefly imagines himself as a female rape victim.[40] Where scholars of the Cold War—as Jaime Harker notes—constructed Faulkner as the creator of "archetypal images of female fecundity" and "a chronicler of virile southern patriarchs," today's critics are routinely attentive to the myriad ways in which "Faulkner's characters transgress gender and sexual norms liberally."[41] James Polchin even reads *Sanctuary* as a "psychosexual text" in which Popeye is a sinister manifestation of Horace's repressed homosexuality, with each playing "out his homosexual desire through Temple Drake's body."[42] Woollcott's boosting of *Sanctuary* thus anticipates twenty-first-century scholarship's concern with Faulkner's subversion of gender and sexual norms and his canon's emphasis upon both queer and perverse sexualities.[43]

As if two reviews were not sufficient—and apparently not put off by the novelist's personal distaste for him—Woollcott continued to publicize *Sanctuary* by regaling readers of his regular column in the *New Yorker* in February 1932 with the hoary tale of the youthful Faulkner's antics as postmaster at Ole Miss.[44] A year later, just prior to the release of *The Story of Temple Drake*, the first film version of *Sanctuary*, Woollcott dashed off an item in the same column suggesting that a better title for this adaptation of "Br'er Faulkner's masterpiece" would be "Mamma Loves Popeye."[45] Again, there is an echo of Woollcott's relationship with Harpo Marx. After the critic's initial review of the Marxes in 1924 and the flourishing of his friendship with Harpo, Woollcott found an excuse "to write something about the Marx Brothers at least once a month."[46] One radio listener even supposedly asked, "How much do the Marx Brothers pay you for being their press agent, Woollcott?"—and reasonably could have posed the same question about Faulkner.[47]

Woollcott's publicity campaign on Faulkner's behalf in the early 1930s established a link between the two writers both in literary culture and in the popular mind that evidently lasted throughout the decade. Some critics clearly considered them equally monstrous or, at least, equally ripe for satire. Sterling North paired Woollcott and Faulkner in a vituperative review of *Pylon* in the *Chicago Daily News* in 1935. "New York critics," he said, "are busy raving about the new Faulkner novel. Raving about Faulkner is the thing to do. Just as repeating the latest insulting wisecrack of Alexander Woollcott is the thing to do. . . . Never mind the thing to do! Faulkner's new book is a sloppy, disgusting nauseating performance."[48] The following year, the *Saturday Review of Literature* carried Timothy Fuller's parody of "The Story of Jack and Jill (As It Might Be Told by William Faulkner, P. G. Wodehouse, and Alexander Woollcott)," implying that of all American authors active in the 1930s, Faulkner and Woollcott possessed both the most instantly recognizable and the most irresistibly imitable prose styles.[49] In the 1930s, then, Faulkner and Woollcott enjoyed renown as flamboyant stylists with a love of the macabre, while naysayers castigated their work as being both overblown and overrated.

If Woollcott had an impact upon Faulkner's sales rather than his writing, one of Woollcott's few extended works—a 1933 play written in collaboration with George S. Kaufman called *The Dark Tower*[50]—clearly demonstrates the influence of the content, mood, and themes of

Sanctuary. The cast includes characters named Miss Temple and Horace, but focuses upon Stanley Vance, a psychopathic Svengali who, like Popeye, "got in some scrape with a woman down in Memphis."[51] Under Vance's evil influence, the play's heroine soon acquires "the unvarying manner of a somnambulist, the monotonous voice, the trance quality,"[52] much like the traumatized Temple after Popeye has raped her. Further, Vance has two dogs named after people—Abelard and Heloise rather than Mr. Binford and Miss Reba—and his descriptions of them echo the insinuations of male impotence that pervade *Sanctuary*: "Your house will not be overrun," Vance assures his host, "Abelard has painfully earned his right to be so called."[53] Reviewers were no less disturbed by the play's heady mixture of evil, violence, salacious suggestion, perverse sex, and dark comedy than initial readers of *Sanctuary*, with one critic castigating its "degenerate verbiage and implication" and its "vaguely foul atmosphere."[54] In addition to the clear debt that *The Dark Tower* owes to *Sanctuary*, the title of its 1934 film adaptation, *The Man with Two Faces*, echoes both Woollcott's shifting sexual personae and the ways in which Popeye acts as Horace's "mirror, reflecting and acting out his own desires."[55]

Although Woollcott seems to have paid little attention to Faulkner's work after *Sanctuary*, he was indirectly instrumental in stimulating the author's sales and reputation in the mid-1940s when the Mississippian was at a particularly low ebb. Biographers and critics rightly credit Malcolm Cowley for the success of *The Portable Faulkner*,[56] but what no one ever acknowledges is that the renowned Viking series was Woollcott's brainchild. In March 1943, just two months after his death, Viking published Woollcott's collection, *As You Were: A Portable Library of American Prose and Poetry Assembled for Members of the Armed Forces and the Merchant Marine*.[57] In compiling this pre-Norton anthology of American literature for overseas servicemen and women, Woollcott polled such authorities as Stephen Vincent Benét, Mark Van Doren, Booth Tarkington, Willa Cather, Thornton Wilder, Carl Sandburg, and E. B. White for nominations (xi). Works by Poe, Twain, Longfellow, Emerson, Thoreau, Whitman, Robert Frost, James Weldon Johnson, Ernest Hemingway, E. E. Cummings, and Willa Cather all made the final cut—alongside less traditionally canonical works by Ruth Gordon, Ogden Nash, Dorothy Parker, Robert Benchley, and of course, Alexander Woollcott—but it contains nothing by Faulkner, a sharp indication of how precarious his literary status had become by the 1940s.[58] Viking promptly adopted the "Portable" brand for what would become a long-running series, beginning with *The Portable Steinbeck* later in 1943. *The Portable Woollcott*—which would serve as a swansong for the once-ubiquitous critic—appeared in April 1946, the very same month as *The Portable Faulkner* reasserted the Mississippi author's importance in twentieth-century American literature, marking the last moment of connection between the two writers: one falling into obscurity, a swiftly forgotten relic of prewar culture, the other rising to the heights of the canon as the grand old man of American letters during the Cold War.

Woollcott—unlike the tenacious Faulkner—is thus part of that long roll call of American modernist authors who were prominent before World War II but whose lives or significant publishing careers did not outlast the 1940s. Thomas Wolfe and James Weldon Johnson both passed away at the end of the 1930s, while such diverse talents as F. Scott Fitzgerald, Nathanael West, Sherwood Anderson, Ellen Glasgow, Gertrude Stein, Willa Cather, Claude McKay, Susan Glaspell, and Margaret Mitchell died in the 1940s, quickly followed by Sinclair Lewis and Edna St. Vincent Millay at the beginning of the 1950s. Zora Neale Hurston published one uncharacteristic novel after 1942 before disappearing into obscurity; Carson McCullers's promising career fell victim to ill health; Eugene O'Neill produced his run of great final plays during World War II, although many of them would not be staged until after his death in 1953; Dorothy Parker virtually abandoned poetry and fiction after the war, even though she lived until 1967; Clifford Odets was persecuted by the House Un-American Activities Committee and wrote only two plays after 1950; Hemingway's *Across the River and into the Trees* (1950)—the author's first novel in a decade—was roundly dismissed as a disaster;[59] and John Steinbeck's credit quickly diminished during the Cold War because of his indelible association with the increasingly unfashionable leftist politics of the 1930s. Faulkner could easily have become part of this sad catalogue—in between his ongoing reliance upon a Hollywood paycheck, decade-long struggle with *A Fable*, and six-year silence after *Go Down, Moses*—but *The Portable Faulkner* and the reception of *Intruder in the Dust* saved him. In retrospect, it is hardly surprising that the New Critics after World War II selected Faulkner as the epitome of American modernist literary achievement: it is not simply that he finally earned the recognition he had long deserved, but that he was also one of very few major American novelists of the 1920s who was still alive and publishing creditable fiction into the 1950s.

Unlike Faulkner, Woollcott was too much a product of the 1920s and 1930s—in both ideological and aesthetic terms—to have prospered during the Cold War, even had he lived. Although the neglect endured by the author of *The Sound and the Fury* and *Absalom, Absalom!* before his postwar renaissance now seems unjust and absurd, Schwartz argues that Faulkner's eventual canonization was as much about politics as artistic quality. The scholars who became influential during the Cold War required a literary poster boy who was not contaminated by either the progressive politics of the 1930s or its attendant emphasis upon prosaic realism and naturalism. In addition, given that so many of the major critics of the postwar era—including Robert Penn Warren, Cleanth Brooks, Allen Tate, and John Crowe Ransom—were proud southerners, Faulkner's regionalism proved, at last, a distinct advantage. In contrast, the new Cold War generation of elite professional literary scholars had little time or respect for the florid writing, widely inclusive aesthetics, unashamedly populist appeal, or the left-wing politics of Alexander Woollcott. When Irving Howe spoke of "shaking off the rubbish of the thirties," he might have been referring to Woollcott as much as the now-unfashionable proletarian and Popular Front authors.[60]

The fate of another American writer, broadcaster, columnist, actor, and raconteur in this period—one much more respected as an artist than Woollcott—suggests that Cold War America was fundamentally inhospitable to certain breeds of "fabbulous monster." James Naremore's account of Orson Welles provides uncanny echoes of Woollcott's talents, emphases, and career. Welles, like Woollcott, flourished in various media—from theater and radio to journalism and cinema—and his work "made hash of highbrow, middlebrow, lowbrow distinctions."[61] He was "a social progressive but also a critic of modernity—an artist who commanded the twentieth century's new media but who was romantically nostalgic for the past,"[62] which was equally true of Woollcott as both radio broadcaster and incurable sentimentalist of yesteryear.[63] Welles was, Naremore concedes, ultimately "more theatrical than writerly" and "must have relished playing [in the film *Black Magic*] an egomaniacal, carnival-show actor who makes everybody believe he has magical powers."[64] Similarly, Woollcott, according to Harpo, was "not a deep thinker or serious writer, but a great, big, wonderful ham,"[65] and he delighted in playing a caricature of himself as an imperious diva in *The Man Who Came to Dinner*. Woollcott also flirted with socialism, counted Eleanor Roosevelt among his close friends, aggressively campaigned for FDR, and railed untiringly against isolationist Middle America during the early 1940s,[66] while Welles was "an important public spokesman for the left" who "enjoyed his most dazzling success in the Roosevelt years" and whose major films of the 1940s "were an outgrowth of his Popular Front activities in the previous decade."[67] Naremore argues that the decline of Welles's filmmaking career was as much about politics as art or commerce, and he suggests that that the director's removal to Europe was motivated primarily by the political climate of the Cold War.[68] It is equally unlikely that Woollcott would have tolerated what became of America during the McCarthy Era, or that it would have tolerated him.[69] Woollcott continued to be ubiquitous for at least a couple of years after his death: *Long, Long Ago* appeared posthumously alongside *As You Were* in 1943, his *Collected Letters* in 1944, and Adams's biography of the author in 1945—but then it is as if he were abruptly erased from the national memory. As Edwin P. Hoyt says, Woollcott was a man "who at the hour of his death was the most powerful literary figure in the English-speaking world and who, a quarter of a century later, was virtually unknown to the general public."[70]

The literary culture of the Cold War proved no less hostile to Woollcott's conception of Faulkner than to Woollcott himself, cleaving the Mississippi author in two and scrupulously distinguishing between the sensationalist popular writer who could sell books and the detached, sophisticated modernist author celebrated in academia's ivory towers. As Schwartz argues, the New Critics and New York intellectuals after World War II had little more respect for popular literature than for Soviet Communism, and they carefully rebranded Faulkner as "the great American avant-garde novelist who represented the dominance of Western humanist values" while presenting themselves and their elevated tastes as the last bulwark against degenerative "*kitsch* and mass culture."[71] Meanwhile, the evolution of cheap paperbacks provided an outlet for a very different Faulkner, one characterized by "popular non-serious qualities: sex, violence, intrigue."[72] There is no more vivid illustration of this bifurcated postwar Faulkner than the manner in which his earlier works were reissued. Random House combined *The Sound and the Fury* and *As I Lay Dying* into a single volume in its esteemed Modern Library series in 1946, at the very moment that the New American Library was licensing *Sanctuary* for a lurid paperback edition that would sell hundreds of thousands of copies.[73] Of course, Faulkner himself established a precedent for this very division in his notorious introduction for the 1932 Modern Library edition of *Sanctuary*, in which he dismissed the novel as "a cheap idea . . . deliberately conceived to make money."[74] Faulkner—unlike Woollcott—was himself occasionally prone to lapse into easy and unexamined assumptions about the distinction between high modernist literature and low popular fiction.

Today, Faulkner is whole again. We have not forgotten the "postwar moralist and symbol of solitary literary genius" bequeathed us by the New Critics, but we have reconciled him with that other Faulkner, the scandalous pop-gothic provocateur immersed in "terror, corruption, barbarism, and decadence."[75] We have redeemed Woollcott's Faulkner, if not Woollcott himself—but the time is certainly ripe for rediscovery and recuperation of the critic who first defined the nature of *Sanctuary*'s genius and who produced some memorable and enduring writing of his own. As Wayne Chatterton notes, "In the history of American letters, the publication of *While Rome Burns* [Woollcott's 1934 collection of essays] has been a neglected landmark—the appearance in the twentieth century of several varieties of belle-lettres that had been highly respected in Old World cultures but that had not held an important place in American literature since the days of Irving and Hawthorne."[76]

Faulkner once dismissed another notorious southern novel of the early 1930s—*God's Little Acre*, by Erskine Caldwell—by suggesting that "Alex Woollcott and Lon Chaney's ghost wrote it."[77] One might equally say that *Sanctuary* reads like a novel written *for* Alex Woollcott, the arbiter of an eclectic cultural middle ground, whose reviews, broadcasts, plays, and essays established that modernism was a complex phenomenon in which great art could be present in hard-boiled descriptions of brutal murders as well as delicate essays on literary appreciation, in *Death Comes for the Archbishop* and *The Maltese Falcon*, Eugene O'Neill and the Marx Brothers, George Bernard Shaw and Walt Disney's *Dumbo*—and in the works of that fabulous monster, Master Faulkner the corncob man, who also happened to be William Faulkner the creator of avant-garde masterpieces.

NOTES

1. See George S. Kaufman and Moss Hart, "The Man Who Came to Dinner" (1939), in *Three Plays by Kaufman and Hart* (London: Methuen, 1981), 207–307. Waldo Lydecker in *Laura*—the 1944 film based upon Vera Caspary's novel—also owes a clear debt to Woollcott. See Howard Teichmann, *Smart Aleck: The Wit, World, and Life of Alexander Woollcott* (New York: Morrow, 1976), 13. Woollcott also appeared in fictional form in two novels by Charles Brackett: briefly as Caleb Bradford in *American Colony* (New York: Horace Liveright, 1929) and then as central character Thaddeus Hulbert in *Entirely Surrounded* (New York: Alfred A. Knopf, 1934). Woollcott also shows up in cartoon form as the presiding "Town Crier" in *Have You Got Any Castles?*, a 1938 Warner Brothers animated short, in which works of literature come to life.

2. Regarding Faulkner's relationship with Dorothy Parker, see Joseph Blotner, *Faulkner: A Biography*, vol. 1 (New York: Random House, 1974), 731, 732, 747; Frederick Karl, *William Faulkner: American Writer* (New York: Weidenfeld & Nicolson, 1989), 459–60; Marion Meade, *Dorothy Parker: What Fresh Hell Is This?* (London: Heinemann, 1989), 217–18; and David Minter, *William Faulkner: His Life and Work* (Baltimore: Johns Hopkins University Press, 1997), 160, 195.

3. Ben Wasson, *Count No 'Count: Flashbacks to Faulkner* (Jackson: University Press of Mississippi, 1983), 120. Wasson's account of Woollcott seems credible given Cornelia Otis Skinner's recollection that, during the regular Sunday brunches Woollcott held at his apartment during this period, he "sat like a Buddha in his pajamas. They were mostly unbuttoned to show the Buddha half of his stomach" (quoted in Teichmann, *Smart Aleck*, 152).

4. Quoted in Samuel Hopkins Adams, *A. Woollcott: His Life and His World* (New York: Reynal & Hitchcock, 1945), 3.

5. Harpo Marx, with Rowland Barber, *Harpo Speaks!* (New York: Bernard Geis Associates, 1961), 170.

6. Ibid., 169, 170.

7. James Thurber bestowed this nickname on Woollcott. See Teichmann, *Smart Aleck*, 226.

8. Quoted in Adams, *A. Woollcott*, 355.

9. Alexander Woollcott, ed., *The Woollcott Reader: Bypaths in the Realms of Gold* (New York: Viking, 1935), ix.

10. Quoted in Teichmann, *Smart Aleck*, 97.

11. Ibid., 126.

12. Edwin P. Hoyt, *Alexander Woollcott: The Man Who Came to Dinner* (London: Abelard-Schuman, 1986), 22.

13. Gilbert Seldes, quoted in Adams, *A. Woollcott*, 257; Hoyt, *Alexander Woollcott*, 267.

14. Joan Shelley Rubin, "'Information, Please!': Culture and Expertise in the Interwar Period," *American Quarterly* 35, no. 5 (Winter 1983): 501.

15. See Lawrence H. Schwartz, *Creating Faulkner's Reputation: The Politics of Modern Literary Criticism* (Knoxville: University of Tennessee Press, 1988).

16. Regarding the vase/spittoon juxtaposition, see Kristin Fujie's essay elsewhere in this collection. For Faulkner's notion of the division between heart and glands, see "The Stockholm Address" (1950), in *William Faulkner: Three Decades of Criticism*, ed. Frederick J. Hoffman and Olga W. Vickery (New York: Harcourt, Brace & World, 1963), 347–48. John N. Duvall discusses Faulkner's involvement with Ellery Queen in another essay in this volume.

17. Studies interrogating the governing assumption that mass culture and Faulkner's modernist literature were essentially antagonistic include Vincent Allan King, "Faulkner's Brazen Yoke: Pop Art, Modernism, and the Myth of the Great Divide," in *A Companion to William Faulkner*, ed. Richard C. Moreland (Malden, MA: Blackwell, 2007), 301–17; Peter Lurie, *Vision's Immanence: Faulkner, Film, and the Popular Imagination* (Baltimore: Johns Hopkins University Press, 2004); John T. Matthews, "Faulkner and the Culture Industry," in *The Cambridge Companion to William Faulkner*, ed. Philip M. Weinstein (Cambridge: Cambridge University Press, 1995), 51–73; Julian Murphet and Stefan Solomon, eds., *William Faulkner in the Media Ecology* (Baton Rouge: Louisiana State University Press, 2015); and Tim A. Ryan, *Yoknapatawpha Blues: Faulkner's Fiction and Southern Roots Music* (Baton Rouge: Louisiana State University Press, 2015). See also the essays by John N. Duvall and Kristin Fujie elsewhere in this collection.

18. Blotner, *Faulkner*, vol. 1, 685, 686, 732. Ben Wasson's memoir features the story of the review and Faulkner's meeting with Woollcott (102–4, 119–20), and Frederick Karl mentions the critic briefly in passing in his *William Faulkner* (460, 469). Other Faulkner biographies simply do not acknowledge Woollcott at all. See, for example, Minter, *William Faulkner*; Stephen B. Oates, *William Faulkner, The Man and the Artist: A Biography* (New York: Harper & Row, 1987); Jay Parini, *One Matchless Time: A Life of William Faulkner* (New York: Harper Perennial, 2005); and Joel Williamson, *William Faulkner and Southern History* (New York: Oxford University Press, 1993).

19. Woollcott is conspicuous by his absence in Schwartz's study, O. B. Emerson's *Faulkner's Early Literary Reputation in America* (Ann Arbor: UMI Research Press, 1984), and Perrin Holmes Lowery's doctoral dissertation, "The Critical Reception of William Faulkner's Work in the United States, 1926–1950" (PhD diss., University of Chicago, 1956). He also does not appear at all in Doreen Fowler and Ann J. Abadie, eds., *Faulkner and Humor: Faulkner and Yoknapatawpha, 1984* (Jackson: University Press of Mississippi, 1986); Doreen Fowler and Ann J. Abadie, eds., *Faulkner and Popular Culture: Faulkner and Yoknapatawpha, 1988* (Jackson: University Press of Mississippi,

1990); or Joseph P. Urgo and Ann J. Abadie, eds., *Faulkner and His Contemporaries: Faulkner and Yoknapatawpha, 2002* (Jackson: University Press of Mississippi, 2004).

20. Hoyt is unique among Woollcott's biographers for quoting from the *McCall's* review of *Sanctuary* (222). Both Hoyt and Wayne Chatterton briefly discuss Fuller's pairing of Faulkner and Woollcott in "The Story of Jack and Jill." See Hoyt, *Alexander Woollcott*, 293, and Wayne Chatterton, *Alexander Woollcott* (Boston: G. K. Hall, 1978), 155. Teichmann mentions Faulkner only once in passing in his biography of Woollcott. See Teichmann, *Smart Aleck*, 164.

21. Adams, *A. Woollcott*, 149, 256.

22. Paul F. Lazarsfeld, *Radio and the Printed Page: An Introduction to the Study of Radio and Its Role in the Communication of Ideas* (New York: Duell, Sloan and Pearce, 1940), 298–99.

23. Marx, *Harpo Speaks!*, 179, 178.

24. Wasson mistakenly identifies this show as the *Town Crier* (102), but Woollcott's broadcasts did not use this title until 1933.

25. Blotner, *Faulkner*, vol. 1, 686, 99n. Woollcott—who was never hesitant to recycle material—used a similar construction when characterizing *The Front Page* by Ben Hecht and Charles MacArthur as being "so profane, derisive, and hard-boiled that, compared with it, *What Price Glory*, its natural forerunner, seems, in gentle retrospect, like a page out of Louisa Alcott." Alexander Woollcott, *The Portable Woollcott* (New York: Viking Press, 1946), 220. In *Writers Gone Wild: The Feuds, Frolics, and Follies of Literature's Great Adventurers, Drunkards, Lovers, Iconoclasts, and Misanthropes* (New York: Perigee, 2012), Bill Peschel claims—without either citation or substantiation—that Faulkner's publisher paid Woollcott five hundred dollars to praise *Sanctuary* on the radio. Other sources and evidence suggest, to the contrary, that the critic steadfastly refused to promote books unless he was genuinely enthusiastic about them. See for example Hoyt, *Alexander Woollcott*, 247.

26. Even an extensive published collection of contemporary reviews—which identifies forty evaluations of *Sanctuary* published in 1931–32—overlooks Woollcott's *McCall's* review. See M. Thomas Inge, ed., *William Faulkner: The Contemporary Reviews* (Cambridge: Cambridge University Press, 1995), 51–64.

27. Chatterton, *Alexander Woollcott*, 85.

28. Alexander Woollcott, "Reading and Writing: Up from Mississippi," *McCall's*, July 1931, 60.

29. Reviews by "B. K. H." and Alex Reynolds Thompson fall into the first camp, and those by Julia Baker, Paul Bixler, Henry Seidel Canby, and Ted Robinson into the second. Philip Wheelwright's detached formalist appreciation, meanwhile, barely acknowledges the book's content. See Inge, ed., *William Faulkner*, 51–64.

30. Florence Dore, "Counting as Decent: Obscenity and Masculinity in William Faulkner's *Sanctuary*," in her *The Novel and the Obscene: Sexual Subjects in American Modernism* (Stanford, CA: Stanford University Press, 2005), 70.

31. Woollcott, "Reading and Writing," 17, 60.

32. Ryan, *Yoknapatawpha Blues*, 128. Lurie also addresses *Sanctuary*'s "Generative Conflict of High and Low" (25).

33. William Faulkner, *Sanctuary*, rev. ed. (1931; repr., New York: Vintage International, 1993), 7.

34. See Adams, *A. Woollcott*, 51, 56, 291, 293, 296–97; Hoyt, *Alexander Woollcott*, 5–6; Marx, *Harpo Speaks!*, 226; and Teichmann, *Smart Aleck*, 32, 53, 54.

35. Teichmann, *Smart Aleck*, 38.

36. Ibid., 46. See also Adams, *A. Woollcott*, 288.

37. Teichmann, *Smart Aleck*, 157, 45. See also Adams, *A. Woollcott*, 40.

38. Robert Dale Parker, *Faulkner and the Novelistic Imagination* (Urbana: University of Illinois Press, 1985), 71–72.

39. Faulkner, *Sanctuary*, 308.

40. Woollcott's generous encapsulation of Horace in the *McCall's* review suggests a sympathetic identification with him: "the one gentle person lingering upon the scene, like a character left over from last night's play. This sole survivor of the old order is chiefly characterized by the delicate futility which so hindered the career of the White Knight whom Alice met on the other side of the looking-glass" (Woollcott, "Reading and Writing," 60).

41. Jaime Harker, "Queer Faulkner: Whores, Queers, and the Transgressive South," in *The New Cambridge Companion to William Faulkner*, ed. John T. Matthews (Cambridge: Cambridge University Press, 2015), 107.

42. James Polchin, "Selling a Novel: Faulkner's *Sanctuary* as a Psychosexual Text," in *Faulkner and Gender: Faulkner and Yoknapatawpha, 1994*, ed. Donald M. Kartiganer and Ann J. Abadie (Jackson: University Press of Mississippi, 1996), 152. See also the discussion of homosocial/homoerotic male bonding in Faulkner's novel in Charmaine Eddy, "The Policing and Proliferation of Desire: Gender and the Homosocial in Faulkner's *Sanctuary*," *Faulkner Journal* 14, no. 2 (Spring 1999): 21–39.

43. In addition to Harker's survey, see Annette Trefzer and Ann J. Abadie, eds., *Faulkner's Sexualities: Faulkner and Yoknapatawpha, 2007* (Jackson: University Press of Mississippi, 2010).

44. Alexander Woollcott (as "Your Correspondent"), Shouts and Murmurs, *New Yorker*, February 13, 1932, 28.

45. Ibid., March 4, 1933, 36.

46. Marx, *Harpo Speaks!*, 180.

47. Adams, *A. Woollcott*, 236.

48. Quoted in Inge, *William Faulkner*, 129.

49. Timothy Fuller, "The Story of Jack and Jill (As It Might Be Told by William Faulkner, P. G. Wodehouse, and Alexander Woollcott)," *Saturday Review of Literature*, December 19, 1936, 10–11. Ernest Hemingway also brought the two writers together in *Men at War: The Best War Stories of All Time* (New York: Crown, 1942), which features Faulkner's "Turn About" alongside two pieces by Woollcott, who had served as a war correspondent for *Stars and Stripes* on the Western Front in World War I.

50. This title, of course echoes Faulkner's "Dark House," his working title for *Light in August* and, later, *Absalom, Absalom!* See Blotner, *Faulkner*, vol. 1, 701, 828–30; Karl, *William Faulkner*, 404, 446n, 492, 513–15; and Minter, *William Faulkner*, 129, 143.

51. Alexander Woollcott and George S. Kaufman, *The Dark Tower: A Melodrama* (New York: Random House, 1934), 136.

52. Ibid., 63.

53. Ibid., 54. Adams reports that one woman who was the object of Woollcott's performative infatuations observed that "Plato wasn't the presiding genius of Aleck's loves. It was Abelard" (291).

54. Quoted in Hoyt, *Alexander Woollcott*, 246. See the contemporary reviews of *Sanctuary* in Inge, *William Faulkner*, 51–64. Similarly, Woollcott's 1932 description of the murder of gambler Herman Rosenthal in Times Square has a distinctly Faulknerian accent. The author describes "that soft, fat body wilting on the sidewalk with a beer-stained tablecloth serving as its pall" and "the fish-belly faces of the sibilant crowd which . . . formed like a clot around those clamorous wounds" (Woollcott, *Portable Woollcott*, 251). This passage is specifically reminiscent of the moment in *Sanctuary* in

which a "knot" of townspeople crowd around the undertaker's parlor "with flattened noses against the glass" to see Tommy's corpse, "the sun-bleached curls on the back of his head matted with dried blood and singed with powder" (Faulkner, *Sanctuary*, 112–13).

55. Rebecca Keane-Temple, "The Sounds of *Sanctuary*: Horace Benbow's Consciousness," *Mississippi Quarterly* 50, no. 3 (Summer 1997): 447.

56. Regarding the significance of Cowley and *The Portable Faulkner* to the author's career, see, for example, Blotner, *Faulkner*, vol. 2, 1187, 1203, 1211; Karl, *William Faulkner*, 704, 707–9, 715, 725–26, 733, 735–38, 743–45; Minter, *William Faulkner*, 207, 210; and Williamson, *William Faulkner and Southern History*, 268.

57. Alexander Woollcott, ed., *As You Were: A Portable Library of American Prose and Poetry Assembled for Members of the Armed Forces and the Merchant Marine* (New York: Viking, 1943). Woollcott had previously edited two other popular literary anthologies for Viking, *The Woollcott Reader* and *Woollcott's Second Reader* (New York: Viking, 1937).

58. It is telling that, in the equally portable series of Armed Services Editions (ASE) in the same era—which featured among its 1,300 titles more than one work each by such diverse contemporary American authors as Steinbeck, Cather, Hemingway, Fitzgerald, Ring Lardner, James Thurber, William Saroyan, Thomas Wolfe, John O'Hara, Walter Van Tilburg Clark, Stephen Vincent Benét, Erskine Caldwell, Sinclair Lewis, Edna Ferber, and Raymond Chandler—there is only a single volume of Faulkner: *A Rose for Emily and Other Stories*. Regarding the ASE series, see Johnny Cole, ed., *Books in Action: The Armed Services Editions* (Washington, DC: Library of Congress, 1984).

59. Schwartz, *Creating Faulkner's Reputation*, 181.

60. Quoted in Schwartz, ibid., 198.

61. James Naremore, *The Magic World of Orson Welles*, rev. ed. (1978, repr., Urbana: University of Illinois Press, 2015), 8.

62. Ibid., 6.

63. Hoyt, *Alexander Woollcott*, 277.

64. Naremore, *Magic World of Orson Welles*, 12, 13.

65. Marx, *Harpo Speaks!*, 179.

66. Adams, *A. Woollcott*, 55, 351; Hoyt, *Alexander Woollcott*, 4–5, 282, 316–18.

67. Naremore, *Magic World of Orson Welles*, 7.

68. Ibid.

69. Woollcott reasonably could have claimed to have discovered Welles, just as Teichmann credits him with discovering Katharine Cornell, Lynn Fontanne, Alfred Lunt, Paul Robeson, and Fred and Adele Astaire (*Smart Aleck*, 21). Not long after boosting *Sanctuary*, Woollcott recommended the young Welles to producer-director Guthrie McClintic, who cast him as Mercutio in a touring production of *Romeo and Juliet*. See Charles Higham, *Orson Welles: The Rise and Fall of an American Genius* (London: New English Library, 1987), 81, 82.

70. Hoyt, *Alexander Woollcott*, 1.

71. Schwartz, *Creating Faulkner's Reputation*, 99, 35.

72. Ibid., 4.

73. Ibid., 55, 56, 58–59.

74. Faulkner, *Sanctuary*, 321–22.

75. Schwartz, *Creating Faulkner's Reputation*, 29, 36.

76. Chatterton, *Alexander Woollcott*, 153.

77. Joseph Blotner, ed., *Selected Letters of William Faulkner* (New York: Random House, 1977), 69.

"A Literary Criticism of Neurotic Literature": The *Saturday Review of Literature* and Faulkner's *Sanctuary*

Sarah E. Gardner

Harold Ross, the *New Yorker*'s founder, famously quipped in the magazine's prospectus that his journal would not be "edited for the old lady in Dubuque." "This is not meant in disrespect," he explained, perhaps disingenuously, "but the *New Yorker* is a magazine avowedly published for a metropolitan audience and thereby will escape an influence which hampers most national publications."[1] Its reviews, especially after New York native and former Simon and Schuster editor Clifton Fadiman took over the books department in the early 1930s, reflected the magazine's urbane and sophisticated wit and often took a critical, if not mocking, look at provincials.

For those not counted among the smart set—for the old lady in Dubuque and the high school teacher in Poughkeepsie, the accountant in Cleveland, and the pediatrician in Raleigh—there was the *Saturday Review of Literature*. Founded by Yale literature professor Henry Seidel Canby in 1924, the *Saturday Review* appealed to middlebrow readers and generally refrained from engaging in the contentious literary culture wars waged by the liberal weeklies such as the *New Republic* and the *Nation* on the one hand and the politically and aesthetically conservative *Bookman* on the other. Genteel in its approach, Canby's magazine attracted those readers who wished to stay current, who might even daringly flirt with writers such as John Dos Passos and Ernest Hemingway on occasion, but whose sensibilities were not mortally offended by the likes of Thornton Wilder and Ellen Glasgow.[2]

Canby held to a set of critical standards that he believed defined "good literature"—standards that William Faulkner violated at nearly every turn. Much like the Progressive Era writers studied by Jaime Harker, Canby held tightly to the idea that "literature contained universal truths that could educate, ennoble, and transform."[3] Not surprisingly, then, he was hardly an experimentalist, and his tastes ran closer to Henry James than to Gertrude Stein. Indeed, Canby pitched his magazine to an audience that "could sit still long enough to enjoy recognized story-tellers."[4] In so doing, he earned rebukes from many of the most prominent literary figures of the interwar years. James Agee, for example, was particularly damning, pithily encapsulating the kinds of criticisms leveled against Canby and his style of reviewing by the likes of Malcolm Cowley and others on the literary Left. In one of his private journals Agee jotted down this line of verse: "Hurrah for our Seidel / Side by Seidel / oleo golden mediocrity." Farther down the page, Agee continued:

> Now, with an eye for the side of bread that's buttered,
> Three loud cheers for the Saturday review,
> Which, with faith good sense has seldom fluttered

As the leading journal of literary criticism during one of the most "vivid and dangerous decades of American life and literary history," the *Saturday Review* failed to meet its obligations to its readers and to authors. "Constantly advancing the safe, the cowardly, the dull-hearted and the evil and as constantly opposing the adventurous, the courageous, the serious and the good," Canby's magazine "blind[ed] and drugg[ed] an audience already blind and drugged." Only the *New York Times Book Review*, Agee added, could match its failings.[5]

Although Agee and others held Canby in contempt for his championing of the safe, unadventurous, and bland, they nevertheless understood the role the *Saturday Review* played in mediating their work to middlebrow book buyers.[6] Authors might have disclaimed any wish of becoming something so hopelessly vulgar as "popular," but few openly professed a desire for their books to remain unsold. Indeed, in what Joseph Blotner has referred to as Faulkner's "misleading, but often quoted introduction" to the Modern Library's reprint of *Sanctuary*, Faulkner claimed the novel "was deliberately conceived to make money,"[7] a point many of Faulkner's detractors, including Canby, later exploited.

This essay explores Canby's mediation of Faulkner's *Sanctuary* to his magazine's middlebrow audience. If Canby's readers needed protecting from that which disturbed and provoked, from that which displayed no discernable moral lesson, then Faulkner's novel about bootleggers, drunkards, murderers, lynchers, prostitutes, and "predatory" debutantes demanded to be quarantined. Think of Canby's review as a literary restraining order. Yet Canby's review of *Sanctuary* reveals more than just his unbending sense of literary aesthetics. Rather, it fit into a larger conversation about recent trends in American literature that played out in the pages of the *Saturday Review* and spilled over to other publications, including the *New Republic* and the *New York Times*. *Sanctuary* stood at the center, serving as the whipping boy for what was seen as the Depression Era's penchant for perversity on the one hand and as the antidote for the cloying sentimentalism and romance of genteel southern letters on the other. Canby understood the *Saturday Review of Literature* could ill afford to ignore *Sanctuary* and novels of its ilk. His readers needed to be kept informed of literary trends, even those he thought pernicious. The space devoted to *Sanctuary*, then, points to Canby's efforts to direct the conversation. He might not be able to shield his readers from what he deemed the literature of the perverse, but he could certainly arm them with the latest theories in order to help them make sense of a changing literary landscape.

During the 1920s and 1930s, the reviewing outlets constantly assessed the state of the field, running editorials and symposia on the criteria of sound literary criticism. Under Canby's stewardship, the *Saturday Review of Literature* saw itself as the standard-bearer, and its editorials reminded readers of the qualities that set it apart from other journals of opinion. Two editorials that ran shortly before Canby reviewed *Sanctuary* are particularly telling. In the first, Canby chided his fellow critics for their reticence. Canby held honesty as the critic's chief virtue, and he brooked no soft-pedaling among his staff. "The critic is neither judge nor jury," he explained. "He does not have the final word; at the most he is an advisor." Thus unburdened, a critic must be willing to pronounce unfavorably on an unsuccessful novel. If he lets a "weakling escape his strictures," he charged, "his function as a sanitary officer is certainly not discharged." This comment is telling, for it reveals Canby's understanding of the critic as a literary eugenicist whose greater function served to protect the literary tradition from corrosive elements. Canby did not demand greater hostility in reviewing, simply the courage of one's convictions. "The critic should not be asked to say neither more nor less than he means," he concluded, "but after deliberation and refinement of the first emotions of predilection or prejudice, to say it with neither favor nor fear."[8]

A few weeks later, Canby showed no fear when he published his editorial, "The School of Cruelty," in which he attempted to make sense of "the sadist strain" in American writing. No longer confined to the writers of gritty urbanism, the trend now extended to regionalists who too seem to "hate their America." "The new books about the old South," he noted ruefully, "are by no means idyllic." Proponents defend this literary trend in the name of "realism"; its eager readers excuse it in the name of "novelty." Canby would have none of it. Its practitioners, he asserted, were cruel—cruel because "they are unhappy, because they do not like the life they live in, and perhaps because they do not like themselves." They were, he continued, "weak men and women incapable of either irony or tragedy." Alas, they were also talented, possessing more skill "than many a better adjusted writer who sees more truly but more dully." Too clever by half, the Hemingways and the Dos Passoses were "impudent," capable of "shrewd realism, but of nothing else." "To tell the truth," Canby confessed to what he imagined to be a sympathetic audience, "we are fed up with them." If those sane but boring writers cannot produce novels worth reading, Canby threatened, "we" shall abandon American writing altogether, turning to the "French or Japanese."[9]

By now, Canby's readers were well primed for his review of *Sanctuary*. Perhaps not surprisingly Canby, by titling this review "The School of Cruelty," telegraphed to his magazine's faithful readers his opinion before they glanced at the notice's first word. The review served as a companion piece to his editorial, giving Canby the space to elaborate and elucidate his position. With Faulkner's latest novel, Canby suggested, American literature had hit bottom. Theodore Dreiser, Hemingway, and Sinclair Lewis paled when held up against the Mississippian, whose cold and calculating cruelty was unrivaled even among his fellow "sadists." Canby conceded that Faulkner possessed talent. Faulkner could write a "still and deadly narrative," at once "vivid and convincing." Yet here too the critic bemoaned the writer's penchant for "omitting explanation and connectives." That was hardly Faulkner's greatest crime, however. "The story!" Canby cried out. "No sane reader," he felt confident, can doubt that "somewhere along the path" followed by Faulkner "lies the end of all sanity in fiction." Here, it is worth quoting Canby at some length. "The emotions are sharpened to a febrile obsession with cruelty, lust, and pain," he wrote, "which exaggerates a potentiality of human nature at the expense of human truth. These debased flappers and hideous mobs in a community which seems incapable of virtue in either the Christian or the Roman sense, are bad dreams of reality which no matter how truly set down are false to everything but accident and the exacerbated sensibilities of the author." Indeed, Canby's chief criticism of *Sanctuary* was its author's singular and disconcerting unconcern with the ways in which people "ought" to act, with "why" they act, and with the meaning that rested behind their actions. Faulkner, the most skilled of the writers of "American sadism," has made "the American scene with all its infinite shadings . . . into something gross, sordid," into something depraved "in which the trivial . . . becomes more horrible than professional evil, while what virtue exists in individuals only throws gasoline on the lyncher's fire."[10]

Still, Canby predicted this hard-boiled era "was headed to the dust heap."[11] He saw encouraging signs from across the pond, where the "war-hurt" generation had begun to mellow, "grow[ing] wiser in life and giv[ing] their work . . . substance." He hoped American writers would soon follow suit. The nation needed rediscovering—"for America has to be rediscovered by every generation"—but it was not the "drunkards, gunmen, politicians, near virgins, will-less youths" who have engaged Faulkner and his ilk but rather "the American scene in all its complexity" that needed rediscovering. "They will never do it," Canby concluded, "while one ounce of sadism, one trace of hysteria remains."

Canby's review, long even for the pages of *The Saturday Review*, was not his magazine's final word on *Sanctuary*, however.[12] The novel's popularity, especially after the Modern Library edition appeared in 1932, prompted Canby to situate *Sanctuary* in what he increasingly came to identify as "the literature of horror," a literature he condemned for its obsession with "with disease, defeat, suffering, frustration, the erotic, cruelty and brutality, and mental ill health in general."[13] Even though Canby considered most of these works "vulgar," "indecent," and "obscene," he nevertheless knew that "they are being read by thousands all over the Western world." As a critic, then, Canby was obligated to take this literature seriously. Such "constant neuroticism in current fiction . . . cannot be dismissed by saying that it is good or bad," he confessed to his readers. "It is a fact with which we have to reckon." "We," he asserted—thus inviting his readers into his ranks—"must understand" this literature "better than do puzzled readers who, if they are conservative damn them for their unblushing frankness, and if they are radical, praise them for their supposed release from Victorian inhibitions." Canby thus positioned the *Saturday Review* as the indispensable guide that would give its readers a critical edge over those confused readers who could only, at best, reach ill-informed conclusions based on gut responses.

Aiding Canby was an unlikely partner, Lawrence S. Kubie, a leading psychoanalyst who later counted among his patients Tennessee Williams. In January 1934, Kubie sent to Canby an unsolicited manuscript that examined Erskine Caldwell's 1933 novel *God's Little Acre*. In it, he proposed to examine "a series of curious social and individual paradoxes" that, he maintained, "must be understood if we are ever to understand or evaluate what goes into the creation and the reception of such a book as this."[14] Canby was so taken with the piece that he asked Kubie to apply his theories to other literary works, including Faulkner's *Sanctuary*.[15] After some back and forth between the two—including an exchange in which Kubie chastised Canby for suggesting that the articles constituted "a psychoanalytically grounded attack on these books" and their writers—the series debuted in the fall of 1934.[16]

Kubie's article on *Sanctuary* ran first. In the introduction that prefaced it, Canby maintained that "even . . . the most hasty reviewers of the erotic, neurotic books which come daily to their desks" must acknowledge that "before judgment begins there are some aspects of this literature that need explaining." Clearly, *Sanctuary* offered "obvious reflections of mental states not clear to the reader, nor," he surmised, "clear to the author." Canby thus believed no literary critic could speak "with absolute confidence until some bedside physician has given him . . . the history of the patient." Kubie was that physician. In presenting Kubie to *Saturday Review* readers, Canby emphasized his skill at "carry[ing] out a psychological analysis of specific books" with "competent control and . . . scientific detachment." Canby was clear: Kubie was not writing literary criticism. Only bad things happen when scientists confuse literary with scientific judgment. Kubie was, however, offering case histories of Popeye, Horace Benbow, and Temple Drake. His diagnoses, however controversial, provided the necessary "preliminaries of a literary criticism of neurotic literature." Any "reputable" literary journal that pronounced judgment without taking into account "available explanations" of the characters' neuroses, Canby had concluded, invited censure and scorn.[17]

Kubie had much to say—more than 4,500 words, in fact—but we can boil down his essay to the argument that a proper and full understanding of the actions and motives of *Sanctuary*'s characters hinged on their fear of genital injury. Although Temple is the novel's only victim, Kubie nonetheless argues that one must examine the men "in these tales of rape for evidence of the nature of this basic fear."[18] What becomes immediately apparent, he maintained, is that these male characters "tend to an extraordinary degree to be figures who are crippled either in a directly genital sense or indirectly through some other form of bodily injury. The crippling produces a state of real or psychic impotence" (218). For Kubie, then, it is no mere accident that Popeye, the novel's "chief villain," is impotent (218). "This was not a device chosen by chance out of many alternatives, merely to intensify the horror," he asserted (218). "It was an inevitable choice; because the whole significance of such horror phantasies is linked to the male's constant subterranean struggle with fears of impotence" (218).

Horace, Gowan Stevens, and even Clarence Snopes and the "lame" prosecutor harbor the same fears and anxieties. "It is as though sophisticated and civilized man is conducting a constant struggle against a sense of impending impotence," Kubie wrote, "a struggle which seems to have in it three direct objects of fear, a fear of women, a fear of other men, and a fear of the community and of society in general" (225). And though they try to evade these fears of powerlessness—by abusing women, by turning with "sour scorn" against the structures of society, by making fun of their own desires—they inevitably fail. "Man cannot," Kubie declared, "free himself from the terror and pain of impotence which break through in horror ridden phantasies" (225). Thus, there is no "sanctuary" for these men. Instead, the title mockingly calls out, "There is no escape from anxiety, no escape from horror; therefore let us make of horror a gay tune to dance and to chortle over; let us roll it under our tongues; let us whistle in the dark to prove that we are not afraid; and let us write books about it, tell our friends, and 'hope they will buy it, too'" (225).

Three weeks later, the *Saturday Review of Literature* published four letters to the editor, two of which were penned by writers likely familiar to the magazine's readers, Van Wyck Brooks and Evelyn Scott, and all of which at some level congratulated Canby for running Kubie's psychoanalytic treatment of *Sanctuary*.[19] That's a lot of attention to a novel that Canby did not particularly enjoy, by an author he did not particularly admire, and that was part of a trend that he feared eroded human dignity. Canby's decision to run the piece in the first place is therefore telling, for Canby could have had the last word—and not a favorable one at that—back in March 1931.

Canby operated in an era of the expert—before blogs, Goodreads, and Amazon.com reviews—when readers turned to book sections for informed and reasoned opinion. As Canby understood it, critics advised readers, writing notices that would hold interest even if the work under consideration failed to meet readers' tastes and predilections. Canby felt qualified to speak on whether a novel met standards of "good art" and, as we have seen, in the case of *Sanctuary*, Canby thought not. It is worth remembering that one of Canby's principal complaints about *Sanctuary* at the time of its publication was its failure to explain why the characters behaved the way they did. Certainly characters behaved badly in classical literature and in the novels of Henry James or Edith Wharton. But Canby believed that Sophocles, Shakespeare, and James illuminated human truths while Faulkner merely wallowed in human depravity. If Faulkner could not explain the motivations behind Popeye's and Temple's behavior, neither could Canby. And so the literary critic relied on the psychoanalyst to elucidate for his readers whether Faulkner's characters acted in a way that proved consistent with the latest psychological thinking. Armed with "knowledge," the readers of the *Saturday Review* were now prepared to render their own judgment on *Sanctuary*'s literary merit.

The question that Kubie's piece could not answer—but that Canby's criticism could—was, according to one reader, whether the literary portrayal of horrific acts "is artistic, whether it enables the refined reader to respond to them with an experience of 'this is beautiful.' . . . The creative artist is in no way different from his fellows in what he [fantasizes]," the reader continued, "only in his capacity to make this a source of pleasure even to those who know him not."[20] And that was Canby's point. Canby's readers could now, the editor felt confident, answer those questions with authority.

Canby continued the conversation by publishing Kubie's analysis of *God's Little Acre* two months later. A brief headnote accompanied the article, urgently reminding readers that Kubie did not pen literary criticism but rather scientific analysis that would "supply a basis for a later literary estimate."[21] Kubie conceded the point, but he made clear he thought little of those who roundly rejected modern literature as obscene. In this sense, Kubie's analysis of modern literature's detractors is more important than his comments on Caldwell. Those same readers who "unprotestingly" accept classical erotica by the likes of Rabelais, Casanova, Boccaccio, and Cellini, Kubie charged, are the ones who "raise the cry that these modern books are deliberately capitalizing the morbid and perverse in human nature. In other words," he continued, "an honest and vivid literature, which is struggling to express the confused problems of sex, arouses such hostile, uncomfortable, and suspicious feelings, that it is attacked as dirty, obscene, sick, useless, [and] ugly" (305). The more pronounced the "vigor" of the art, the more powerful the sense of resentment and the firmer the denunciations of obscenity (305). Although some readers might experience "therapeutic relief" from works like *Sanctuary* and *God's Little Acre*, Kubie admitted, the jury was still out on their benefit to society at large (312). For some readers, such novels will "break up inhibited and bigoted ideas about the body" (312). For others, Caldwell and Faulkner will merely confuse. But as the field of psychoanalysis develops, Kubie predicted, and "subjects" itself to the "needs of art," much of the confusion will dissipate (312). Kubie ended his essay by reminding readers that the search for beauty "leads through strange fields; and that to touch the deep chords in human nature . . . might have subtler values than it is possible as yet to characterize" (312).

To be sure, Canby gave over to Kubie a great deal of space in his magazine. But he did not allow Kubie to have the final word, either. A year later, the *Saturday Review of Literature* published an essay by Ellen Glasgow that redirected the conversation once again. The Virginia novelist, once considered something of a literary renegade, had by the 1930s found herself more closely aligned with the southern literary conservatives. Appalled by what she termed "Faulkner's Raw-Head and Bloody-Bones" school of fiction, a phrase she would return to repeatedly during the mid-1930s, Glasgow purposefully set out to publish a novel that countered those penned by the social realists and the writers of the grotesque. In the two years leading up to the publication of *Vein of Iron* (1935), she explained to dozens of correspondents her intent.[22] Early in 1933, for example, she informed Allen Tate that her work in progress examined the poor, but not as a class. "I have seen so much destitution among educated people in this depression," she noted, that she had decided to write about those whom "the breadline seldom reaches."[23] Glasgow earnestly hoped that the tide "of materialism, of cruelty, of vulgarity" would soon turn but recognized that the new era in literature had to be ushered in by "some writer, some critic, who has the ideas and the power to convey their meaning . . . that civilization does not end in noise and many inventions."[24] On the eve of *Vein of Iron*'s publication, she partnered with Canby to announce publicly her assault on prevailing literary trends, thus ensuring that the right author and the right critic led the way.

Orchestrating the entire affair was Glasgow's publisher, Alfred Harcourt, who had invited his author to deliver an address to the Friends of Princeton Library in the spring of 1935.[25] Glasgow's talk, later reprinted as "Heroes and Monsters" in the *Saturday Review*, served as an explanatory note for her latest work. In it, she excoriated both the southern "realists" and those northern critics who embraced them as tellers of the "truth." Glasgow dismissed William Faulkner, Erskine Caldwell, and other darlings of the literati as inconsequential and bristled at critics so easily seduced. Like other southern literary conservatives, Glasgow thought the situation dire. "Few things are more certain than this," she pronounced: "The literature that crawls too long in the mire will lose at last the power of standing erect. On the farther side of deterioration lies the death of a culture."[26]

The *New York Herald-Tribune*'s Lewis Gannett gently chastised Glasgow for this last comment, reminding readers that her career had once been "a protest against refusal to look into the slums of a society and the individual human nature."[27] The former rebel had renounced the old fight, he regretted, and rebuked those who had taken her place. Glasgow responded to Gannett, taking the opportunity to elaborate on her position, for "there isn't much one can say, you know, in ten minutes."[28] She considered the "dark obsession" of the realists as "sensationalism, pure and simple."[29] Pointing to Faulkner's introduction to *Sanctuary*, Glasgow affirmed her comment about the dangers of crawling in the mire. In so doing, she distinguished her earlier literary battles from those of the social realists. "For you must admit that 'to touch mire,' is one thing," she prompted, but "to crawl in slime" is quite another story.[30] "One may touch to destroy, but one crawls too long only for pleasure or profit."[31] Confessing her profound skepticism, she told Gannett, "I remain to be convinced that our latest horror-mongers are angels of light that have fallen by accident in to popular fashion."[32]

Hamilton Basso's comments on Glasgow's address, which appeared in the *New Republic*, were much sharper than Gannett's. In a three-page survey of southern literature, Basso summarily dismissed Glasgow's analysis as uninformed. Like Gannett, Basso found profound irony in Glasgow's rejection of the realists of the 1930s, for she had once castigated Thomas Nelson Page and other writers of the "moonlight and magnolia school" of southern fiction for their "evasive idealism." Now, Glasgow and her ilk claimed that "only the traditionalists have any real and vital connection with the Southern past." If we viewed "the culture of the South as a river," Basso wrote caustically, "we would find them as fresh and gushing tributaries while the realists, who have questioned established authority, would be nothing but dank and smelling swamps breading monsters and malaria." Basso, however, charted the river differently. The South belongs to William Faulkner and Erskine Caldwell as much as it belongs to the traditionalists, he asserted. "The Southern past . . . can be a dead weight or a living instrument." In the hands of the traditionalists, who retreat into the past "as if into some half-lit acropolis away from all sight and sound of the outside world," the past is a burden. The realists, however, use the past to "understand the South today—which is," Basso believed, "the most important part of our inheritance."[33]

Not surprisingly, Basso's article irritated the traditionalists. "Doubtless you've seen the particularly stupid article . . . by Hamilton Basso," Allen Tate wrote to one of his correspondents.[34] He recoiled at Basso's characterization of the traditionalists and affirmed Glasgow's position that the realists wreak great violence "to the art of the novel."[35] Tate charged these iconoclasts with confusing sociology and fiction, noting they were not particularly skilled at either. Stark Young, for his part, initially feared that Basso's article might impugn Glasgow's character. The essay was so badly written, though, "that I don't think the point got out, save to a few who want to think it. It was all too poorly done to work you much harm," he comforted Glasgow.[36] Moreover, Basso, who had attended Glasgow's lecture, behaved abominably. He "drew funny pictures, talked, made faces . . . did dumb shows," thus ruining the talk for everyone at his table.[37] Basso's behavior and his article did not merely offend, however. If Young believed it did little harm to Glasgow's reputation, he did regard it as doing great damage to the South. Basso "slipped into their ears the things they want to think of the South and divers[e] Southern authors," he wrote novelist Caroline Gordon.[38] Young conceded one point, however: "I *will* say this for Basso," he wrote snidely, "he understands the *New Republic*'s South better than any Southern writer I know."[39]

Others weighed in. That same year, Gerald Johnson published "The Horrible South," a follow-up to his 1923 article "The Congo, Mr. Mencken," in which he had prophesized that the South would respond to Mencken's attack by emphasizing the primitive. "It could not be otherwise," he asserted, for it "has the pulse of the tom-tom in its veins, the scents of the jungle its nostrils."[40] Southern literature might be "gorgeously barbaric," he speculated (201). "It may be in some manifestations tremendously evil—it may even wallow in filth, but," he concluded, "it will not dabble in dirt" (201). Johnson believed that the literary careers of Erskine Caldwell, William Faulkner, and Thomas Wolfe had borne out his predictions. To be sure, writers who belonged to an older, more genteel tradition of southern letters continued to ply their trade, "but they remain outside the main current of southern writing" (203). North of the Potomac and west of the Mississippi, Johnson explained, "the impression is general that the characteristic Southerners are the horror-mongers" (203).

Johnson applauded both his prescience and the development in southern fiction. "I find myself able to swell with patriotic pride as the show proceeds," he confessed (216). But he knew that all did not share his enthusiasm. No matter. Those who decried recent literary outputs, he charged, saw "only the lame, the halt, and the blind; the morons, the perverts, the idiots, the murders, the satyriasis and nymphomania" (216). They overlooked "the horror and the pity" that had inspired the region's most talented minds (216). They overlooked "the burning indignation that such things should be in the land we love, and the fierce determination that the South shall see at any cost, shall see although her soul is sickened, shall see in spite of the thick crust of prejudice, hypocrisy, laziness, arrogance, and fear; shall stand, like Faust, for her own soul's salvation, gaze into perdition" (216). Johnson conceded that if the "horror mongers were the South's last word," he might have cause for concern (217). But this group of writers will hardly be the last to wrestle with the South's problems. Rather they will force others to see and to act. "Dixie, far from standing aghast, ought to hail this uproar with the triumphant shot of the Father broadcasting the return of the Prodigal Son; for her youth 'was dead and is alive again, was lost and is found'" (217). A decade into the southern renaissance, Johnson's heady optimism seemed warranted.

The literary landscape looked different at midcentury, however. Even Kubie had come to regret the publication of his articles, although not because he shared the southern traditionalists' revulsion toward neurotic literature. By the 1950s, Kubie wondered whether he had done a disservice to the authors whose works he had scrutinized. "I began to ask myself whether it was fair to do this at all," he explained to R. W. B. Lewis, "whether it was possible to dissect unconscious fantasies in a living author's writings without at least giving the impression that one was holding the man himself up to public analysis. Therefore I broke off the series and have never resumed them; although it has often had a tantalizing lure for me."[41] He made a similar confession to Norman Cousins a few years later.[42] The timing of Kubie's reassessment of his earlier work is telling, for it occurred at moments when Faulkner's and Caldwell's careers were enjoying renaissances. Lewis had requested permission to reprint Kubie's essay in an anthology of Faulkner criticism designed to capitalize on the popularity of all things Faulkner following his Nobel Prize in Literature in 1950. Near the decade's end, United Artists released a cinematic version of *God's Little Acre*, prompting Kubie to raise concerns about the studio's advertising campaign. Because he no longer believed his brand of "literary" analysis valid, he wished to suspend any use of his article in the film's promotion.[43]

If Kubie had disclaimed the validity of a psychoanalytical reading of neurotic literature, midcentury middlebrow readers had reason to see Faulkner as something other than neurotic. In 1946 Viking published Malcolm Cowley's *Portable Faulkner*. In it, Cowley presented not the Faulkner who trafficked in the grotesque but rather the Faulkner who illuminated abiding questions of the human condition. True, the collection contains an excerpt from *Sanctuary*, but it is brief and dwarfed by the other selections. In Cowley's deft hands, Faulkner became not an exponent of sadism and nihilism but a moral fabulist for the nuclear age. A lot had changed in twenty years, including the mediation and reception of William Faulkner. Caroline Gordon, Robert Penn Warren, and Cleanth Brooks might seem to be unlikely champions of the once-maligned "horror-monger," but no more so than Lawrence S. Kubie, who, for a while, was one of Faulkner's most talked-about critics.

NOTES

1. Ross quoted in Ben Yagoda, *About Town: The "New Yorker" and the World It Made* (New York: Scribner's, 2000), 39.

2. Norman Cousins, *Present Tense: An American Editor's Odyssey* (New York: McGraw-Hill, 1967), 3–4. See also Henry Seidel Canby, *American Memoir* (Boston:

Houghton Mifflin, 1947), 267–420. As Jaime Harker has explained, middlebrow readers expected "an emphasis on plot," "formal choices that didn't alienate," and characters and situations with which they could identify. See Jaime Harker, *America the Middlebrow: Women Novelists, Progressivism, and Middlebrow Authorship between the Wars* (Amherst: University of Massachusetts Press, 2007), 19.

3. Harker, *America the Middlebrow*, 13.

4. Cousins, *Present Tense*, 4.

5. Michael A. Lofaro and Hugh Davis, eds., *James Agee Rediscovered: The Journals of "Let Us Now Praise Famous Men" and Other New Manuscripts* (Knoxville: University of Tennessee Press, 2005), 306–7.

6. Harker, *America the Middlebrow*, 16–18. See also Joan Shelley Rubin, *The Making of Middlebrow Culture* (Chapel Hill: University of North Carolina Press, 1992); Janice A. Radway, *A Feeling for Books: The Book-of-the-Month Club, Literary Taste, and Middle-Class Desire* (Chapel Hill: University of North Carolina Press, 1997); and Gordon Hutner, *What America Read: Taste, Class, and the Novel, 1920–1960* (Chapel Hill: University of North Carolina Press, 2009).

7. See Joseph Blotner's notes in William Faulkner, *Sanctuary*, rev. ed. (1931; repr., New York: Vintage International, 1993), 321–22.

8. Henry Seidel Canby, "Reluctant Reviewers," *Saturday Review of Literature*, January 10, 1931, 513.

9. Henry Seidel Canby, "The School of Cruelty," *Saturday Review of Literature*, February 21, 1931, 609.

10. Ibid., March 21, 1931, 673–74.

11. Ibid., 674.

12. As Joseph Blotner has pointed out, the *Saturday Review of Literature* "devoted more space to *Sanctuary* than it had to any three books since the magazine's founding." See Blotner, *Faulkner: A Biography*, vol. 1 (New York: Random House, 1974), 685.

13. Henry Seidel Canby, "Introductory Essay," *Saturday Review of Literature*, October 20, 1934, 217.

14. Lawrence S. Kubie to Henry Seidel Canby, January 29 and February 24, 1934, MS 61720, Lawrence S. Kubie Papers, Library of Congress, Washington, DC (hereafter LOC).

15. Henry Seidel Canby to Lawrence S. Kubie, February 21, 1934, MS 61720, Lawrence S. Kubie Papers, LOC.

16. See, for example, Lawrence S. Kubie to Henry Seidel Canby, September 20, 1934, and enclosure, "Comment's on Dr. Canby's Preface," MS 61720, Lawrence S. Kubie Papers, LOC.

17. Canby, "Introductory Essay," 218. Kubie, anxious to protect himself from accusations of libel, had an attorney read over his draft and suggest revisions. See Robert S. Samuels to Lawrence S. Kubie, May 22, 1934, and "Inserts for Review of Sanctuary," undated TS, MS 61720, Lawrence S. Kubie Papers, LOC. At least one reader commented to Kubie on Canby's introduction: "Incidentally, I thought Canby's introduction, aside from his insistence that you were not being called upon to express artistic judgment, very fine." See Irena to Lawrence S. Kubie, undated, MS 61720, Lawrence S. Kubie Papers, LOC.

18. Lawrence S. Kubie, "William Faulkner's *Sanctuary*," *Saturday Review of Literature*, October 20, 1934, 218. Hereafter cited parenthetically in text.

19. Letters to the Editor, "Four Correspondents on 'The Literature of Horror,'" *Saturday Review of Literature*, November 10, 1934, 272, 280. Kubie received many complimentary letters, too. The sentiments expressed in this letter from a friend were typical: "It was a rare experience to read such a careful, penetrating, graceful, inoffensive review

of a book like 'Sanctuary.' You left nothing unsaid, but you did it all with a rare delicacy of feeling and expression. I congratulate you most heartily." See Sue to Lawrence S. Kubie, October 29, 1934, MS 61720, Lawrence S. Kubie Papers, LOC.

    20. Letters to the Editor, "Four Correspondents," 272.

    21. Lawrence S. Kubie, "God's Little Acre: An Analysis," *Saturday Review of Literature*, November 24, 1934, 305. Hereafter cited parenthetically in text.

    22. See, e.g., Ellen Glasgow to Allen Tate, January 30, 1933, and March 11, 1933; Ellen Glasgow to Stark Young, July 28, 1934; Ellen Glasgow to Irita Van Doren, September 8, 1933; Ellen Glasgow to Bessie Zaban Jones, January 8, 1935; Ellen Glasgow to Edwin Mims, July 1, 1935. All reprinted in Blair Rouse, ed., *Letters of Ellen Glasgow* (New York: Harcourt, Brace, 1958), 126–28, 129–30, 143–44, 158–59, 171–72, and 186–87, respectively).

    23. Ellen Glasgow to Allen Tate, January 30, 1933, in *Letters of Ellen Glasgow*, ed. Blair Rouse (New York: Harcourt, Brace, 1958), 128.

    24. Ellen Glasgow to Allen Tate, March 11, 1933, in *Letters of Ellen Glasgow*, ed. Blair Rouse (New York: Harcourt, Brace, 1958), 129–30.

    25. Alfred Harcourt to Ellen Glasgow, March 20, 1935, in *Letters of Ellen Glasgow*, ed. Blair Rouse (New York: Harcourt, Brace, 1958), 174.

    26. Ellen Glasgow, "Heroes and Monsters," *Saturday Review of Literature*, May 4, 1935, 4.

    27. Lewis Gannett, "Books and Things," *New York Herald-Tribune*, June 7, 1935, 15.

    28. Ellen Glasgow to Lewis Gannett, July 12, 1935, in *Letters of Ellen Glasgow*, ed. Blair Rouse (New York: Harcourt, Brace, 1958), 189. Gannett and Glasgow were on friendly terms. After T. S. Stribling won the Pulitzer Prize for fiction in 1933, Gannett wrote a column in the *Herald-Tribune* arguing that Glasgow's *Sheltered Life* was the better novel and should have won. Glasgow sent Gannett a short note of thanks, declaring, even then, that although she was "imperfectly reconciled to a world in which the noisy, the timely, and the second best almost invariably wins in the race, I have learned, after thirty years of watching, that the race itself is far from important. Nothing really matters but to reserve, at cost, one's own sense of artistic integrity." See Ellen Glasgow to Lewis Gannett, May 25, 1933, in *Letters of Ellen Glasgow*, ed. Blair Rouse (New York: Harcourt, Brace, 1958), 135–36.

    29. Ellen Glasgow to Lewis Gannett, July 12, 1935, in *Letters of Ellen Glasgow*, ed. Blair Rouse (New York: Harcourt, Brace, 1958), 189.

    30. Ibid.

    31. Ibid.

    32. Ibid.

    33. Hamilton Basso, "Letters in the South," *New Republic*, June 19, 1935, 163.

    34. Allen Tate to John Peale Bishop, July 3, 1935, in *The Republic of Letters in America: The Correspondence of John Peale Bishop and Allen Tate*, ed. Thomas Daniel Young and John J. Hindle (Lexington: University Press of Kentucky, 1981), 118.

    35. Ibid.

    36. Stark Young to Ellen Glasgow, September 2, 1935, in *Stark Young: A Life in the Arts: Letters, 1900–1962*, ed. John Pilkington, vol. 1 (Baton Rouge: Louisiana State University Press, 1975), 637.

    37. Ibid., 636.

    38. Stark Young to Caroline Gordon, undated, Correspondence Files, Caroline Gordon Papers, Princeton University Library, Princeton, NJ.

    39. Ibid.

40. Gerald Johnson, "The Horrible South," *Virginia Quarterly Review* 9 (Winter 1935): 201. Henceforth cited parenthetically in text. See also Gerald Johnson to Lambert Davis, March 24, 1934, and Lambert Davis to Gerald Johnson, March 27, 1934, both in the Papers of the *Virginia Quarterly Review*, 1925–1935, Albert and Shirley Small Special Collections Library, University of Virginia, Charlottesville.

41. Lawrence S. Kubie to R. W. B. Lewis, May 17, 1951, MS 61720, Lawrence S. Kubie Papers, LOC.

42. Lawrence S. Kubie to Norman Cousins, April 16, 1958, MS 61720, Lawrence S. Kubie Papers, LOC.

43. Ibid.

Building the Brand: Faulkner at Random

JAY SATTERFIELD

At Dartmouth College's Rauner Special Collections Library, we pride ourselves in open access to a phenomenal collection. We have a beautiful space, collections that have been developed over nearly 250 years, and a commitment to seeing that the collections are used. During the 2014–2015 academic year, 126 different classes accounting for 220 sessions used the collections directly. These classes came from 30 different departments and brought in over 1,800 students on a campus with only 4,200 students. That is over 40 percent of the student body just for classes. One such class was American Writers between the World Wars. One of the major assignments was to take a prominent novel from the interwar period and use the material artifact of the book, the advertisements for the book, and the publishing context that produced the book to write about how it may have been perceived in its first year. *The Great Gatsby* is a wonderful example. With its cover art that Fitzgerald saw before he finished the novel and, in his words "wrote in," it has the glitter and excitement of the Jazz Age but with the pathos of the novel superimposed over it.[1] And then there is the back of the jacket: boldly stated across the top is "Perilously Near a Masterpiece."[2] It has to be one of the best blurbs ever. Is the book almost a masterpiece, or do they say that just because Fitzgerald will be shelved perilously near Faulkner and Hemingway? It is a great assignment that helps students to think about the materiality of their reading, canon formation, and the impact of a text's cultural context on its reception in a specific historical time and place. It is book history, and that is my specialty. I am not a Faulkner scholar but a book historian, so I am going to address Faulkner's works in that context: as commodities in a marketplace to be bought and sold and the implications of their being a commodity on reception and perception.

In 1933 Bennett Cerf, publisher of the Modern Library and cofounder of its then-recently established subsidiary, Random House, met with Eugene O'Neill, whose publisher, Horace Liveright, had just gone bankrupt. Cerf was keen to bring O'Neill into the small but growing stable of writers at Random House. O'Neill was an author who bore the promise to be the Holy Grail for a new company bent on creating attractive books of lasting value and selling them for a profit: he was popular enough to ensure healthy sales and also possessed tremendous cultural capital with the literati. Cerf followed up his visit with a four-page proposal: "What the Modern Library Can Offer Mr. O'Neill." Not only would Random House hire O'Neill's longtime editor Saxe Commins to be "at Mr. O'Neill's service," but Cerf also promised beautiful books. "All limited editions of Mr. O'Neill's books will, in the future, be handled in the most efficient manner possible and . . . the typography will be supervised by the best printers in the country."[3] It went on, though, to offer more, a kind of vertical integration new to the field: "The fact that Random House and the Modern Library are parts of the same corporation will mean that any reprint editions of Mr. O'Neill's books will be completely cared for, and in short, every possible kind of edition of the books—the limited editions, trade editions, and reprint editions— will be the responsibility of the same firm."[4] His pitch worked. O'Neill was wooed not only by Cerf's "drive and enthusiasm, coupled with keen shrewdness," but also by Cerf's ambitions beyond the normal expectations of trade publishing.[5] O'Neill noted that Cerf has "a love of beautiful books, an appreciation for good literature, an ambition to keep his firm above the level of the others, to expand only along lines of distinction."[6] And finally, "Cerf has two unique things—[the] Modern Library and Random House."[7]

A few years later, in 1936, Random House made the first of many major acquisitions that would one day make it a giant in literary publishing. It absorbed the young but decidedly literary firm of Smith & Haas, making Robert Haas a one-third partner in Random House and bringing a host of new writers under the imprint, including William Faulkner. Cerf did not need to sell Random House to Faulkner as aggressively as he did to the free agent O'Neill, but he had already used the Modern Library reprint series to open conversations with him.[8] It is hard to imagine he did not court his stable's new horse without zeal. Cerf is known for that—wildly enthusiastic, infectiously personable, and forever selling. Sometimes he was a bit over the top and perhaps not as dignified as what one might expect in a literary publisher, but he possessed a keen sense of how to promote authors' reputations and sell their books.[9] He may have lacked the level of cultural prestige enjoyed by Alfred Knopf at the time, but more than any other publisher, Cerf had the potential to take a literary author and push his or her works to the vast, affluent American middle class without ever tainting the author with crass commercialism.

Faulkner's relationship to Random House from the merger of Smith & Haas with Random in 1936 to just before he won the Nobel Prize was crucial to the development and maintenance of his reputation. The period included the publication of *Absalom, Absalom!* in 1936, *The Unvanquished* in 1938, *The Wild Palms* in 1939, *The Hamlet* in 1940, *Go Down, Moses* in 1942, and *Intruder in the Dust* in 1948. His first years with Random House were a prolific time in Faulkner's career, but a period of low productivity and artistic struggle followed. When Faulkner came to Random House in 1936, he had the potential to bring new prestige to the relatively young imprint. But the energetic young publishers he had joined had much to offer Faulkner as well. Through skillful and timely marketing strategies, Random House reestablished the Faulkner brand—a brand that would later help to cement his place in the American literary canon.

According to Cerf, Faulkner "had a firm belief that the author writes the book and the publisher publishes it. He would bring in a manuscript, and I'd say, 'Bill, do you have any ideas about the book jacket and the advertising?' Bill would say, 'Bennett, that's your job. If I didn't think you did it well, I'd go somewhere else.'"[10] Cerf went on to say that they lavished extra attention on Faulkner's books to "prove to him that he was right" in trusting them.[11] And Faulkner had every reason to trust them.

Cerf approached the selling of books differently than most American publishers. His introduction to the business was working for the brashly commercial Horace Liveright at Boni & Liveright, the firm that invented the book launch party and knew that any publicity (especially a sensational book banning) was good publicity.[12] Cerf nurtured his commercialism at Boni & Liveright, but he also sought to emulate the prestige-minded Alfred Knopf. He said of Knopf, "His Borzoi books were my dream of the ways books should look. To me, everything he did represented publishing at its best."[13] The huckster and the distinguished gentleman, Cerf tried to marry these two distinct personalities with his own gregarious self to create the perfect publishing monster. Of course, he wasn't alone at Random House. His initial partner, Donald Klopfer, was a shrewd businessman who managed the production and distribution side of the firm. Without his level head, Cerf may have tended more toward Liveright's flashy persona at the cost of the firm's prestige. And with the Smith & Haas merger, his marketing skills were taken to a new level by Robert Haas—a cofounder of the Book-of-the-Month Club. The three partners, with the talented Saxe Commins on the editorial staff, balanced each other and created a publishing colossus.

Important for Faulkner's time at Random was Cerf's view of advertising. For years most people in the publishing industry had dismissed the notion that advertising was an effective way to sell books. It was considered a kind of necessary evil to appease authors' egos. They argued that books were not soap and could not be marketed with the same techniques.[14] Modern advertising was not designed to sell a single item. It would not behoove Ivory Soap to run ads in national magazines to convince someone to buy one bar of soap. Modern advertising was predicated on the idea of establishing a brand and creating a market dedicated to that brand. So Ivory might spend a lot of money to get customers to buy one bar of soap, but they were really setting them up to become repeat buyers. If they liked the soap, they were likely to buy another bar—and then another each week for the rest of their lives. The modern ad campaign worked because it created long-term repeat buyers.[15]

People in the book trade reasoned that they could devote the same advertising dollars to get you to buy a copy of a novel, but then the return would abruptly stop. How likely is it that someone will buy the same book again? Well, if she really loves it, she might buy a copy for a friend, but for the most part, it is a one-and-done situation. But Cerf, Knopf, and a few other rising publishers knew better. They knew they could develop advertising strategies to sell the line. Here is Knopf in 1923 touting his Borzoi books:

> When a writer brings us a manuscript that we think the public should have a chance to read, we publish it. We do not permit its sales possibilities to influence our judgment one way or another. We hope it will register with the Cash Register, but we will publish it in any event so long as it "registers" as a book! Most of our books are financial successes for the author, some of them achieve large sales, but all of them are productions of merit, for we will never put the BORZOI imprint on anything else. Buy a BORZOI BOOK Today. Its label is the label of merit.[16]

While Knopf's claim that he ignored the bottom line when selecting titles seems dubious, his assertion of his brand held weight. When most readers see that little emblem of Knopf's Borzoi, or Random House's stone mansion, or the Modern Library's Promethean torchbearer on a book, they *know* it is good.

Think about how differently you might approach a Penguin classic as opposed to a Harlequin romance: those brands have been developed, promoted, and protected, and they matter. They affect the way people read. Consider, for instance, the following two books, featuring almost the same title: one is William Lee's *Junkie: Confessions of an Unredeemed Drug Addict* (New York: Ace Paperback, 1953) and the other is William Burroughs's *Junky* (New York: Penguin Book, 2003). One is an Ace paperback at 35 cents published *dos-à-dos* with *Narcotic Agent*. You finish *Junky*, flip the book over, and you get *Narcotic Agent*. Lurid cover art on both sides suggests sex, drugs, and violence, and the book is published in the standard pulp fashion of the 1950s. The other is a Penguin. Billed as the "50th anniversary definitive edition," it has a modern, sophisticated cover design and an introduction by Oliver Harris. In addition to the introduction (with footnotes), there are seven appendices, one by Allen Ginsberg, another by Carl Solomon, another a variant of chapter 28, and a glossary. The packaging and branding of these books are shaping a reader's perception (see Figures 1, 2, and 3).

Now imagine yourself reading the Ace paperback. You get to a sentence or paragraph that you do not really understand. What is your reaction? Most likely you will declare that the book is trash and poorly written by a hack writer. Now imagine reading the Penguin. By the time you get to the text, you have been pounded over the head with its importance. It is in the Penguin line, and it is by an author who, the book has told you, has been a major literary influence over the past half century. If you come to a passage that you do not understand (and with Burroughs that will probably happen), well, what is your response? Not everyone, but most of us will feel we are inadequate. We are not up to the task of understanding this great work of art.

There is a critical difference here. In one case, the onus is on the book. It has to prove itself worthy of the reader and the reader's time. If any part fails, even momentarily, it is the author's fault. In the other case, the onus is on the reader. The reader has to rise to the level of the novel. The Penguin is encrusted with cultural capital, the Ace is stripped of it. Now both of these are commodities in a marketplace, and they both sold, but they have been branded much differently. One is presented as a work of lasting literary merit, the other as an ephemeral, throwaway read. What makes this particular instance so remarkable is that in both cases it is the same text. The Ace paperback is the first edition of William Burroughs's *Junky*—published under a pseudonym with the only publisher he could get to touch it. Fifty years later, it is presented as a modern masterpiece on its way to becoming a classic.

The editorial staff at Random House understood this dynamic, and they also understood that brand names matter. They sought to build off the Modern Library's cultural cachet to make their brand a guarantee of quality, and they cultivated their list to reflect that ethos. They wanted their books to get the benefit of the doubt from readers—culturally speaking, the reader needed to come to them. At the same time, they wanted to sell as reliably as Ivory Soap.

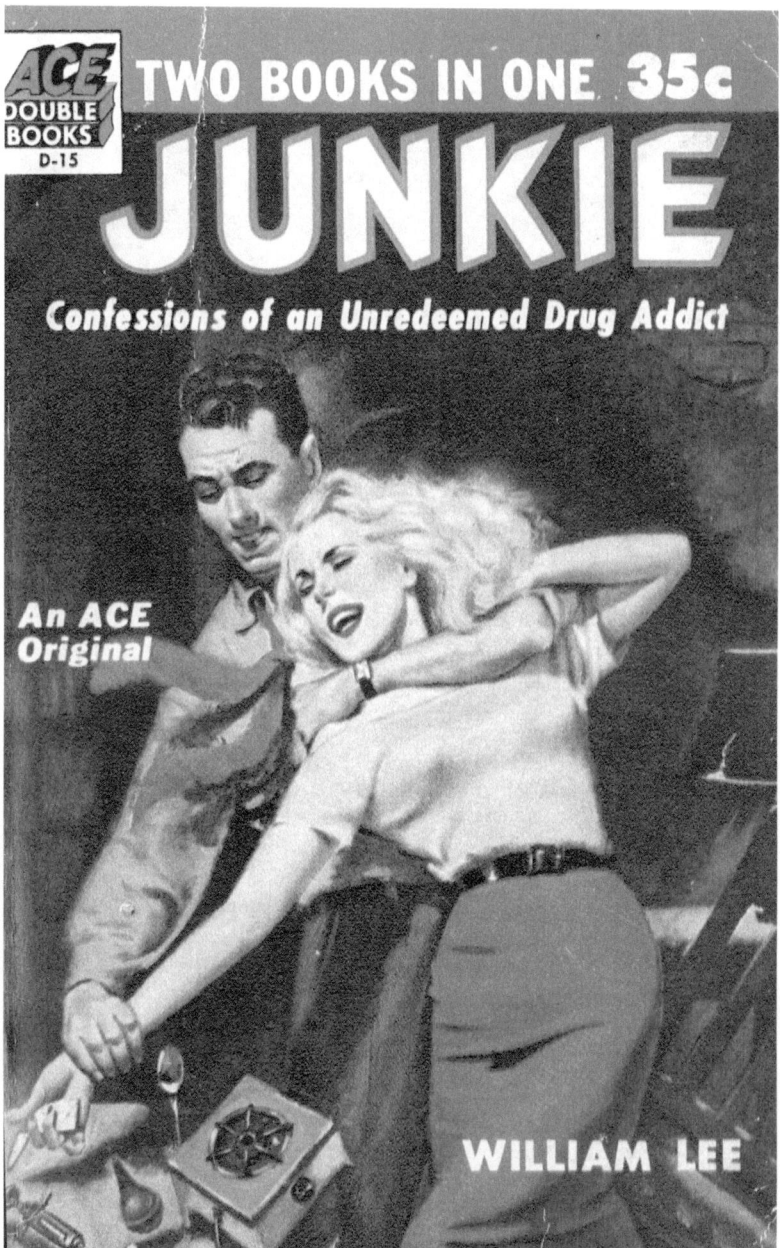

Fig. 1

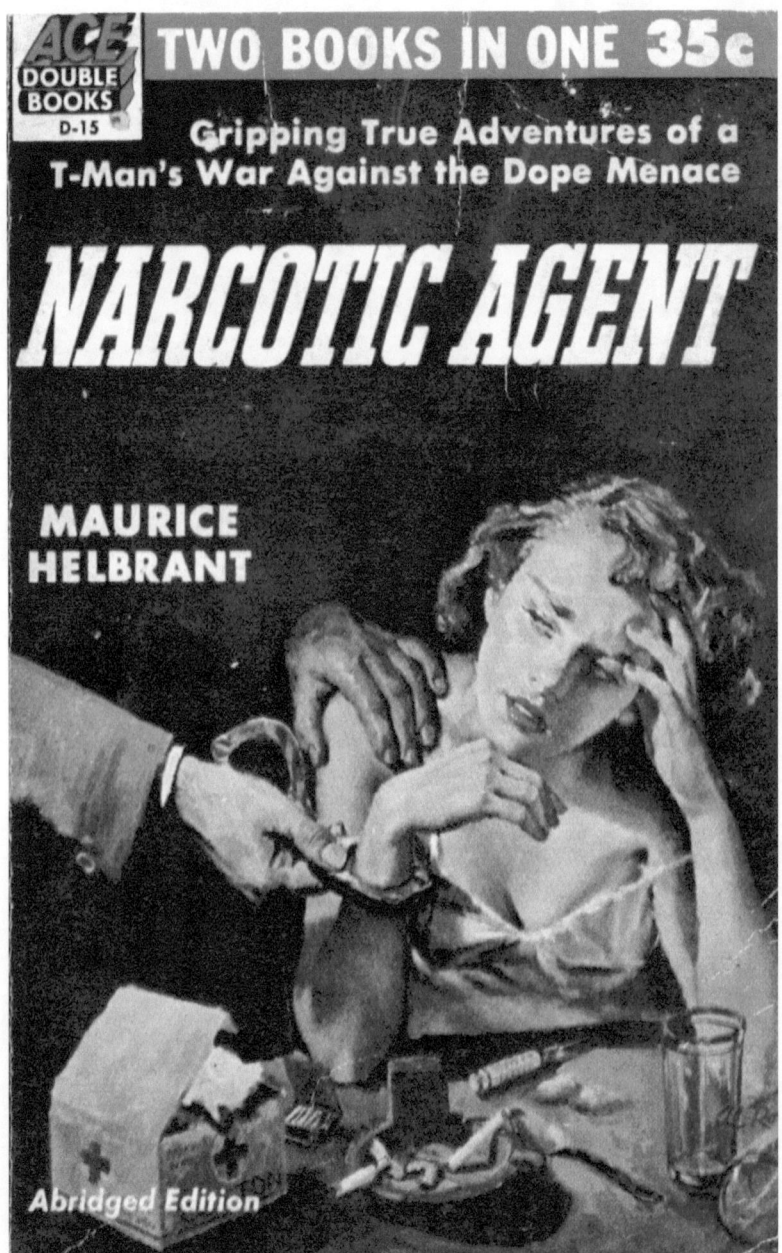

ACE DOUBLE BOOKS D-15

TWO BOOKS IN ONE 35c

Gripping True Adventures of a
T-Man's War Against the Dope Menace

NARCOTIC AGENT

MAURICE HELBRANT

Abridged Edition

Fig. 2

Fig. 3

In 1932 Random House took out an ad in *Publishers' Weekly* (the trade journal for publishers and booksellers) depicting a woman in a bathtub surrounded by copies of Modern Library books floating among the suds: *The Magic Mountain*, *Droll Stories*, *Of Human Bondage*, *Swann's Way*, and Faulkner's *Sanctuary*. "They Float" screamed the headline, in reference to Ivory Soap's then-famous slogan. The ad sells the Modern Library, and in this case Faulkner, like soap. It deemphasizes the Modern Library as literature and pushes it as profitable merchandise for booksellers.[17] Cerf was, of course, ridiculing the industry's claim that books aren't soap. The floating books are grouping individual titles under a single heading, the Modern Library, to emphasize the power of a brand name and its potential for creating repeat sales. The ad is not selling any individual book but selling the line. And it is so clever. "They Float" had been advertised to the point where every American knew the phrase— but unstated in this ad is the rest of the slogan: "99 44/100ths Percent Pure." Cerf was wooing booksellers by claiming that the Modern Library was editorially pure and as dependable as soap in a drugstore.[18]

Cerf *never* would have put an ad like this in the popular press where actual book buyers would see it. That would risk undermining the brand's reputation and, as a result, cheapening the product in the eyes of book buyers. When people buy a novel by Proust, they do not want to think they are succumbing to clever marketing—they are having a sacred moment. They are exercising their personal choice to enjoy a cultural masterpiece fitted to their elevated tastes in art and literature. They see themselves as being cool in an intellectual, cultured sort of way. They do not walk away embarrassed by their purchase but proud and hoping someone notices. Cerf's ads to the public show something very different than his ads to the trade: the ads were based on the assumption that his readers were daring, intelligent individuals. They did not appeal to reader insecurity as the Harvard Classics often did.[19] Instead, they used rational arguments that emphasized the book buyer's inherent good taste and freedom of choice.[20]

Here is a gratuitous example of Cerf's cavalier attitude with the trade, but it illustrates his playful, joking ways (he was the author of many joke books and a regular on *What's My Line?*, after all) and his clever use of not-so-subtle humor. When Macmillan was making a killing on Kathleen Winsor's sensational historical romance *Forever Amber* in 1944, she was featured on the cover of *Publishers' Weekly*.[21] Her personality and looks made her a natural on the book tour, and Macmillan had no scruples about using her physicality to sell a notorious and scandalous bodice ripper—remember that this was even before the era of *Mad Men*, and the old boys at the publishing office were decidedly unliberated in their thinking about gender. Cerf was undaunted. He responded by taking out a full-page ad in *Publishers' Weekly* a few weeks later that proclaimed "Shucks, we've got glamour girls, too!" under a picture of decidedly frumpy Gertrude Stein and Alice B. Toklas.[22] It is an interesting ad. It is a clear snubbing of the nose at Macmillan's handling of Winsor, but by featuring an avant-garde writer and her partner, it was also a definite assertion of Random House's cultural superiority. Just what does "glamour" mean anyway? Random House offers the glamour of the mind, not the body. Still, it is hard to imagine Cerf ever publishing this ad in a place where Stein's readers would have seen it.

So how did this approach play out with Faulkner? Random House started with zeal. The first Faulkner title under the imprint was *Absalom, Absalom!* in 1936. Random not only sold the book with direct advertising but also pushed Faulkner's name. In an August 30, 1936, ad in the *New York Times Book Review*, Random House leads off its fall 1936 authors list with Faulkner—an author who had yet to publish a book with Random but one they hoped to elevate in their ranks.[23] Another display ad from May 23, 1937, places Faulkner squarely in the company that was making Random House a "Rising Star." Faulkner is featured with Eugene O'Neill, James Joyce, and Proust. The text here is worth quoting at length:

> The first book to bear the imprint of Random House appeared in 1928. In the past five years, more Random House books have been chosen by the "Fifty Books of the Year" juries for typographic excellence than those of any other publisher in America, though a dozen firms publish more books in a month than Random House publishes in a season. The editorial content of Random House books is consistent with the beauty of their format. Featured on this page are only some of the books that Random House has sponsored in the nine years of its existence.[24]

The word *sponsored* (rather than published or sold) hides Random's commercialism behind a shroud of patronage. The ad goes on to remind readers that Random House publishes the Modern Library and had successfully fought to lift the American obscenity ban on James Joyce's *Ulysses*. The imprint is presenting itself as a classy new joint in town where Faulkner has just become a regular.

Random House launched *Absalom, Absalom!* with four ads in the *New York Times* in November and December of 1936.[25] Two of these ads pushed the line by featuring other books in the Random House fall list, but Faulkner gets top billing in one of them. The other two are devoted exclusively to his new novel. Random House knew it did not have a *Gone with the Wind*, that year's runaway best seller, on its hands, but it still devoted a solid chunk of advertising change on a book without much commercial potential, and it used that advertising money to assert Faulkner as a major literary talent.

Contrast this with the way Random presented *Absalom, Absalom!* to the trade: pushing the novel to the top of a four-page list that included the *Theater Guild Anthology*, Gertrude Stein, Stephen Spender, Pushkin, and John Strachey, among others, a 1936 ad in *Publishers' Weekly* touts sales potential: "10,000 copies are the least that have been sold of any Faulkner novel published during the past six years. *Absalom, Absalom!*—the story of the rise and disintegration of a strange southern family—is an exciting and saleable successor to *Sanctuary* and *Light in August*."[26] There is nothing about the novel being a good book, nothing about Faulkner as a major voice in American literature, and no catchy blurbs. This ad is about exciting the sales force by emphasizing units and giving the bookseller talking points. The book, however, did not live up to the sales of earlier books, selling a disappointingly low eight thousand copies. [27]

The physical book itself got the usual lavish attention that Random House prided itself on. The trade edition sold for $2.50 and featured artwork by George Salter, one of the most creative and adventurous book jacket designers in the business at the time. The printing included the added expense of the two-color foldout map reproduced from a drawing by Faulkner. Random also used the back cover to enmesh Faulkner within a burgeoning canon by again associating him with Havelock Ellis, Marcel Proust, Herman Melville, James Joyce, and Eugene O'Neill: the jacket copy advertises these authors as part of "a LIFETIME Library."[28] The books are made to last a lifetime, but the texts within justify the production—these are books readers will want to return to again and again.

Simultaneously, Random brought out a limited edition at double the price: $5.00 (the equivalent to $85.00 in 2015). The limited edition used the exact same printing plates but was printed on bright rag paper with untrimmed deckle edges. It was issued without a dust jacket; instead, it was protected by a green and gold paste-paper binding. And of course, it contained a limitation statement (three hundred copies) signed by Faulkner. An author signature and a limitation statement can do something to a book. They elevate the book and the author. The book was touched, the hand of the author is directly involved. In an age of mechanical reproduction, this has the aura of the original. At the same time, it suggests that the author is an artist—his signature means he has deemed this book true to him and his vision.

This basic marketing strategy was employed through the remainder of the 1930s, though with each successive book, a little less attention was given to Faulkner, whose sales were disappointing. Random House kept up a chatter about Faulkner's literary importance, but the company seemed to have accepted, at least temporarily, that his books would probably represent a loss.[29] This is not that unusual. Literary houses often subsidize authors in exchange for the prestige they may bring to the brand. Still, the extent of Random's patience with a demanding and temperamental author who failed to earn back his advances is notable, especially when it's considered that Faulkner was not at that time achieving the level of critical acclaim we now take for granted.

The war years disrupted the publishing industry on nearly all fronts: paper supplies were unpredictable, the market for books shifted, Armed Services Editions changed the look and feel of books, and publishers and authors found themselves in the military. The trade did not take a hiatus like many others, but marketing was toned down, and a certain retrenchment occurred in the field. Random House did not take out a single ad in 1942 or 1943 for *Go Down, Moses* in the *New York Times*, an indication of the expectation of sales but also of a period of stress in the industry.

But when the war was finally over, publishers recognized the potential for new sales—returning GIs fed on Armed Services Editions would be hungry for more books, especially those returnees entering college on the GI Bill. Families had newfound disposable income to spend (and a temporary dearth of consumer products on the market). There was a chance to expand vastly the size of the book-buying public, and publishers were willing to push books more aggressively and try new marketing strategies.[30] For Faulkner, this meant that he needed to produce something new. With so much of his attention in Hollywood, Random House needed to coax him to write—ideally something popular—to cash in on the new potential market. This became far more urgent after 1946. That year Malcolm Cowley worked with Viking Press on *The Portable Faulkner*, a reintroduction of Faulkner to a new generation of avid readers. Cerf and Random House saw the opportunity and worked to free Faulkner from other obligations so he could produce a new book.[31] It was slow in coming. Faulkner had been struggling through the war years and hadn't published a novel since *The Hamlet* in 1940 or a book with Random House since *Go Down, Moses*, a collection of short stories, in 1942. Finally, in 1948, Random House got something close to what it wanted, *Intruder in the Dust*, a book that had the potential to expand Faulkner's audience.

Intruder was announced to the trade with a flourish in *Publishers' Weekly*. Random House boasted a "Banner List" for 1948. Topping the list of authors was William Faulkner. The next page featured a full-page ad: "first new novel in 8 years," "*An event of importance in American letters!*"[32] Indulging in some hyperbole, the ad states that "William Faulkner's reputation has grown immeasurably in the eight years since his last book."[33] To the public, Random House pushed the novel as "an event in American Literature" that "has no American rival" and is "a triumphant work of art."[34] Faulkner's name, boldly printed in a large typeface, nearly overshadows the title of the book in the ad. Among the cool things we have at Dartmouth's Rauner Special Collections Library is a copy of Shakespeare's first folio from 1623. The iconic title page, with its portrait of Shakespeare and emphasis on his authorship, asserts his standing and his importance as a writer in a way that is a quantum leap from how he had ever before appeared on a title page. On a lesser scale, the Random ad follows up the *Portable Faulkner* and is Faulkner's "folio" for Random House. He is a force, he is important, and he is a must read. He has no rival since Melville or James, his work is a second cousin to *Huckleberry Finn*, he has "hypnotic verbal intensity," he *is* America's major novelist.[35] There is a quotation from Malcolm Cowley that actually has nothing to do with the book being advertised, though it is pulled out of context to seem like it does: "Faulkner performed a labor of imagination that has not been equaled in our time. . . . No author has a higher standing among his fellow novelists. . . . At his best—sometimes at his worst—he has a power, a richness of life and intensity to be found in no other American novelist of our time."[36] The passage is from Cowley's introduction to the *Portable Faulkner* of two years earlier, but in this context, surrounded by other blurbs about *Intruder in the Dust*, the typical reader would have reasoned that Cowley was writing about the novel being advertised.

This ad is not really about *Intruder in the Dust*. It is about Faulkner. It is an attempt to grab the cultural capital Cowley lent to Faulkner with the *Portable Faulkner* and transform it into an unabashed assertion of Faulkner's literary standing at a point when he is being reintroduced to an American reading public that was made much larger and more affluent by the war years. It is timely—the hiatus of the war and the hiatus in Faulkner's publishing gave Random the opportunity to reintroduce him as the author the company wanted him to be—both popular and a literary genius—as opposed to the Faulkner who limped (at least commercially) through his first twelve years at Random.

The book, with its film noir cover and eerie dust jacket, is described in the jacket blurb as "a study of murder and the mass mind," "distinguished for its penetration, subtlety, and gripping narrative power."[37] In other words, it's a literary work that's also a page-turner. The back of the jacket sold the line, but not Random's line: Faulkner's. It presents Faulkner as a brand name. Interestingly, he is a brand that no longer appears to need blurbs from critics or other writers nor the association of other, better-known writers. Instead, the *Intruder* jacket simply lists "Books by William Faulkner." Random House was presenting Faulkner as an established force in American letters. Perhaps this was true in the firm's mind and certainly in Cowley's, but it was not quite true yet to most of the American reading public. Through the 1930s and 1940s, his books continually disappointed Random and Faulkner himself with sagging sales. Cowley certainly made the claim for Faulkner's importance, but it was a claim yet to be taken up by many others. It seems that Random House wanted to assert it as a given as in the *Publishers' Weekly* ad: "*An event of importance in American letters!*" The book itself speaks this way—there is a kind of unquestioned assumption of the literary worth of the novel and of Faulkner's writing.

Sales figures for *Intruder in the Dust* were more respectable than for Faulkner's other works at Random. The novel sold twenty-three thousand copies and finally made Faulkner a break-even author for Random House. The sales figure dwarfed the eight thousand copies for *Absalom, Absalom!*, the seven thousand for *The Hamlet*, and the mere four thousand copies for *Go Down, Moses*. *The Wild Palms* topped the early Random years with twelve thousand copies.[38]

On November 10, 1950, Faulkner was awarded the Nobel Prize in Literature. *Intruder in the Dust* had finally made Faulkner a profitable author for Random House after years as a loss to the firm. The Modern Library list included *Sanctuary* and *Light in August*. An *Absalom, Absalom!* reprint was planned for 1951. The brand was established, and Random House and Faulkner were poised to turn years of patient marketing into profit—they could leverage the cultural capital they had created to produce more tangible capital. The kind that pays the rent.

Interestingly, it does not appear that any of this went as planned. Random appears to have seen in Faulkner an opportunity to build its own brand by using his growing literary status to lend prestige to the Random imprint. But as Faulkner faltered in the 1940s and Random's brand ascended, the company could combine its prestige with that of the Modern Library and the Viking Portable series to keep Faulkner's name and work current. Without all of that, would the Nobel committee have given him the recognition it did in November 1950? I am not sure, but I suspect not. I am going to leave this open because this is where it would be nice to be a full-fledged Faulkner scholar instead of a book historian. But I hope that further discussion brings forth another series of influences on Faulkner and his reputation at a critical time in his career. The

Random touch built his brand over a period of lax productivity and carried his work far enough forward that other markers of distinction could be added to his name. Those in turn brought more attention in critical circles and with the general reading public to help make Faulkner the revered author he is today.

NOTES

1. F. Scott Fitzgerald to Maxwell Perkins, August 27, 1924, quoted in Matthew J. Bruccoli, ed., *F. Scott Fitzgerald: A Life in Letters* (New York: Scribner's, 1994), 79.

2. F. Scott Fitzgerald, *The Great Gatsby* (New York: Scribner's, 1925), dust jacket.

3. "Report to O'Neill," June 27, 1933, Random House Archives, Columbia University, New York.

4. Ibid.

5. Eugene O'Neill to Saxe Commins, May 31, 1933, quoted in *"Love and Admiration and Respect": The O'Neill-Commins Correspondence*, ed. Dorothy Commins (Durham, NC: Duke University Press, 1986), 159–60. For further discussion of Random House's wooing of O'Neill, see Jay Satterfield, *"The World's Best Books": Taste, Culture, and the Modern Library* (Amherst: University of Massachusetts Press, 2002), 114–15.

6. Ibid.

7. Ibid.

8. See Frederick R. Karl, *William Faulkner: American Writer* (New York: Weidenfeld & Nicolson, 1989), 468–70, and Bennett Cerf, *At Random: The Reminiscences of Bennett Cerf* (New York: Random House, 1977), 129.

9. Thomas B. Morgan, "The Long Happy Life of Bennett Cerf," *Esquire*, March 1964, 112–13.

10. Cerf, *At Random*, 129.

11. Ibid.

12. See Tom Dardis, *Firebrand: The Life of Horace Liveright* (New York: Random House, 1955).

13. Cerf, *At Random*, 55.

14. O. H. Cheney, *Economic Survey of the Book Industry, 1930–1931* (1931; repr., New York: R .R. Bowker, 1960), 285.

15. Satterfield, *"World's Best Books,"* 38–41.

16. Alfred Knopf advertisement, *New York Times*, April 28, 1923.

17. Modern Library advertisement, *Publishers' Weekly*, May 14, 1932, 2015.

18. Satterfield, *"World's Best Books,"* 78.

19. For an excellent discussion of the Harvard Classics' marketing strategies, see Joan Shelley Rubin, *The Making of Middlebrow Culture* (Chapel Hill: University of North Carolina Press, 1992), 93–147.

20. Satterfield, *"World's Best Books,"* 38–64.

21. *Publishers' Weekly*, September 9, 1944, cover.

22. *Publishers' Weekly*, October 28, 1944, inside front cover.

23. Random House advertisement, *New York Times Book Review*, August 30, 1936, 24.

24. Random House advertisement, *New York Times Book Review*, May 23, 1937, 105.

25. The four Random House advertisements appeared in the *New York Times* or the *New York Times Book Review*, December 13, 1936, 23; December 10, 1936, 25; November 15, 1936, 20; and November 9, 1936, 17

26. Random House advertisement, *Publishers' Weekly*, August 22, 1936, 560.

27. Lawrence H. Schwartz, *Creating Faulkner's Reputation: The Politics of Modern Literary Criticism* (Knoxville: University of Tennessee Press, 1988), 20.

28. William Faulkner, *Absalom, Absalom!* (New York: Random House, 1936), dust jacket.

29. For an excellent discussion of Faulkner's ups and downs with Random House, see Schwartz, *Creating Faulkner's Reputation*, 38–72.

30. For a good summary, see John Tebbel, *A History of Book Publishing in the United States*, vol. 4, *The Great Change, 1940–1980* (New York: R. R. Bowker, 1981), 50–61.

31. Schwartz, *Creating Faulkner's Reputation*, 45–47.

32. Random House advertisements, *Publishers' Weekly*, June 26, 1948, cover and inside pages.

33. Ibid.

34. Random House advertisement, *New York Times Book Review*, October 24, 1948, 14.

35. Ibid.

36. Ibid.

37. William Faulkner, *Intruder in the Dust* (New York: Random House, 1948), dust jacket.

38. Schwartz, *Creating Faulkner's Reputation*, 20, 63.

Gearing Up for War: Faulkner's "Two Soldiers" and the *Saturday Evening Post*

JENNIFER NOLAN

"Two Soldiers" appeared as the lead item in the March 28, 1942, issue of the *Saturday Evening Post* less than two months after Faulkner's agent, Harold Ober, received it.[1] Both the placement of the story and the rapidity with which it appeared suggest the high value that the magazine placed upon it—a fact perhaps more striking when set against the history of Faulkner's relationship with the *Post*, which as James Meriwether has noted, rejected far more of his stories than it ever published.[2] The fact that this is the only one of Faulkner's eighteen stories published in the magazine during his lifetime to occupy the lead position in an issue provides further support of the *Post*'s regard. The story's timely focus on a young boy's reaction to his brother's decision to enlist in the US military after Pearl Harbor is likely to have played an important role in this placement, given that the story appeared within four months of the entrance of the United States into World War II, but it is only by considering what was happening at the magazine itself that we gain a complete understanding of what this story signified for the *Post* and its audience.

When offered at all, critical responses to "Two Soldiers" have traditionally been cursory, at best tepid, and more often excoriating. As Shawn Miller encapsulates well in his 2012 reappraisal of the story, "It has been called [among other things] embarrassing, soupy, shameless, and crass . . . slick, offensive, gushing, and cute by people who matter."[3] A common thread throughout this criticism is a dismissal of the story as, to quote Hans Skei, a "strongly patriotic and rather sentimental reaction to the new war."[4] Miller attributes this disdain largely to the story's commercial and popular success and cites several critics who denounce "Two Soldiers" for its proximity to things written by "dismal hacks" and for its pecuniary value. In a particularly harsh assessment, Frederick Karl concludes that "knowing what the *Saturday Evening Post* wanted and being able to produce such copy was a form of literary prostitution, for the stories were not only inferior, they were turned out knowingly inferior."[5] However, as I will show, in overemphasizing the commercial nature of the story, critics have oversimplified its purpose as well. While it is true that "Two Soldiers" is responding to its historical moment, it does so in a way that subtly challenges the rapid editorial repositioning occurring at the *Post*, which itself was reflective of immediate and overwhelming calls for patriotism throughout the nation in early 1942, and in doing so, the story offers essential and increasingly rare breathing room for its readers.

The purchase and publication of Faulkner's story occurred during a period of editorial and ideological upheaval at the *Post*. In the years preceding Pearl Harbor, the prevailing editorial stance was largely isolationist and was espoused most regularly by anti–New Deal "editorial writer in chief," Garet Garrett.[6] In one of his last editorials written before—but published after—Pearl Harbor, Garrett encapsulates his position succinctly, even as he admits that it is no longer tenable: "Whether the noninterventionists were right or wrong is now a question that belongs to history. Their cause is lost. But they were never confused, never involved in a moral dilemma. It was not our war. . . . The place to defend American freedom was here, not in Europe, Asia, or Africa."[7] Just a little over three months later, on March 7, 1942, the tone of the editorial page was markedly different. Though Garrett and editor-in-chief Wesley Stout would not officially announce their resignation at the *Post* until a few days later on March 12, Garrett's time as editorial writer in chief had ended.[8] In an editorial section titled "That Was Then and This Is Now," the *Post* outlined its new ideological and editorial stance. The editorial begins with the mention of an article from October 1939, "I Think I'll Sit This One Out," which argued strongly against involvement in the war. It continues as follows: "That was then and this is now. Three months after Pearl Harbor, is there any American so deluded as to suppose that he can sit this one out? There are many, we gather, and we pity them. . . . If you do not like the way this war is being prosecuted, it is your privilege and your duty to use all lawful pressure on your representatives to correct it. But if it is merely that you do not like this war, then you can lump it."[9] While the editorial alludes to the *Post's* former stance expressed consistently and repeatedly by Garrett, there is no direct mention of him, though the echoing of his December editorial seems unlikely to be coincidental: "The *Post* fought the Administration's foreign policy steadily up to the moment war became a fact. Once we were at war, the question of whether we could or should have stayed out was referred to history."[10]

Two facts are relevant here to understanding just how and where "Two Soldiers" figured in this editorial transition. The first is that editorials

went to press approximately one month prior to the magazine's publication date, meaning that this editorial went to press during the first week
of February 1942.[11] Further support for this conclusion comes from a
letter written by Garrett on February 6, 1942, in which he explains that
he has "stopped writing for the editorial page of the *Saturday Evening
Post*."[12] The second salient fact is that Faulkner's story was accepted on
Thursday, February 5, 1942, which means that it likely was purchased
the same week that the magazine's editorial shift was occurring.[13]

This pro-war rebranding was evident elsewhere in the magazine as
well. Throughout 1941, as military-related manufacturing increased in
response to the Lend Lease Bill passed in March, which authorized the
president to supply munitions in support of countries deemed vital to
the defense of the United States, war-related coverage and advertising
was present in the *Post*, but it also demonstrated the relatively minor
role that the war played in average American lives. For example, in the
December 6, 1941, issue, the last published before the attack on Pearl
Harbor, the war is mentioned on a little less than 20 percent of the
pages: in one article, one editorial, one work of fiction, and a few advertisements. Even the Army Recruiting advertisement originally printed
on page 90 of the magazine reveals how the war was framed in early
December: not as a crisis requiring sacrifice but as a way to advance one's
future prospects (see Figure 1). The focus of the advertisement is on the
"amazing opportunity" enlistment offers men to prepare themselves "for
a thrilling, well paid job in aviation," and it emphasizes the "training"
that such a "BIG opportunity" will provide for a "career." The absence
of any mention of fighting on what we now know to be the eve of Pearl
Harbor might be surprising to a present-day audience, but it reveals how
most Americans still viewed the war at this stage. Contrast this with the
advertisement for rubber that appeared on February 21, 1942, by which
time even everyday activities like driving were being discussed in terms
of sacrifice for the war effort (see Figure 2). Particularly telling is the
formulation of the obligations of car owners as a "creed," complete with
a profession of faith in the importance of using their vehicles responsibly
for the greater good. The repetition of "I Will" works both visually and
textually to reinforce this message. Visually, the calligraphy-inspired font
is evocative of the US Constitution, while textually repeating "I Will"
mirrors the Army Oath of Enlistment, which read as follows during the
1940s: "I, A.B., do solemnly swear (or affirm) that *I will* support and
defend the Constitution of the United States against all enemies, foreign
or domestic; that *I will* bear true faith and allegiance to the same; that
I take this obligation freely, without any mental reservation or purpose
of evasion; and that *I will* well and faithfully discharge the duties of the

office on which I am about to enter. So help me God" (italics added).[14]

Within a space of less than three months, the war went from being an opportunity for men who chose to join to, now, a global struggle requiring vigilance from all Americans. The war had now entered American homes. Nowhere is this more clear than in an advertisement cosponsored by fifty-four electric companies that immediately faced the table of contents in the February 21, 1942 issue, which situated the "all out job of giving arms to Democracy" squarely at the supper table (see Figure 3). The table of contents itself also reflected this rapid shift: four of the five articles are directly about the war, including one ("Wilderness Defense") that the publishers redacted at the behest of the Office of Censorship.[15]

By March 28, 1942, when "Two Soldiers" appeared as the lead story, the *Post's* pro-war rebranding was complete. It is this very rebranding and the speed with which it was accomplished that make the story interesting in terms of its audience. Looking beyond the text to the paratext, the advertisements, articles, and even poetry inundate the audience with evidence of and calls for patriotism. Immediately opposite the first page of "Two Soldiers," for instance, is another army recruiting ad, though this one is quite different from its prewar predecessor (see Figure 4). No longer relegated to one column near the back of the magazine, the full-page advertisement emphasizes service rather than personal

Fig. 1. US Army recruiting advertisement in the *Saturday Evening Post*, pre–Pearl Harbor

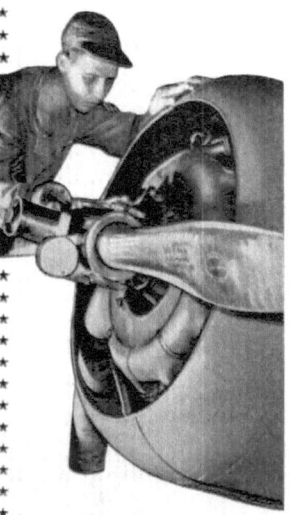

Fig. 2. "The Car Owner's Creed" (February 21, 1942)

gain. The "opportunity" that enlistment represents for young men is now reframed as the chance to provide the "spirit" the "country needs . . . in its fighting men as never before," and readers are prompted to "call the nearest Army Recruiting Station" to "get full details on how you can best serve your country."[16] While the prewar recruitment advertisement focused on training with no mention of fighting, the March 28 advertisement foregrounds the need for a "First-Class Fighting Man" in both word and image, depicting a line of smiling soldiers rushing into battle with their rifles and bayonets ready. In a noteworthy parallel with Faulkner's story, in which an almost twenty-year-old Pete voluntarily enlists after Pearl Harbor, the advertisement emphasizes that "men 18 and 19 years old, with keenness, enthusiasm, and daring, are especially desired."

The war-oriented content continues throughout the remainder of the story as well. The article immediately following the first pages of the story, "Heroes—Wholesale," focuses on the US Army's aviation training program and describes how "Uncle Sam sets out to find the men to man the planes."[17] Perhaps more strikingly, every subsequent page

Jim eats breakfast at the SUPPER table now!

It's a screwy schedule. Jim downs a man-sized dinner while Mom's doing the breakfast dishes, sleeps the day away, and gets breakfast at the family supper table! *He's on the midnight shift at the munitions plant.*

The night is bright with light when Jim goes to work. Machines that have been humming 24 hours a day scarcely pause as fresh men take over the all-out job of giving arms to Democracy.

CONTINUOUS production makes tremendous demands on men, machines, *and on the electric service that powers practically every operation.*

But the power is always there—day and night—Sundays and holidays—365 days a year. The electric industry was *ready* when the crisis came—ready to turn the eager wheels of almost every arms factory—ready to meet *new* needs with new construction. 1941 saw more than 2½ *million more horsepower* installed—enough to light *one-fourth of all the homes in the U. S. A.!*

America's electric companies have been able to accomplish this by good business management—by producing about ⅔ of the nation's electric power and making it available almost anywhere, over carefully interconnected systems.

We're glad we can make this report—and glad to pledge our unending effort to supply millions of Jims with all the electric power they need to make America POWERFUL!

Fig. 3. Advertisement in *Saturday Evening Post*, cosponsored by fifty-four electric companies demonstrating how the war had entered the home (February 21, 1942)

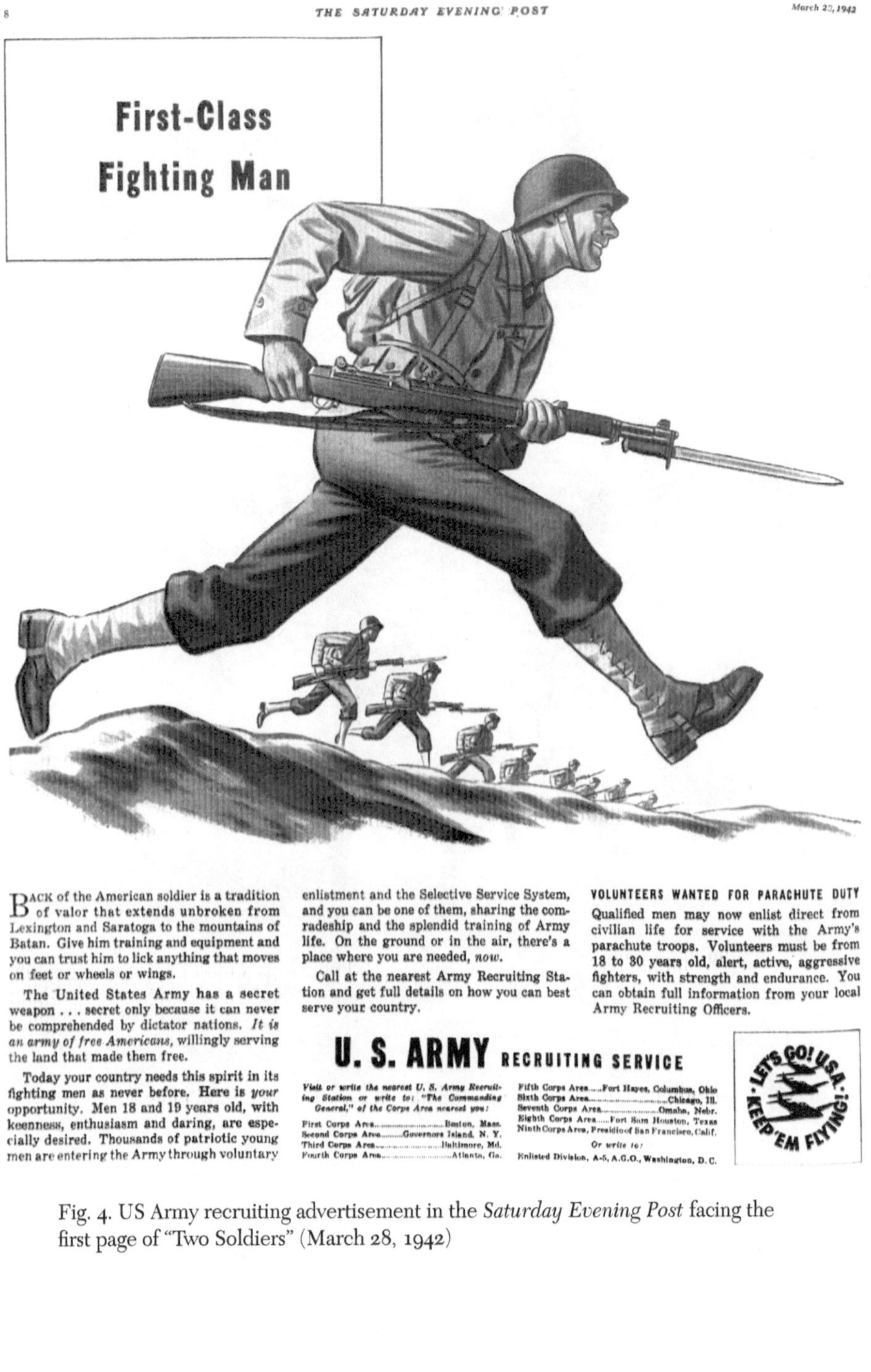

First-Class Fighting Man

BACK of the American soldier is a tradition of valor that extends unbroken from Lexington and Saratoga to the mountains of Batan. Give him training and equipment and you can trust him to lick anything that moves on feet or wheels or wings.

The United States Army has a secret weapon . . . secret only because it can never be comprehended by dictator nations. *It is an army of free Americans,* willingly serving the land that made them free.

Today your country needs this spirit in its fighting men as never before. Here is *your* opportunity. Men 18 and 19 years old, with keenness, enthusiasm and daring, are especially desired. Thousands of patriotic young men are entering the Army through voluntary enlistment and the Selective Service System, and you can be one of them, sharing the comradeship and the splendid training of Army life. On the ground or in the air, there's a place where you are needed, *now.*

Call at the nearest Army Recruiting Station and get full details on how you can best serve your country.

VOLUNTEERS WANTED FOR PARACHUTE DUTY
Qualified men may now enlist direct from civilian life for service with the Army's parachute troops. Volunteers must be from 18 to 30 years old, alert, active, aggressive fighters, with strength and endurance. You can obtain full information from your local Army Recruiting Officers.

U. S. ARMY RECRUITING SERVICE

Visit or write the nearest U. S. Army Recruiting Station or write to: "The Commanding General," of the Corps Area nearest you:

First Corps Area............................Boston, Mass.
Second Corps Area..........Governors Island, N. Y.
Third Corps Area......................Baltimore, Md.
Fourth Corps Area..........................Atlanta, Ga.

Fifth Corps Area.....Fort Hayes, Columbus, Ohio
Sixth Corps Area.................................Chicago, Ill.
Seventh Corps Area..................Omaha, Nebr.
Eighth Corps Area.....Fort Sam Houston, Texas
Ninth Corps Area, Presidio of San Francisco, Calif.

Or write to:
Enlisted Division, A-5, A.G.O., Washington, D. C.

Fig. 4. US Army recruiting advertisement in the *Saturday Evening Post* facing the first page of "Two Soldiers" (March 28, 1942)

of Faulkner's story is surrounded by war propaganda. On page 35, for instance, the text of "Two Soldiers" appears immediately across from an advertisement outlining how keeping Chevrolet trucks in good repair is "vital to victory."[18] Embedded in the next page of the story is a sappily patriotic poem, "The Saga of Johnny the One," who "won't march home until the job is done."[19] The poem includes stanzas such as

> *Oh, Johnny was young and strong and free*
> *Holding his head courageously*
> *America's youngest son was he*
> *Marching to keep her liberty.*[20]

And the final full page of the story, on page 38, is across from a Buick advertisement explaining how the company's workers "relish their opportunity to prove that when Uncle Sam needs better war goods, Buick men can build them."[21]

Thus, in a space of less than four months the *Post* entirely reframed its outlook on the war and seemingly expected its audience to do so swiftly and easily as well. What is absent in the overwhelmingly patriotic clamor is any consideration of the "dreadful uncertainty that must have suffused post–Pearl Harbor America," the very thing that Shawn Miller argues that Faulkner addresses.[22] Miller provides an important corrective to scholarly dismissals of "Two Soldiers" by suggesting that a lack of close reading has resulted in a failure "to recognize that the story is not merely Faulkner's contribution to unexamined flag-waving (or even to a kind of nationalism we like), but an inquiry into war-time patriotism" that "establishes radical, heart-rending loss as the impetus for what otherwise might be viewed as altruistic or self-sacrificial patriotic expression."[23] In Miller's more complex reading, both Pete and his brother are reacting out of desperation to the absolute upheaval of the world as they have known it.[24] What attention to the context and paratext allows us to see is precisely why such a message would have resonated so strongly with the *Saturday Evening Post* audience at this time. Within this context, "Two Soldiers" provides a rare and much-needed expression of Americans' complex and conflicted feelings about having recently entered the war. Rather than argue as Miller does that the story is deserving of scholarly attention despite its "appeal to the *Post*'s unrefined audience," I argue that Faulkner's nuanced appeal to this audience is itself a compelling reason why the story deserves further consideration.[25]

The very swiftness with which Americans were expected to shift their attitudes toward the war is in fact one of the topics that "Two Soldiers" addresses, as a brief outline makes clear. The story begins with the narrator, an eight-year-old boy, and his nineteen-year-old brother, Pete, listening to reports of the attack on Pearl Harbor from outside a neighbor's window. After several nights of restless sleep, Pete decides to enlist, tells his parents the next morning, and sets off for Memphis the following day. That night, the narrator sets off to join Pete and, after many twists and turns, locates him, only to be sent home once again. The time from Pete's decision to enlist to the narrator's return home alone—that is, the time it takes for the narrator's world to be completely upended—is three days.

The narrator's initial reaction to hearing about the bombing of Pearl Harbor reveals how quickly things are changing. The beginning of the story repeatedly notes his confusion about what is happening. When he first hears the news, he responds, "What? Japanese? What's a pearl harbor?," and as the boys settle into bed that night, despite several attempts by his older brother to clarify things, the boy is still feeling befuddled: "I still couldn't understand where it was, and Pete told me again—the Pacific Ocean."[26] Given the European focus of most war coverage throughout 1941, including in the pages of the *Post*, the narrator's disorientation likely captures some of what the audience was feeling as well.

His parents' reactions also give voice to the conflicting feelings people had at a time when the wisdom and meaning of US involvement in the war was far from certain—and this uncertainty may have been particularly acute for readers of the formerly isolationist *Post*. It's not difficult to see how the mother's reaction must have reflected how mothers all over the country were feeling: "'No,' she said, crying, 'I don't want him to go. I would rather go myself in his place, if I could. I don't want to save the country. Them Japanese could take it and keep it, so long as they left me and my family and my children alone'" (10). However, the father's reaction is perhaps more interesting. While his argument is inherently "ridiculous," as Miller has pointed out,[27] what he's expressing—that is, doubt over how much Americans want to expend in another European war—was not an uncommon sentiment at the time, and indeed was one only recently espoused by the *Post*.

"To the war?" he said. "Why, I just don't see a bit of use in that. You ain't old enough for the draft, and the country ain't being invaded. Our President in Washington, D.C., is watching the conditions and will notify us. Besides, in that other war your ma just mentioned, I was drafted and sent clean to Texas and was held there nigh eight months until they finally quit fighting. It seems to me that that, along with your Uncle Marsh who received a actual wound on the battlefields of France, is enough for me and mine to have to do to protect the country, at least in my lifetime." (10)

The narrator's reactions to the nation's rapidly changing outlook on the war are also expressed symbolically through his descriptions of the bus to Memphis. As Cathryn Halverson has pointed out, despite the lack of scholarly attention to the bus in American literary and cultural studies, "its resonances are highly distinct."[28] Among those resonances most familiar is the bus as a transformative mode of transportation for "the small-town boy," as Halverson aptly describes: "A bus rolls up to a rural crossroads and a single passenger embuses to set off for college or the military; life will never be the same."[29] The narrator's description of the bus that takes Pete away both fits into this familiar trope and emphasizes the overwhelming speed of change: "Then we see the lights of the bus coming and I was watching the bus until it come up and Pete flagged it, and then, sho enough, there was daylight—it had started while I wasn't watching" (11). The effect is reinforced by the narrator's own bus ride into Memphis to find Pete. Though exhausted from his overnight walk, he will not allow himself to sleep: "When the bus got to going good, I found out I was jest about wore out for sleep. But there was too much I hadn't never saw before. . . . I was jest about plumb wore out for sleep, but I couldn't resk it" (36). As Miller has noted, the most conspicuous use of repetition in the story involves "variant(s) of the clause *I got to go*" by both Pete and the narrator, which Miller reads as an indication of their compulsion to act.[30] As regards the narrator, at least, I want to suggest that Faulkner additionally uses repetition to convey his attempts to come to terms with the dizzying speed of the upheaval he is experiencing. In this case, the repetition of "wore out for sleep" followed by "but" emphasizes his utter exhaustion at trying to contain the "resk" that anything else might happen "while [he] wasn't watching." When he is finally reunited with Pete, just one day after the latter has left, the bus continues to feature prominently as a symbol of the alarming rate of the changes the boy is experiencing: "He looked jest like he did when he got on the bus yestiddy morning, except it seemed to me like it was at least a week, so much had happened, and I had done had to do so much traveling. He come in and there he was, looking at me like he hadn't never left home, except that here we was in Memphis, on the way to Pearl Harbor" (36, 38). Though Pete looks "just like he did when he got on the bus yestiddy morning," all is not the same because the bus has taken them both to Memphis and Pete will soon be leaving. As the narrator remarks when the bus pulls away with Pete, everything "was going fast" (11).

The story concludes with another expression of the overwhelming feelings brought on by the swiftness with which things were changing in post–Pearl Harbor America. Though the narrator returns home in a car, the bus remains on his mind, as indicated by his description of the journey "back on the same highway the bus run on this morning" (40). The most prevalent image in the final passage is that of speed, which both echoes the earlier descriptions of the bus and features its own internal repetitions:

> Then we was *running* again between the fields and woods, running fast now, and except for that soldier, it was like I hadn't never been to Memphis a-tall. *We was going fast now.* At this rate, before I knowed it we would be home again, and I thought about me riding up to Frenchman's Bend in this here big car with a soldier *running* it, and all of a sudden I begun to cry. I never knowed I was fixing to, and I couldn't stop it. I set there by that soldier, crying. *We was going fast.* (40; italics added)

While this passage certainly indicates, as Miller suggests, "the inevitable defeat the rest of the boy's journey has merely delayed," the emphasis is clearly on the speed with which both defeat and journey have taken place.[31] Not only are "running" and "fast" each mentioned three times, but the final sentence emphasizes not the boy's grief but how quickly the world is changing. Such a message was sure to resonate with an audience inundated with calls for patriotism from a magazine that had been espousing isolationism just four months before and with a populace being asked for sacrifice by a government so recently promising opportunity to military enlistees.

In his 1937 *Saturday Review of Literature* article "Writing for Money," Bernard DeVoto argues that "the historian is going to recover the surface of American life—at least of middle-class life—much more fully and with less distortion from the slicks than from the novel of our day."[32] Rather than an expression of blind patriotism, as some critics have labeled it, "Two Soldiers" emphasizes the bewildering speed of change that all Americans—the Petes, the Maws, the Pas, and the children—were being asked to accept in the first few months after America's entrance into World War II. This becomes stunningly clear upon examination of the changing content of the *Post* between the bombing of Pearl Harbor and the publication of Faulkner's story. Isolating this story (and others published in the slicks) from the advertisements, articles, and other documents that surrounded it removes important evidence of Faulkner's nuanced responsiveness to the social context of his time and to the magazines where he placed his work.

NOTES

1. For more on the publication history of and critical responses to "Two Soldiers," see Diane Brown Jones, "Two Soldiers," in her *A Reader's Guide to the Short Stories of William Faulkner* (New York: G. K. Hall, 1994), 64–72.

2. According to Meriwether, though Faulkner published many more stories in the *Post* "than in any other magazine," "perhaps even more impressive is the number of stories which he submitted to the *Post*, but which were rejected." See James Meriwether, "Faulkner's Correspondence with the *Saturday Evening Post*," *Mississippi Quarterly* 30, no. 3 (1977): 461. Like many, Faulkner was attracted to the *Post* for its generous fees, but he could not command the magazine's highest prices. See Susan Donaldson, "Dismantling the *Saturday Evening Post* Reader: The *Unvanquished* and Changing 'Horizons of Expectations,'" in *Faulkner and Popular Culture: Faulkner and Yoknapatawpha, 1988*, ed. Doreen Fowler and Ann J. Abadie (Jackson: University Press of Mississippi, 1990), 182–85.

3. Shawn Miller, "Returning to Faulkner's 'Two Soldiers,'" *Southern Literary Journal* 44, no. 4 (2012): 38.

4. Skei quoted in Jones, "Two Soldiers," 67.

5. Karl quoted in Miller, "Returning to Faulkner's 'Two Soldiers,'" 40.

6. For more on these editorials, see Bruce Ramsey, ed., *Defend America First: The Antiwar Editorials of the "Saturday Evening Post"* (Caldwell, ID: Caxton Press, 2003). While Ramsey's book is hampered by its own political agenda, it nonetheless provides a useful introduction to Garrett's position as espoused in the editorial pages of the *Post*.

7. Garet Garrett, "Review," *Saturday Evening Post*, December 20, 1941, 24. As Ramsey explains, editorials went to press approximately one month before their publication date, meaning that this editorial was submitted in late November (16, 247).

8. This change is reflected on the editorial page of the March 7, 1942, issue, where Garrett is listed among a number of associate editors rather than as editorial writer in chief, as he had been in the previous issue on February 28, 1942. Stout handed in his resignation on March 12, effective as of Monday, March 16. See "Wesley W. Stout Resigns: *Saturday Evening Post* Editor Differed over Policy," *New York Times*, March 13, 1942, 21.

9. "That Was Then and This Is Now," *Saturday Evening Post*, March 7, 1942, 26.

10. Ibid.

11. Ramsey, *Defend America First*, 16.

12. Ibid., 261.

13. Jones, "Two Soldiers," 64. These facts also suggest that there is something disingenuous about Stout's "associates [who] professed themselves to be completely surprised by his resignation," as reported in "Wesley W. Stout Resigns."

14. "Oaths of Enlistment and Oaths of Office," *US Army Center of Military History*, last modified June 14, 2011, http://www.history.army.mil/html/faq/oaths.htm.

15. Of these articles, two ("Food is a Weapon" and "Postmarked London") concerned British wartime efforts, one ("We Learn the Hard Way") discussed "our Pacific war," and "Wilderness Defense" appeared in scrubbed form after facing the Office of Censorship as a result of its focus on defense projects being developed in the Pacific Northwest.

16. US Army recruiting advertisement, *Saturday Evening Post*, March 28, 1942, 8.

17. Richard Thruelsen, "Heroes—Wholesale," *Saturday Evening Post*, March 28, 1942, 12.

18. Chevrolet advertisement, *Saturday Evening Post*, March 28, 1942, 34.

19. Le Roux, "The Saga of Johnny the One," *Saturday Evening Post*, March 28, 1942, 36.

20. Ibid.

21. Buick advertisement, *Saturday Evening Post*, March 28, 1942, 39.

22. Miller, "Returning to Faulkner's 'Two Soldiers,'" 47.

23. Ibid., 41. On the critical discussion of patriotism in the story, see also Jones, "Two Soldiers," 66–67. Though not explicitly mentioned by Miller, Thomas Nordanberg's three-paragraph analysis provides a good example of how a cursory examination of "Two Soldiers" lends itself to overly simplistic readings of the story's "outspoken patriotism" and "unquestioning" acceptance of the war. See Thomas Nordanberg, *Cataclysm as Catalyst: The Theme of War in William Faulkner's Fiction* (Stockholm: Almquist and Wiksell, 1983), 119, 152.

24. See Miller, "Returning to Faulkner's 'Two Soldiers,'" 47–48.

25. Ibid., 47. To be fair, it should be noted that Miller argues strongly against "the tired notion that fiction with mass appeal is artistically middling or worse," a view that, "like all snobbery . . . inhibits, rather than invites, rigorous inquiry" (40). While he has disdain for critics who dismiss commercially successful and popular works out of hand, however, his own labeling of the *Post's* audience as "unrefined" perhaps accounts for his conclusion that "the story has merits that surmount the writer's aims" (47) rather than considering that Faulkner's aims in writing for this audience may have been both more complex and indeed more in line with Miller's own reading of the story than he allows.

26. William Faulkner, "Two Soldiers," *Saturday Evening Post*, March 23, 1942, 9. Hereafter cited parenthetically.

27. Miller, "Returning to Faulkner's 'Two Soldiers,'" 42.

28. Cathryn Halverson, "John Steinbeck's Sweetheart: The Cosmic American Bus," *College Literature* 35, no. 1 (2008): 85.

29. Ibid.

30. Miller, "Returning to Faulkner's 'Two Soldiers,'" 41.

31. Ibid., 46.

32. Bernard DeVoto, "Writing for Money," *Saturday Review of Literature*, October 9, 1937, 20.

An Error in Canonicity, or
A Fuller Story of Faulkner's Return
to Print Culture, 1944–1951

John N. Duvall

It's often easy to forget that William Faulkner, Nobel Laureate, canonical High Modernist, always was keenly aware of genre fiction and pulp
magazines. In his library, one finds mystery novels by the likes of "John
Dickson Carr, Ellery Queen, Rex Stout, Agatha Christie, and Dorothy
Sayers."[1] As for pulp magazines, they show up regularly in Faulkner's
writing. In chapter 5 of his 1932 novel, *Light in August*, the supremely
alienated Joe Christmas is a reader of pulp fiction. On the day that he
confronts his estranged lover, Joanna Burden, for the final time, Joe
leaves his cabin and takes with him only his shaving things (razor, brush,
shaving soap) and a "magazine of that type whose covers bear either
pictures of young women in underclothes or pictures of men in the act of
shooting one another with pistols."[2] Later in the morning, Joe reads "the
magazine straight through as though it were a novel" (111). His choice
of reading material speaks to his sense of masculine identity. Joe tries
to embody the magazine's hard-boiled masculinity with its attendant
misogyny, but we subsequently learn that this masculinity is but a sham
performance that he deploys to hide from his trauma as an orphan and a
victim of child abuse who can never know his racial identity in a culture
predicated on the color line.

An even more extended treatment of the pulps occurs in Faulkner's
1939 novel that was originally published as *The Wild Palms* but is now
known by Faulkner's intended title, *If I Forget Thee, Jerusalem*. Com-
prised of two novellas that are told in alternating chapters, the central
male characters of both narratives have an intimate relation to the pulps.
The Tall Convict in "Old Man" is a naive reader of pulp fiction. At the
start of the narrative, he is at the state penitentiary in Parchman, Mississippi, for a comically failed train robbery that leaves him with "rag-
ing impotence" directed toward the writers whom he believes to be

criminally ignorant of their subject matter.[3] The Tall Convict expected useful representations. He plotted his attempted robbery by reading pulp westerns about the likes of Diamond Dick and Jesse James

> for two years, reading and rereading them, memorising them, comparing and weighing story and method against story and method, taking the good from each and discarding the dross as his workable plan emerged, keeping his mind open to make the subtle last-minute changes, without haste and without impatience, as the newer pamphlets appeared on their appointed days as a conscientious dressmaker makes the subtle alterations in a court presentation costume as the newer bulletins appear. And when the day came, he did not even have a chance to go through the coaches and collect the watches and the rings, the brooches and the hidden money-belts, because he had been captured as soon as he entered the express car where the safe and the gold would be. He had shot no one because the pistol which they took away from him was not that kind of a pistol although it was loaded; later he admitted to the District Attorney that he had got it, as well as the dark lantern in which a candle burned and the black handkerchief to wear over the face, by peddling among his pine-hill neighbors subscriptions to the *Detectives' Gazette*. (21–22)

What the Tall Convict doesn't realize is that his close study of western pulps had not prepared him to rob trains but actually might have enabled him to write pulp fiction himself, something that Harry Wilbourne, his counterpart in the novel's other half, "Wild Palms," might have told him. In order to earn money to support his adulterous affair with Charlotte Rittenmeyer, Harry writes for the pulp confessional magazines

> stories beginning "I had the body and desires of a woman yet in knowledge and experience of the world I was but a child" or "If I had only had a mother's love to guard me on that fatal day"—stories which he wrote complete from the first capital to the last period in one sustained frenzied agonising rush like the halfback working his way through school who grasps the ball . . . and runs until the play is completed—downed or across the goal line, it doesn't matter which. (103)

But despite the football metaphor, Harry's writing, like the Tall Convict's reading, troubles his gendered identity. Both have their masculinity challenged by their relation to the pulps. If the Tall Convict's reading makes him comparable to a dressmaker, Harry's writing turns him into a househusband. Because he writes in their apartment (as opposed to Charlotte, who works outside their home), Harry does most of the domestic labor in the relationship. In writing stories of transgressive female sexuality,

Harry thinks of himself in the kind of light bondage so common to pulp fiction cover art: "I had tied myself hand and foot in a little strip of inked ribbon" (114). It's hard not to read Harry's relationship to writing as commenting on Faulkner's own sense of the limitations of his authorship. At the time Faulkner published *If I Forget Thee, Jerusalem*, his domestic responsibilities increasingly made him need to turn to other forms of work (particularly Hollywood scriptwriting) in order to pay the bills, precisely because his modernist novels did not sell. As Harry complains, "It's not avocation that elects our vocations, it's respectability that makes chiropractors and clerks and bill posters and motormen and pulp writers of us all" (114).

Although there's much more to be said about Faulkner's representations of pulp magazines, I'd like to turn to an element of material culture—the appearance of Faulkner's fiction in pulp formats. If Faulkner used pulps to signal gender trouble in his fiction, the gendered space of the pulps, one that looks almost campy to the contemporary eye, may have helped save Faulkner's fiction for posterity. At the end of World War II, the status of William Faulkner within print culture was at its lowest point. With the exception of a 1942 Avon paperback reprint of *Mosquitoes*, his novels, including those that we think of as major modernist achievements—*As I Lay Dying*, *The Sound and the Fury*, *Light in August*, *Absalom, Absalom!*, and *Go Down, Moses*—were out of print. Of this midcentury moment, John Earle Bassett succinctly notes, "Booksellers, librarians, and publishers all apparently had little interest in [Faulkner]."[4]

But 1946 was a watershed year in which one particular publication began to turn things around. Now I know many will think that I'm going to name Malcolm Cowley's Viking *Portable Faulkner* as that publication, but that would be wrong. Not that I in any way wish to devalue the significance of Cowley's heroic effort to bring Faulkner back to the American reading public's attention. After all, in its obituary of Cowley in 1989, the *New York Times* flatly states, "It was Mr. Cowley who rescued William Faulkner from possible early oblivion."[5] Faulkner himself had already authorized the *Times* claim when he said, "I owe Malcolm Cowley the kind of debt no man could ever repay."[6] Nevertheless, I would like to speak about the work of a different author, editor, and critic who published and reprinted Faulkner and who argued for the significance of Faulkner's fiction from the mid-1940s through the early 1950s. Of whom am I speaking? Ellery Queen. Laugh if you want to, but Queen introduced Faulkner to a new, broadly popular readership—and not just when Faulkner's short story "An Error in Chemistry" appeared as a second-prize winning story in the June 1946 issue of *Ellery Queen's Mystery Magazine* (*EQMM*).

Fig. 1. Cover of *Ellery Queen's Mystery Magazine*, June 1946. Copyright © 2017 by Penny Publications/Dell Magazines (TheMysteryPlace.com). Reprinted with permission of the publisher. Cover image by George Salter. Used by permission of Janet Salter Rosenberg.

Ellery Queen was the pen name of two Russian Jewish cousins from Brooklyn, Frederic Dannay (1905–1982) and Manfred Bennington Lee (1905–1971), who began writing detective fiction together in 1928. But their pen name is only one layer of their constructed identity; their desire to assimilate into American culture is signaled by their earlier name changes: Dannay was born Daniel Nathan; Lee, Emanuel Benjamin Lepofsky. By 1946 Dannay and Lee had authored twenty-one mystery novels and three collections of their stories. Additionally, Ellery Queen had edited twelve anthologies of other writers' detective fiction. Their book sales during this period totaled over fifteen million. Dannay and Lee may have been the first authors to fully grasp how the electronic media could enhance their brand. Complementing their pulp print empire, their radio drama, *The Adventures of Ellery Queen*, was broadcast from 1939 to 1948 before becoming a television series with the same title, which ran from 1950 to 1952. Between 1935 and 1942, ten of their books were made into B movies. Although Dannay and Lee wrote their fiction together, Dannay was responsible for editing *EQMM*, which began in 1941.[7] That Dannay's magazine in the 1940s was a pulp is clear from its price (25 cents), its cheap paper quality, and its cover art. *EQMM* covers highlight violent and eroticized desires. The most frequent subject matter of these cover images is a woman about to be or recently murdered.

However, despite its pulp packaging, Dannay had aspirations for his magazine, aspirations that he repeatedly made clear not only in his headnotes, which he wrote for each and every story his magazine published, but also in the several works of criticism he published as Ellery Queen. Dannay felt that detective fiction was unfairly disparaged and marginalized by the literary establishment. On the cover of each issue of *EQMM*, Dannay promised readers "the Best Detective Stories, New and Old." Only about 40 percent of the stories, however, were new. The rest Dannay reprinted from book collections, mainstream magazines (such as *Collier's*, *Harper's*, and *Cosmopolitan*), as well as from other pulp magazines (such as *Black Mask*). In this regard, *EQMM* was a queer publishing space, one mixing the gendered subgenres of detective fiction—stories in the classical, ratiocinative tradition favored by the domestically appropriate slicks appearing alongside the masculine hardboiled stories of other pulps. Intermixed with these were stories by more recognizably literary authors. In his magazine's first five years, Dannay reprinted fiction not only by Dorothy Sayers (creator of the aristocratic dilettante crime solver, Lord Peter Wimsey) and Dashiell Hammett (with his manly noir detective, Sam Spade), but also by O. Henry, Mark Twain, Jack London, H. G. Wells, E. M. Forster, Theodore Dreiser,

Graham Greene, and other significant modernist authors. In a special
All Nations issue (August 1948) commemorating the formation of the
United Nations, *EQMM* included a translation of Jorge Luis Borges's
"The Garden of Forking Paths," which is notable for being the first
time that Borges was published in the United States. Unlike Faulkner, a
runner-up in the 1946 contest, Borges won the 1948 *EQMM* contest.[8]

This is not to say that *EQMM* did not publish some highly forgettable
fiction by pulp writers. But unpacking a bit of the history of Dannay's
magazine dovetails with what Paula Rabinowitz has argued—that from
the late 1930s to the early 1960s, "the story of American pulp is the story
of American modernism."[9] For Rabinowitz, pulp magazines and books

> were dynamic media, akin to our digital world of interactive electronics. Their
> pervasiveness achieved a kind of blanketing of culture that brought the words
> of thinkers and writers of every stripe into a vibrant relationship, through
> intense visual and linguistic stimulation, with an enormous mass of people. . . .
> This demotics of reading occurred by way of a handy object—packaged for
> portability, designed to allure, priced to sell—establishing pulp as an interface
> among the masses, the author, and the thing itself.[10]

My argument is that the postwar recuperation of Faulkner's literary
reputation occurs on two fronts, culminating in Faulkner's receiving the
Nobel Prize for literature in 1950. The first front is the one we know
best: the construction of literary (or high) Faulkner through such publications as Cowley's *Portable Faulkner* in 1946 (with its excerpts from *The
Sound and the Fury*, *Light in August*, and *Go Down, Moses*) and *Collected Stories of William Faulkner* in 1950. The second front we might
call pulp Faulkner, the writer of detective fiction, as evidenced by the
1948 novel *Intruder in the Dust* and a different collection of stories,
Knight's Gambit, which appeared in 1949, both of which feature Gavin
Stevens and his nephew, Chick Mallison. If the *Collected Stories* essentially announces to the reader "Here is literary Faulkner," the stories of
Knight's Gambit (which reprints "An Error in Chemistry") say, "Enjoy
pulp Faulkner." But this distinction between literary and pulp Faulkner
has always been a false one, because Faulkner's high modernist novels
so often operate squarely within the conventions of the genre of crime
and detective fiction.[11] If the lawyer Gavin Stevens plays detective in the
short stories not included in the *Collected Stories*, isn't there another
lawyer in *Sanctuary* who tries to exonerate his client by discovering who
really murdered Tommy? Horace Benbow may spectacularly lose his
case, but that doesn't change the fact that he tracks down the key witness in a Memphis brothel.[12] Don't two college students in *Absalom*,

Absalom! obsess in their dorm room over the evidence in a cold case, finally revealing a motive that makes full historical and psychological sense of Henry Sutpen's murder of Charles Bon? And isn't the violent death of a woman at the heart of *Light in August*? Recalling that the British title of Cowley's *Portable Faulkner* was *The Essential Faulkner*, the more you look at it, the more the essential Faulkner bears a striking resemblance to Faulkner's nonessential detective fiction.

To get at a fuller sense of Ellery Queen's role in promoting Faulkner's fiction, I want to look at how the pulp context of the publication of "An Error in Chemistry" serves as an important but overlooked piece of the puzzle in our understanding of Faulkner's reemergence in print from the mid-1940s through the early 1950s. This may seem a heavy burden for a lightly regarded story about a former magician, Joel Flint, who would have gotten away with the murder of his wife and father-in-law by impersonating the father-in-law but who gives himself away when Gavin Stevens sees Flint incorrectly make a cold toddy: Flint fails to mix the sugar and water before adding the whiskey, an error that his father-in-law never would have made.[13] But the story's pulp publication is ultimately more significant than the narrative content.

This story actually appeared twice in 1946: first, in the June issue of *EQMM* and again in November in *The Queen's Awards, 1946*, an anthology of the prizewinning stories from the first Ellery Queen crime and detective story competition. We can certainly understand why Faulkner would have submitted to Queen's magazine. "An Error in Chemistry" had failed with his preferred top-paying venues. Faulkner had sent the story to his agent Harold Ober in November 1940, with a self-congratulatory note saying that he thought it was "a pretty good Who-done-it,"[14] but the story was rejected in short order by the *Saturday Evening Post*, *Collier's*, and six other magazines. In 1945 Faulkner was desperate for money because of various family obligations and a contract dispute with Warner Bros. By submitting "An Error in Chemistry" to the mystery magazine, Faulkner could potentially double dip, so to speak. If the editors liked the story, it would appear in *EQMM*, a publication paying $300, and then be eligible for the 1946 contest that boasted a first prize of $2,000 (which in 2015 dollars would be $24,074).

Someone who plunked down a quarter for the June 1946 issue of *EQMM* would have first been greeted by a cover image by the illustrator George Salter. The image shows a woman (and we know it's a woman because of the hand's red fingernails) reaching out in desperation as a man finishes walling her up "Cask of Amontillado" style. The German-born Salter, who immigrated to the United States in 1934, revolutionized book jacket design and is best-known for his striking illustrations of numerous modernist classics, including *Absalom, Absalom!* and *The Hamlet*. But like *EQMM* itself, Salter is a figure who helps bridge the divide between modernism and mass culture. Salter was hired as the artistic director of Mercury Publications in 1938, and he illustrated all of the covers for *EQMM* throughout the 1940s. Thomas S. Hansen notes that despite the subject matter with which Salter had to work, the *EQMM* covers show Salter seeking a middle ground between his "loyalty to the tradition of fine art" and the "lurid excesses" that typify the majority of pulp detective magazine covers.[15] His subject matter is still recognizably pulp, but there is a degree of restraint.

Opening the June 1946 issue of *EQMM*, the reader finds Faulkner's "An Error in Chemistry" as the lead story. In his headnote, which is identical in both the magazine and the book collection, Dannay explains that Faulkner failed by a single vote to win the magazine's first detective story contest and that two of the five judges found that "An Error in Chemistry" represented "the most distinguished writing" of the 838 manuscripts that were submitted. But beyond the information about the contest, Dannay identifies Faulkner, along with Ernest Hemingway, John Steinbeck, and John Dos Passos, as one of the "four outstanding contemporary novelists in America."[16] Dannay goes on to place Faulkner in the tradition of Poe and Ambrose Bierce.

But as important as Ellery Queen's headnote is to burnishing Faulkner's aura is the company in which Faulkner found himself in the June 1946 issue. "An Error in Chemistry" was followed by one of Agatha Christie's Hercule Poirot stories, "Four and Twenty Blackbirds." Unlike Faulkner, Christie never struggled with being out of print. According to her estate's official website, she is the best-selling author of all time.[17] Her books are like the McDonald's hamburgers of fiction—over two billion served, which means that she's only behind the Bible and the works of Shakespeare in the number of books sold. My point is that it matters mightily to the public perception of Faulkner that Dannay juxtaposes the modernist experimenter with Christie, a popular entertainer valued more for her ingenious plots than for her literariness. If we thought Faulkner was the anti-Christie, their side by side pairing in Queen's magazine goes a long way to bridging the great divide between modernism and mass culture. And it should be clear that a different set of readers, one unlikely to be impressed by a favorable *New York Times* review, receives the clear impression that if Ellery Queen endorses Faulkner and places his work next to Christie's, maybe, just maybe, they should read some more Faulkner!

Turning from the pulp magazine to the collection of prize-winning stories, *The Queen's Awards, 1946*, we again see a broadening of the cultural context of Faulkner's reception. The table of contents reveals that Faulkner actually shared second place with five other authors—Manning Coles, T. S. Stribling, Philip MacDonald, Helen McCloy, and Anthony Gilbert. While Coles, MacDonald, McCloy, and Gilbert were established genre writers, Stribling was at the time arguably the more famous southern writer in America. His 1932 novel, *The Store*, the second in his trilogy of the Vaiden family, won the Pulitzer Prize in 1933. A tale of miscegenation and social climbing in the Reconstruction-era South, *The Store* achieved the kind of literary recognition that Faulkner's fiction covering the same matter had yet to find.

"An Error in Chemistry" appears second in Queen's volume, preceded only by the contest winner, written by a figure best-known prior to the contest for forms of mass cultural narrative even less respected than the genre of detective fiction. Manly Wade Wellman won for his story of the Native American detective David Return in "A Star for a Warrior."[18] Wellman had been a newspaper reporter in Wichita, Kansas, who turned to writing for sci-fi pulps in the late 1930s, regularly contributing to *Weird Tales*, *Wonder Stories*, and *Astounding Stories*. But in the early 1940s, he was heavily involved in comic books, producing "a tremendous volume of work, inventing characters and writing stories for all the major and most minor outfits, including such notable comic heroes as Captain Marvel, Prince Ibis, the Spirit, Blackhawk, Green Lantern, Plasticman, Captain America, Aquaman, and countless others."[19] Like Faulkner's proximity to Christie in Queen's magazine, Faulkner's linkage to Wellman in the anthology further helps to democratize modernism and disseminate Yoknapatawpha County to a new audience. And make no mistake—Ellery Queen envisioned a different audience for the book than for the magazine. If the magazine only cost a quarter, the handsome hardback book published by Little, Brown would set you back $2.75 (about $33.50 today). People who might have felt pulp magazines were beneath them could enjoy the same content in the more culturally prestigious and collectable form of the book.

Faulkner's association with the publishing juggernaut that was Ellery Queen is not exhausted, however, by his sharing second prize in the 1946 contest. "An Error in Chemistry" was neither Faulkner's first nor his last appearance in *EQMM*, a fact that has escaped the notice of Faulkner scholars. Two and a half years earlier, Faulkner's story "The Hound" appeared in the January 1944 issue. This story of Ernest Cotton's ambush murder of a wealthy neighbor named Houston is material that Faulkner would rework in *The Hamlet* as Mink Snopes's murder of Jack Houston. The story was originally published in *Harper's* in August 1931 and reprinted in Faulkner's 1934 collection *Dr. Martino and Other*

Fig. 2. Cover of *Ellery Queen's Mystery Magazine*, January 1944. Copyright © 2017 by Penny Publications/Dell Magazines (TheMysteryPlace.com). Reprinted with permission of the publisher. Cover image by George Salter. Used by permission of Janet Salter Rosenberg.

Stories. In his headnote to "The Hound," Dannay notes that "when William Faulkner turns his dark pen to a tale of murder, it is not easy to forget" and compares the feeling of "prickling horror" he experienced reading "The Hound" to that of reading "A Rose for Emily."[20]

Dannay again reprinted Faulkner in the October 1947 issue of *EQMM*.[21] This time the story was "Smoke," another narrative focusing on Gavin Stevens's detective work, which (like "An Error in Chemistry") Faulkner then reprinted in *Knight's Gambit*. In "Smoke," Stevens uses conjecture and courtroom trickery to get Granby Dodge to confess to the murders both of his uncle and subsequently of the judge who was delaying the execution of the uncle's will. In his headnote to this reprint, Dannay returns to a point that he had made in announcing Faulkner's second prize a year earlier, namely, an affinity Dannay sees between Faulkner's Gavin Stevens stories and the Uncle Abner detective stories of Melville Davisson Post.[22] As is the case in a number of Post's stories, "Smoke" shows that Gavin Stevens is not above a little extralegal trickery to get a suspect to reveal his guilt. Post's lawyer-detective solved crimes in rural western Virginia before the Civil War. Post was a popular author whose stories regularly appeared in the *Saturday Evening Post* during the second decade of the twentieth century. He collected his detective stories in a 1918 volume titled *Uncle Abner, Master of Mysteries*. What is strikingly similar is that it is Abner's nephew who narrates his cases, just as Gavin Stevens's cases (with the single exception of "Smoke," which has an anonymous first-person narrator) are told from the angle of vision of his nephew. Whether Dannay is correct in speculating that Faulkner modeled his detective stories on Post's, one might wonder whether Faulkner, who surely received copies of *EQMM* in which his stories appeared, got the idea for collecting his Uncle Gavin stories in *Knight's Gambit* from Dannay's headnote.

But these three stories in *EQMM*, along with Faulkner's appearance in the anthology of prizewinning stories from the 1946 contest, do not represent the end of Dannay's editorial relation to Faulkner. In 1946 Dannay edited another anthology of crime fiction, *Murder by Experts*, that once again reprints "The Hound." I cannot overemphasize how consistently Faulkner scholars have gotten the publication history of "The Hound" wrong. The consensus's erroneous claim is that after Faulkner's long out of print collection *Dr. Martino and Other Stories*, "The Hound" became unavailable to readers for forty-five years until Joseph Blotner reprinted the story in *Uncollected Stories of William Faulkner*, published by Random House in 1979.[23] This misses both reprints that were authorized by the Ellery Queen brand. *Murder by Experts*, however, was a little different from Dannay's other edited collections. For this volume,

Fig. 3. Cover of *Ellery Queen's Mystery Magazine*, October 1947. Copyright © 2017 by Penny Publications/Dell Magazines (TheMysteryPlace.com). Reprinted with permission of the publisher. Cover image by George Salter. Used by permission of Janet Salter Rosenberg.

Dannay invited other leading crime writers to select and introduce their favorite stories. Faulkner's story was chosen by Margaret and Kenneth Millar, wife and husband, who each wrote popular detective fiction. Although Margaret Millar was known for the psychological depth of her women characters and was initially the more successful of the two, her fame was eventually eclipsed by that of her husband, who is better-known under his pen name, Ross Macdonald. Macdonald was the author of the popular Lew Archer detective novels and is one of the few genre writers to receive attention from academics, in part because his interest in Freudian psychoanalysis resonated with critical concerns during the Cold War. In their introduction to "The Hound," the Millars begin with the following claim: "Though he helped to write the screen play of *The Big Sleep*, William Faulkner is not usually thought of when mystery authors are mentioned. The fact is that he has made a more original and imaginative contribution to mystery form than anyone since Poe," particularly in the "strange and wonderful novel, *Sanctuary*."[24] The Millars go on to call Faulkner the best American fiction writer and predict that people will still be reading his fiction in a hundred years. Like Dannay's, the Millars' perspective shows the respect detective writers had for Faulkner at a time when Yoknapatawpha's sole owner and proprietor supposedly had been largely forgotten.

In the final paragraph of their introduction, the Millars speak of their personal impressions of Faulkner. In the summer of 1945, Margaret, like Faulkner, was under contract at Warner Bros., and they struck up a friendship. The reason I mention this is that nowhere in any of the biographies of William Faulkner (not Joseph Blotner's, not Frederick Karl's, not David Minter's, not Jay Parini's) is there any reference to the Millars or Ross Macdonald, which seems of a piece with the desire that many Faulkner scholars have to not link Faulkner in any way to genre fiction.

But Dannay was not done promoting Faulkner. In 1951 Dannay published *Queen's Quorum*, a history of the detective short story from Hawthorne and Poe through Faulkner. Dannay's discussion focuses on *Knight's Gambit*, and he speaks with irritation about its place in print culture:

> The publication, advertising, and critical reviews of Faulkner's *Knight's Gambit* have emphasized once more the shameful literary snobbishness that has always existed, and still exists in America. Too many publishers and critics regard detective stories as the illegitimate children of literature, to be treated with arrogance and disdain. For example, the publishers of *Knight's Gambit*, anticipating in 1949 Faulkner's winning the Nobel Prize for literature (the

award was not officially made until November 10, 1950), advertised the book as the author's first "detective story." First? What was Faulkner's *Intruder in the Dust* (1948) if not a detective story?[25]

Dannay's observation returns us to a point I made earlier, namely, that most of Faulkner's novels deploy conventions of crime and detective fiction.

If Faulkner profusely thanked Cowley for his editorial work, Faulkner essentially spat in Dannay's face. In a letter to his agent, Harold Ober, Faulkner wrote: "Thank you for the Ellery Queen check. What a commentary. In France, I am the father of a literary movement. . . . In America, I eke out a hack's motion picture wages by winning second prize in a manufactured mystery story contest."[26] And yet Dannay's magazine, which had a monthly readership of over two hundred thousand, presented Faulkner to far more people than Cowley's *Portable Faulkner*.

Whether we privilege Malcolm Cowley's or Ellery Queen's editorial efforts to revive Faulkner's reputation, one thing is clear: Faulkner's novels came back into print. Certainly, Cowley's work was largely responsible for the 1946 Modern Library one-volume hardback edition incorporating *The Sound and the Fury* and *As I Lay Dying*.[27] However, what Faulkner novels came back into print the soonest as *paperbacks*, and where they were published, suggest Queen's world, not Cowley's. Between 1947 and 1951, the New American Library reprinted seven Faulkner books in its pulp Signet paperback series.[28] Signet's motto was "Good Reading for the Millions," and the series was instrumental in pulping modernism, in making modernist texts available to the masses in cheap paper form. In that five-year period, Faulkner's Signet reprints sold nearly 3.3 million copies at 25 cents a pop.[29] (By contrast, in roughly the same time period, *The Portable Faulkner* only sold twenty thousand copies.[30]) Signet focused on Faulkner at his pulpiest—*Sanctuary*, *Wild Palms*, *Old Man*, *The Unvanquished*, *Intruder in the Dust*, *Knight's Gambit*, and *Pylon*—all printed on pulp paper and packaged with pulp covers. Signet, incidentally, was at this time also Mickey Spillane's paperback publisher. Author of the Mike Hammer detective novels, Spillane's fiction is full of sex and extreme violence. But if you were the kind of reader who selected books on the basis of their covers, you'd probably have a hard time distinguishing pulp author Spillane from High Modernist Faulkner![31] My point is that pulp publisher Signet was likely at least as impressed by the Faulkner that Ellery Queen championed as by the Faulkner that Malcolm Cowley claimed for the pantheon of literature with a capital "L." By showing that there was a Faulkner who could move the "merch," Signet paved the way for the paperback reprinting of the novels that we most often teach and write about today.[32] Like Faulkner, Faulkner critics have for too long overlooked or dismissed the Nobel Laureate's second-prize award in Ellery Queen's 1946 detective fiction contest. But far from disparaging pulp Faulkner, we should acknowledge the crucial role genre fiction played in bringing a forgotten author back to the attention of millions. So why don't we just admit it—Faulkner readers and scholars owe Ellery Queen a debt none of us can ever repay.

NOTES

1. C. Hugh Holman in *"Absalom, Absalom!*: The Historian as Detective," *Sewanee Review* 79, no. 4 (1971): 542–53, argues that *Absalom, Absalom!* is strongly influenced by the tradition of detective fiction and notes that in Faulkner's library there were books by thirty-one detective writers, including the ones here identified (544).

2. William Faulkner, *Light in August* rev. ed. (1932; repr., New York: Vintage International, 1990), 110. Hereafter cited parenthetically.

3. William Faulkner, *The Wild Palms* (later known as *If I Forget Thee, Jerusalem*) (1939; repr., New York: Vintage International, 1995), 22. Hereafter cited parenthetically.

4. John Earle Bassett, *William Faulkner: The Critical Heritage* (New York: Routledge and Kegan Paul, 1975), 26.

5. Albin Krebs, "Malcolm Cowley, Writer, Is Dead at 90," *New York Times*, March 29, 1989.

6. Faulkner, quoted in ibid.

7. No full-length biography of Dannay and Lee exists, but an overview of their joint career may be found in John L. Bren's *A Shot Rang Out: Selected Mystery Criticism* (Vancleave, MS: Surinam Turtle Press, 2008), 105–10. Additional biographical information about the cousins appears in the introduction to Francis M. Nivins Jr.'s *Royal Bloodline: Ellery Queen, Author and Detective* (Bowling Green, OH: Bowling Green University Popular Press, 1974), 1–14.

8. In *American Pulp: How Paperbacks Brought Modernism to Main Street* (Princeton, NJ: Princeton University Press, 2014), Paula Rabinowitz devotes chapter 6 to Borges's appearance in *EQMM*. As Rabinowitz notes, Borges won the magazine's third annual detective story contest (160).

9. Ibid., 27.

10. Ibid., 41.

11. Speaking specifically of *Sanctuary*, David M. Earle, in *Re-Covering Modernism: Pulps, Paperbacks, and the Prejudice of Form* (Burlington, VT: Ashgate, 2009), suggests that "Faulkner looked to the pulps as a model for salability at a time when his career was floundering, both critically and economically" (197).

12. In his preface to the 1932 French translation of *Sanctuary*, the novelist André Malraux saw "the intrusion of Greek tragedy into the detective story" (translated and quoted in Joseph Blotner, *Faulkner: A Biography* [New York: Random House, 1984], 349).

13. Jay Watson is one of the very few critics to comment on "An Error in Chemistry." He does so in the context of reading *Knight's Gambit* as more about the power of conversation than about classic detective ratiocination. See *Forensic Fictions: The Lawyer Figure in Faulkner* (Athens: University of Georgia Press, 1993), 142–47.

14. Joseph Blotner, ed., *Selected Letters of William Faulkner* (New York: Random House, 1977), 137.

15. Thomas S. Hansen, *Classic Book Jackets: The Design Legacy of George Salter* (New York: Princeton Architectural Press, 2005), 44.

16. Ellery Queen [Frederick Dannay], "Second-Prize Winner: William Faulkner," *Ellery Queen's Mystery Magazine*, June 1946, 4.

17. See Agatha Christie, Agatha Christie Limited, http://www.agathachristie.com (accessed May 11, 2016).

18. As Jeremiah Rickert explains, there was a four-member panel of judges for the contest: Dannay, Lee, Howard Haycroft, and Christopher Morley. Faulkner, Stribling, and Wellman each had the unqualified support of one of the judges as the best. The detective writer Rex Stout was brought in to break the tie. Stout read the three deadlocked stories and picked Wellman's. See Jeremiah Rickert, "Genre Fiction: Manly Wade Wellman," *Oregon Literary Review* 2, no. 2 (2007), http://orelitrev.startlogic.com/v2n2/OLR-rickert .htm#faulkner (accessed October 5, 2015). Unfortunately, individual issues of the journal are no longer accessible at this site.

19. Ibid.

20. Ellery Queen [Frederic Dannay], untitled headnote to William Faulkner's "The Hound," *Ellery Queen's Mystery Magazine*, January 1944, 51.

21. As was the case in the 1946 issue, Faulkner's stories in the 1944 and 1947 issues of *EQMM* appear along with stories by Agatha Christie.

22. Ellery Queen [Frederic Dannay], untitled headnote to William Faulkner's "Smoke," *Ellery Queen's Mystery Magazine*, October 1947, 50.

23. Although hardly alone in the error, Hans Skei typifies the failure of Faulkner critics to credit the Ellery Queen reprints of "The Hound." See Hans Skei, *Reading Faulkner's Best Short Stories* (Columbia: University of South Carolina Press, 1999), 96.

24. Margaret Millar and Kenneth Millar, headnote to "The Hound," in *Murder by Experts*, ed. Ellery Queen (Chicago: Ziff Davis, 1946), 99.

25. Ellery Queen [Frederic Dannay], *Queen's Quorum* (Boston: Little, Brown, 1951), 108–9.

26. Blotner, ed., *Selected Letters*, 217–18.

27. As Lawrence Schwartz notes in *Creating Faulkner's Reputation: The Politics of Literary Criticism* (Knoxville: University of Tennessee Press, 1988), Cowley was actually not happy with the timing of the Modern Library publication, fearing that it would under-cut sales of *The Portable Faulkner*. See Schwartz, *Creating Faulkner's Reputation*, 56.

28. In 1947 *Sanctuary* was first reprinted as a Penguin paperback, but shortly there-after, when New American Library broke off from the British firm Penguin Books and became a publisher in its own right, *Sanctuary* became a New American Library title.

29. In *American Pulp*, Rabinowitz cites a New American Library interoffice memo from 1951 for this sales number (272).

30. Schwartz, *Creating Faulkner's Reputation*, 55.

31. As Earle notes, quoting André Schifflin, "If you did not look at the title, you would be hard pressed to know whether what you had in your hand was by Mickey Spillane or William Faulkner" (*Re-Covering Modernism*, 197).

32. In 1954 Random House released in paperback its 1946 hardback pairing of *The Sound and the Fury* and *As I Lay Dying*. For fuller discussions of this publication his-tory and pertinent scholarship, see Charles A. Peek and Robert W. Hamblin, eds., *The Companion to Faulkner Studies* (Westport, CT: Greenwood, 2004), 302n61.

Hard-Boiled Faulkner?
Gender, Art, and Commerce
in William Faulkner's *Knight's Gambit*

ERIN A. SMITH

In late 1944, William Faulkner was in Hollywood working on the screen-play for the 1946 film *The Big Sleep*, an adaptation of Raymond Chandler's 1939 novel of the same name. He and Howard Hawks, the director, got into an argument over a plot point: who had killed the Sternwood's chauffeur, Owen Taylor? They wired Chandler, who was working as a screenwriter at a nearby studio, to ask him. Chandler reportedly thought about it and wired back that he hadn't the faintest idea.[1] The story is testimony to how complicated the plots of many hard-boiled detective stories are, unlike the carefully plotted mysteries of Arthur Conan Doyle or Agatha Christie. It is also, however, a fitting anecdote to open this essay, because it is about a conversation between Faulkner and Chandler about detective fiction, a conversation that I argue shaped Faulkner's own mystery stories.

Faulkner's detective stories, collected in 1949 into the volume *Knight's Gambit*, are part of a larger cultural conversation about authorship, liter-ary commerce, and detective fiction. Chandler published his self-serving historiography of the detective story as an essay called "The Simple Art of Murder" in *Atlantic Monthly* in 1944. In it he made claims about the ways that good detective stories—"realistic" detective stories—were intimately enmeshed with ideas about gender, social class, and nation. Faulkner's title story, "Knight's Gambit," was originally a short story he finished and unsuccessfully tried to get published in the early 1940s. He finally published it in 1949 as a long story, revised and expanded after he had been immersed in working on the screenplay for *The Big Sleep*. "Knight's Gambit" is—in part—an answer to Chandler's "Simple Art of Murder" and the hard-boiled detective stories it celebrated. Faulkner rehearses some of Chandler's premises but ultimately undermines the gendered binaries on which they are based.

Pulps and Slicks
Detective Fiction and the Marketplace

Mysteries were the first mass-market category of fiction in the United States. Like all modern genres—mysteries, romances, westerns, science fiction—they arose from pulp magazines in the 1920s and solved a stubborn problem for publishing houses. Unlike each box of Kellogg's Corn Flakes, each book published by Simon and Schuster was different. How could one effectively advertise and market such goods? Genres provided the solution, offering publishers a way of selling similar stories to the same audience again and again. For example, the number of subscribers to *Ellery Queen's Mystery Magazine* provided a decent estimate for the number of copies of a particular mystery novel to publish and a uniquely effective place to advertise the new book to likely purchasers. Genre fiction made the business of publishing much more predictable and profitable. Its blatantly commercial origins, however, often compromised its reputation for literary merit.[2]

This was certainly how Faulkner thought about it. After his agent informed him that his story, "An Error in Chemistry" (which had appeared in 1946 in *Ellery Queen's Mystery Magazine*), had won second prize in a contest, he snapped back a testy reply: "What a commentary. In France, I am the father of a literary movement. In Europe I am considered the best modern American and among the first of all writers. In America, I eke out a hack's motion picture wages by winning second prize in a manufactured mystery story contest."[3] Faulkner's brother John recalled that "when Bill received word he had won the Nobel Prize, I fully believe he was about written out. He had said years ago that if that happened, he'd turn to writing mystery stories. One thing about them, he said, was that once you found a formula that worked, you could keep on using it over and over, by simply changing names and places."[4] Faulkner's disdain here is for mystery stories generally, but the literary field for detective fiction was actually more complicated. Mystery readers make a distinction between "classic" mysteries written by authors like Arthur Conan Doyle, Agatha Christie, and Dorothy Sayers and hard-boiled detective stories written by authors like Dashiell Hammett and Raymond Chandler. A classic mystery—the prototypical English county house murder—is often called a "cozy." As W. H. Auden argued in his 1948 essay, "The Guilty Vicarage," such mysteries involve a closed community—an extended family at an ancestral home, a small town, a college—whose Edenic peace is ripped apart by a brutal murder. These books are intellectual puzzles in which a detective uses rational means to explain a crime, identify the single individual responsible for it, and ultimately restore the prelapsarian social order by expelling that individual from the larger community.[5] These stories offer reassurance that we live in a just, rational society in which evil is the result of single individuals rather than corrupt social institutions.[6]

Hard-boiled stories are tougher and more violent. Their detectives rely as much on brawn and tough talk as on their brains. Hard-boiled worlds are often overrun by systemic crime—gangsters, crooked cops, ruthless political machines. In many of these stories, "Whodunit?" seems beside the point given the large-scale corruption that characterizes the cities in which they are typically set. Hard-boiled heroes are usually working men of little means who are fighting the good fight in a world gone to hell. Moreover, these stories frequently have complicated plots (like *The Big Sleep*) that fail to live up to the logical, carefully crafted chain of clues that readers of Christie or Doyle might expect.

The differences are the result of the varied conditions of literary production out of which these stories arose. That is, the English country house murder and the mean streets murder have distinct literary genealogies marked by gender, social class, and national origins. These literary genealogies profoundly shaped what it meant to read or write mystery stories in the twentieth century. In general, the structuring binary was between the masculine, proletarian pulp magazines where hard-boiled detective stories first appeared in the 1920s and the feminine, consumerist slick-paper magazines where classic detective stories left their mark. Although the binary is too simple, it was embraced and policed by writers on either side of the divide in the 1920s, 1930s, and beyond.[7]

The slick-paper mass-market magazine appeared on the scene in 1893, when Frank Munsey cut the price of *Munsey's Magazine* from twenty-five cents to ten cents and replaced its genteel content with articles of interest to middle-class readers. The low price attracted a mass audience, which lured advertisers, who subsidized the high production costs of the magazine. This formula—low price, large circulation, lots of advertising—was taken up by a whole generation of entrepreneurs, including George Horace Lorimer of the *Saturday Evening Post* and Edward Bok of the *Ladies' Home Journal*. By slashing prices and shaping editorial content for a mass audience, mass-market magazines increased circulations tenfold, from one hundred thousand or less to a million or more by 1900. This was "the magazine revolution." These magazines—mass-market magazines—required high quality, glossy or "slick" paper for the reproduction of images in their ads. Because the paper was so expensive, most mass-market magazines were one-half to two-thirds ads to underwrite the substantial production costs. Since advertisers targeted women as "purchasing agents" for their families, estimating that 85 percent of consumer purchases were made by women, most of these slicks were implicitly "women's magazines."[8]

These "slicks" were critical to the success of English country house, classic mystery stories. Sherlock Holmes made his debut in America in the pages of *Collier's* in 1903–1905, and the immense success of these stories set off a flood of copycats. *Collier's, Liberty, McClure's,* and the *Saturday Evening Post* all ran one classic mystery story after another between the wars. In the late 1920s, Agatha Christie and Mary Roberts Rinehart were serialized in the *Post*.[9] Because of their association with mass-market magazines that targeted women, this fiction was deemed bourgeois, feminine, and consumerist.

Juxtaposed with these slick mass-market magazines were pulp magazines, named for the cheap, wood-pulp paper on which they were printed. Pulp magazines featured 128 pages of densely packed print with simple line drawings in black and a few ads in separate sections in front and back—mostly for correspondence schools, body-building plans, elocution lessons, and work clothes. Pulps needed to grab the attention of passersby of the newsstand (there were few subscription sales), so they had lurid covers featuring men with guns and women in skimpy clothing. Instead of being paid for a story, pulp writers were paid by the word. This is to say that they were piecework prose producers. Pulp writer Erle Stanley Gardner described himself not as an author but as a "fiction factory." Authors often wrote under multiple pseudonyms and the names were often owned by the company, with several writers publishing under a single name. Most studies maintained that pulp audiences were marginal to literary culture—young, working-class, poorly educated, and often immigrant. Librarians and social workers fretted that "the proletariat" read mostly pulp magazines.[10]

The most important pulp magazine for hard-boiled detective stories was *Black Mask*, founded in 1920. Although *Black Mask* initially featured all kinds of fiction, it rapidly specialized in "masculine" westerns and detective stories. By 1926 it was subtitled "The He-Man's Magazine." In a 1933 column, editor Joseph Thompson Shaw described the ideal *Black Mask* reader: "He is vigorous-minded, hard . . . responsive to the thrill of danger, the stirring exhilaration of clean, swift, hard action. . . . [He] knows the song of a bullet. The soft, slithering hiss of a swift-thrown knife, the feel of hard fists, the call of courage."[11]

This binary between artisanal, masculine pulp fiction and consumerist, feminine slick-paper fiction was self-consciously played out in the 1920s and 1930s in both the pulps and the slicks. Frank Gruber, a prolific pulp magazine writer, described the slick-paper magazine stories:

"Most of them were terribly effeminate . . . and I was more at home with the virile, masculine type of story."[12] Harold Hersey, who edited pulp magazines between the wars, insisted that "one is not afflicted in the fiction magazines with an infinite variety of copy relating to female complaints and perplexities."[13]

Not only were these publications gendered, they were also deeply imbricated with social class. The slicks disdained sensational pulp magazines. *Vanity Fair* featured an exposé of pulp magazines in June 1933 called "The Pulps: Daydreams for the Masses." It denigrated pulp writers as hacks, characterized pulp readers as "those who move their lips when they read," and deemed these magazines "gaudy, blatant, banal."[14] Joseph Thompson Shaw, editor of *Black Mask*, pushed back in a subsequent editorial column defending his writers, his magazine, and his audience. He also disparaged the average *Vanity Fair* reader as being "the society matron who considers it smart to have on her table the so-called class magazine with its illustrations regardless of its text."[15] In Shaw's telling of it, the status-seeking, effeminate readers of the slicks were easily seduced by pretty pictures but had no literary taste whatsoever.

The distinctions between artisanal, masculine hard-boiled detective stories and effeminate, genteel classic tales got obfuscated in the paperback book market. The paperback appeared on the scene in 1939, when Pocket Books launched a series of twenty-five-cent books to be sold and distributed like magazines at newsstands, drugstores, train stations, and bus depots instead of trade bookshops. American paperback mysteries from either tradition most often featured lurid, pulp-magazine-inspired covers, and they shared space on the same book displays. Although the classic mysteries and the hard-boiled ones were promiscuously mingled in the 1940s paperback market, these genealogies mattered immensely— to Raymond Chandler and to William Faulkner.

"The Simple Art of Murder"
Chandler Maps the Literary Field

In Raymond Chandler's article "The Simple Art of Murder,"[16] Chandler claimed that good detective fiction was "realistic." He then spent a lot of time ridiculing as *un*realistic best-selling examples of the classic mystery by A. A. Milne, E. C. Bentley, Agatha Christie, and Dorothy Sayers. Next he installed Dashiell Hammett as the father of the good, realistic, hard-boiled school. Finally, he offered a model of the detective hero that implicitly placed his own work at the center of the field. All of this rhetorical work dividing the detective-story sheep from the goats was articulated through the categories of class, gender, and nation.

Chandler's essay described quality novels sitting neglected on the shelf while "old ladies" pushed and shoved to get at mysteries titled *"The Triple Petunia Murder Case* or *Inspector Pinchbottle to the Rescue"* (3). These silly novels were written during the so-called Golden Age of detective stories between the World Wars, although Chandler insisted that two-thirds to three-quarters of the detective stories published still adhered to the same old "arid formula" (5, 12). Here is Chandler's sarcastic summary of the classic mystery prototype:

> The same careful grouping of suspects, the same utterly incomprehensible trick of how somebody stabbed Mrs. Pottington Postlethwaite III with the solid platinum poniard just as she flatted on the top note of the "Bell Song" from *Lakmé* in the presence of fifteen ill-assorted guests; the same ingénue in fur-trimmed pajamas screaming in the night to make the company pop in and out of doors and ball up the timetable; the same moody silence next day as they sit around sipping Singapore slings and sneering at each other, while the flatfeet crawl to and fro under the Persian rugs, with their derby hats on. (10)

These books really got Chandler down. "This," he declared, "the classic detective story, has learned nothing and forgotten nothing. It is the story you will find almost any week in the big shiny magazines, handsomely illustrated, and paying due deference to virginal love and the right kind of luxury goods" (10). Note that—for Chandler—this ridiculous fiction was enabled by the advertising-supported slick magazines that were full of sentimental, effeminate claptrap and consumerist propaganda. Although he spent most of the essay ridiculing British writers (whom critics preferred), Chandler insisted there were plenty of preposterous, badly plotted American novels as well.

Having dismissed the classic mystery and the slick-paper magazines in which it was found, Chandler turned to the world of pulp magazines, where hard-boiled fiction first appeared. Chandler argued, in the most quoted passage of the essay, that Dashiell Hammett "gave murder back to the kind of people that commit it for reasons, not just to provide a corpse; and with the means at hand, not hand-wrought dueling pistols, curare, and tropical fish" (14). Hammett did this with a signature "style" that Chandler described as "the American language" (15). Good detective fiction, then—the realistic type—was "American," although Chandler conceded that this "American language" was not exclusively American anymore. Terse, tough talk spoken just about anywhere could qualify as "American" by virtue of its distinctive style and tone.

Hammett's canonization required some additional defense. The "old ladies" from earlier in the essay made an encore appearance when

Chandler defended Hammett from those who claimed that he did not write detective stories at all—merely tough novels with a little mystery thrown in for interest. Chandler characterized such critics as "the flustered old ladies—of both sexes (or no sex) and almost all ages—who like their murders scented with magnolia blossoms" (16).

Like the national categories, the gender categories here are quite fluid. The enemies (of either sex) are women. The bad "British" fiction of ridiculous plots and impossible gentility (whether authored by Englishmen or not) is feminine (whether women write it or not), and the good "American" fiction (whether authored by Americans or not) is masculine (whether men write it or not) by virtue of its realism.

At the conclusion of the essay, Chandler argued that Hammett, "realistic" as he was, had neglected a more important artistic principle, a quality that Chandler called "redemption." It is worth quoting at length: "But down these streets a man must go who is not himself mean, who is neither tarnished nor afraid. The detective in this kind of story must be such a man. He is the hero; he is everything. He must be a complete man and a common man and yet an unusual man. He must be, to use a rather weathered phrase, a man of honor" (18).

In Chandler's account, good detective stories do not concern themselves with silly British ladies or folks who read slick, shiny women's magazines, but instead with heroic American men like those in the pulps. Slick-paper magazines and the classic detective fiction they published placed women, women's ways of knowing, and the consumption in which middle-class women engaged at the center of American life. Pulp magazines and the hard-boiled fiction they marketed placed the disappearing artisanal world of men in the position of privilege. The war of words between the pulps and the slicks, then, was part of a larger debate over the ways mass consumption would change how ordinary people experienced the world.

Faulkner, Magazines, and Detective Stories

In an April 1929 letter to his publishers, Faulkner described the print culture of Oxford: "I live in a complete dearth of print save in its most innocent form. The magazine store here carries nothing that has not either a woman in her underclothes or someone shooting someone else with a pistol on the cover."[17] There was plenty of commercial culture in Faulkner's world—pulps and slicks—and he engaged with both in his life and in his fiction.

Faulkner paid the bills with magazine fiction and screenwriting in Hollywood. In 1929 he self-consciously took a financial approach to fiction, studying the best-seller list to identify the characteristics these stories shared so that he could write one to order. He sold to the *Saturday Evening Post, Collier's*, and many other slick-paper magazines and often directly tailored his stories to their specifications, but he also dismissed these stories as "trash." He complained that he had to write them because "first class stories fetch no money" in the United States, and his novels were not going to pay the bills.[18]

The most important slick for Faulkner was the *Saturday Evening Post*. He began sending the *Post* stories in the mid-1920s and finally had one published in 1930. Between 1930 and his death in 1962, the *Post* published eighteen of his stories, more than any other magazine, although it did reject many more of his stories than it accepted. For example, between 1930 and 1932, he sent them thirty-two stories; they accepted five. Faulkner initially submitted at least five of the six stories in *Knight's Gambit* to the *Post*.[19]

By the 1920s, the *Post* was an American institution. For thirty-seven years (until 1936), it was edited by George Horace Lorimer, who knew how to put the "mass" in mass-market magazines.[20] Leslie Fiedler describes it as the most popular of the family slicks.[21] Lorimer's *Post* was characterized by what Susan Donaldson calls "a penchant for romance, fast-paced adventure, resolution, unity, and reassurance about the goodness of American life."[22] Frank Luther Mott, a historian of American magazines, repeats the most frequent criticism of *Post* fiction—its "crass materialism." He summarizes, "Thus business success, romance, sports, humor, and public affairs were said to constitute the *Post* Pattern; and short stories, serials, and articles were alleged to be created and repeated according to a few variants of a successful formula, thus killing originality, new ideas, and the art impulse in general."[23] The formulaic happy endings drew scorn from writers in the 1920s and 1930s, but they kept sending in stories (Faulkner included) because the *Post* paid better than anywhere else—sometimes two to four times as much. In 1940 Faulkner complained to his editor, "I wrote six short stories . . . trying to write the sort of pot boilers which the Post pays me $1,000.00 each for, because the best I could hope for good stories is 3 or 4 hundred, and the only mag. to buy them is Harper's etc."[24] Moreover, Faulkner thought quite self-consciously about art and commerce, about mass culture and magazines in many of his stories. Popular magazines (pulps and slicks) appear in *Light in August, Pylon, The Wild Palms*, and *Knight's Gambit*.

Although he engaged all kinds of popular forms—aviation pulps, flapper stories, tales of gangsters and gun molls—the detective story was his favorite.[25] Faulkner was a lifelong fan of detective stories, although he grew increasingly reticent about that fact in public interviews later in his life. His friends and family recall that he read them in his leisure time and that they talked with him about his favorites. He and Howard Hawks bonded over their mutual fandom. Faulkner's library included at least twenty-five titles—by Rex Stout, Georges Simenon, John Dickson Carr, Dashiell Hammett, Ellery Queen, Mary Roberts Rinehart, E. C. Bentley, Agatha Christie, Dorothy Sayers, G. K. Chesterton ("Father Brown"), Edgar Allan Poe, and Wilkie Collins, in addition to uncatalogued stacks of paperbacks.[26]

Faulkner engaged specifically with hard-boiled writing culture and the pulps. He and Frederick Faust, a prolific writer of western pulps under the name Max Brand, worked together in Hollywood and became friends.[27] He and Dashiell Hammett—both southerners—met in Hollywood and became what Leslie Fiedler describes as "mutually destructive drinking buddies."[28] Fiedler and Walter Wenska have convincingly argued that *Sanctuary* follows closely two installments of Hammett's *The Dain Curse*, which was serialized in the November and December 1928 issues of *Black Mask*.[29] Moreover, Faulkner revised *Sanctuary* in page proofs to have a more objective, "hard-boiled" narrative voice rather than the original version's Jamesian focalization through Horace Benbow.[30]

Faulkner's deepest engagement with hard-boiled writing culture, however, was his stint as a screenwriter adapting Raymond Chandler's *The Big Sleep* for the silver screen. Faulkner's chess-playing knight-errant, Gavin Stevens, owes an immense debt to Chandler's chess-playing knight-errant, Philip Marlowe, and "Knight's Gambit" is Faulkner's dialogue with Chandler and hard-boiled writing culture about just what a "man of honor" should look like.[31]

Knight's Gambit
Faulkner's Conversation with Raymond Chandler

In November 1948, Faulkner wrote to his editor, Saxe Commins, at Random House,

> I am thinking of a "Gavin Stevens" volume, more or less detective stories. I have four or five short pieces, averaging 20 pages, in which Stevens solves or prevents crime to protect the weak, right injustice, or punish evil. There is one more which no one has bought. The reason is, it is a novel which I tried to compress into short story length. It is a love story, in which Stevens prevents a crime (murder) not for justice but to gain (he is now fifty plus) the childhood sweetheart which he lost 20 years ago.[3]

This collection became *Knight's Gambit*, a compilation of five previously published short stories arranged in chronological order by publication date and the lengthy original title story. Faulkner first circulated the twenty-page short story version of "Knight's Gambit" in the early 1940s, revised it significantly in 1942 and 1946 (before and after his work on *The Big Sleep*), and saw it rejected twelve times by nine different magazines before recalling it to become the concluding tale. The collection was published in 1949 by Random House and in a Signet paperback by New American Library in 1950.[33] The paperback had the requisite lurid cover—a man with a gun and an embracing couple, the woman in a low-cut dress. It promised "TALES OF CRIME, GUILT, AND LOVE" and reminded readers that Faulkner was the "Author of SANCTUARY," his paperback claim to fame.

The idea of collecting his short stories came from one of Faulkner's editors, but Faulkner embraced it. Originally, they imagined the Stevens stories as a section of his *Collected Stories*, but Faulkner decided on a separate volume. He believed that even a collection of stories needed to have a shared focus and single organizational principle to unify it.[34] *Knight's Gambit* is unified by a number of elements. First is genre—it is a collection of detective stories; Gavin Stevens is the lawyer-detective in all of them. Second, the stories celebrate a kind of redemptive agrarianism. In all of them, "outsiders"—folks from the backwoods or Memphis or the North or some foreign country—disrupt the peaceful, agrarian ways of Yoknapatawpha County (usually by interfering with the transfer of family property or by abusing the land and traditions), and Stevens solves the case and restores the peace.[35] Third, all of the stories celebrate community storytelling and/or gossip, since this frequently provides the knowledge necessary to solve the crime, and ignorance of it frequently trips up the criminal. As some critics complained, Stevens does very little detecting. Mostly, he just chats and the necessary knowledge comes to him (or gets brought to him by Charles, his equally chatty nephew).[36]

Stevens is no hard-boiled hero. One critic not inaccurately characterizes him as a "high minded egghead."[37] He is a Phi Beta Kappa from Harvard and has a PhD from Heidelberg. In his spare time, he plays chess and translates the Old Testament back into classic Greek. He is the Mississippi version of Dorothy Sayers's Lord Peter Wimsey or S. S. Van Dine's garrulous Philo Vance. In place of terse, tough talk, and fistfights is a lot of chatting with everybody about just about everything. Stevens "could discuss Einstein with college professors and . . . spent whole afternoons among the squatting men against the walls of country stores, talking to them in their idiom."[38] In Chandler's terms, he is effeminate, aristocratic, and "British." His mysteries follow the "arid formula" of the classic mystery, although the closed community whose Edenic peace he is restoring is small-town Mississippi rather than a family estate in rural England. These stories are puzzles (and not very good ones, the critics would add).[39] Also—like the closed communities of classic British fiction—they represent the disturbance of an established world by an ill-intentioned outsider, who is convicted for his crime. Afterward, justice is restored. Perhaps most important, all of the short stories first appeared in those effeminate slick-paper magazines.[40]

Many sources have been hazarded for Gavin Stevens—fellow southerner, creator of the locked-room mystery, Edgar Allan Poe; S. S. Van Dine's Philo Vance (identified in Chandler's essay as a "junior varsity" dreary detective); Dorothy Sayers; G. K. Chesterton's Father Brown mysteries; Irvin S. Cobb's "Judge Priest" tales; and most importantly, the "Uncle Abner" stories of Melville Davisson Post, "the highest paid magazine writer in America," serialized in the *Post* nearly two dozen times between 1911 and 1928.[41] What these sources have in common, however, is that they are all classic, English country-house fiction—unrealistic, effeminate, and consumerist in Chandler's terms.

And Faulkner knew it. Again and again, he cast his writing (particularly his commercial writing) as feminizing. He wrote to his agent from Oxford in 1936 that "since last summer I seem to have got out of the habit of writing trash but I will still try to cook up something for Cosmopolitan. Maybe I can get hold of one of the magazines and take a story that they will buy and change locale and names, etc. That's probably hard work too and requires skill, but I seem to be so out of touch with the Kotex Age here that I cant seem to think of anything myself."[42] This phrase, "the Kotex Age," suggests—like Chandler's petulant complaints about the slicks—the unfortunate dominance of women, women's concerns, and mass-marketed commodities and the ill luck of the manly geniuses like Chandler and Faulkner who must try to navigate this treacherous literary field in order to make a living. After eight consecutive rejections from the *Post*, Faulkner approvingly quoted a correspondent who complained about living "in an age when all magazines appear to be edited by and for women."[43]

In a letter to Malcolm Cowley, Faulkner characterized "art" in the South as "really no manly business."[44] As Susan Donaldson points out, in the aborted introduction to *The Sound and the Fury*, Faulkner wrote about just this question. The male artist in the South, he argued, was "forced to choose, lady and tiger fashion, between being an artist and being a man."[45] How, then, could Faulkner simultaneously sell classic mysteries to effeminate slick-paper magazines and assert his real manhood? "Knight's Gambit"—the concluding tale—was his solution. In it he heaps scorn on slick-paper magazines and feminized consumer culture more generally, but—more importantly—his chatty, intellectual detective wins the girl away from a fine specimen of hard-boiled manhood.

The most obvious connections between Chandler's *The Big Sleep* and Faulkner's "Knight's Gambit" are chess and chivalry.[46] *The Big Sleep* opens as Philip Marlowe, Chandler's hard-boiled private eye, appears at the home of General Sternwood to take a case. The Sternwood mansion has a stained-glass window in the front hall "showing a knight in dark armor rescuing a lady who was tied to a tree and didn't have any clothes on but some very long and convenient hair. The knight had pushed the vizor of his helmet back to be sociable, and he was fiddling with the knots on the ropes that tied the lady to the tree and not getting anywhere. I stood there and thought that if I lived in the house, I would sooner or later have to climb up there and help him."[47] The other scene, which marks Marlowe as a knight-errant out of his league among his corrupt clients, occurs when Carmen Sternwood shows up naked in his bed to seduce him. He talks to her calmly while he studies a chess problem laid out on a card table under a lamp. "I couldn't solve it," he said, "like a lot of my problems. I reached down and moved a knight." Two pages later, he recognizes his mistake: "I looked down at the chessboard. The move with the knight was wrong. I put it back where I had moved it from. Knights had no meaning in this game. It wasn't a game for knights."[48]

"Knight's Gambit" starts with Stevens and his nephew, Charles, peacefully playing chess around ten o'clock one night, when the Harriss siblings (Max and his unnamed sister) burst in demanding that he do something to stop the Argentine playboy whom they met on their international travels, Sebastian Gualdres, from marrying their mother, Melisandre Backus Harriss, for her money. Max does not "intend that a fortune-hunting Spick shall marry my mother" (144), but he is also angry and jealous because the Argentine is a better swordsman, athlete, horseman, and lover than he is. In his sister's telling of it, "Sebastian always beat him. At everything" (190). The Harriss daughter is in love with Gualdres herself and fears her angry, jealous brother will murder her beloved. She interrupts the chess game again later that night with a farmer's daughter in tow, claiming that Gualdres had seduced the girl away from Max, to whom the girl was secretly betrothed. Everyone is hyperaware that the Harriss daughter is trafficking in a well-worn cultural narrative—the lord of the manor-peasant's daughter love story she identifies as being straight out of "Scott or Hardy or somebody else" (191).

The long story/legend of the Harriss family—narrated in the third person, but focalized through Charles—is shot through with a cultural

logic that echoes Raymond Chandler's. There are masculine and feminine narrative modes. The "masculine" narrative modes include chess (a
game of pure logic that Stevens is teaching Charles to play) and the classics (Greek and Latin being the exclusive domain of men of privilege).
In his spare time, Stevens is translating the Old Testament back into
classic Greek, and his kin know better than to interrupt him when his
study door is shut and he is at work on the project. Moreover, the Harriss
family legend includes a benevolent patriarch who whiled away the long
summer afternoons reading Roman poets in the original Latin on the
porch, his dog asleep next to his chair (150). Both of these endeavors are
now spectacularly unfashionable; the young folks go to the movies and
read mass-market magazines instead.

The "feminine" narrative modes come into play when Faulkner provides the back story on the Harriss family. It is a soap opera—melodramatic, sentimental, and "feminine" to the core. The story is passed down
to Charles not through the male line, but from his mother, grandmother,
and the "spinster aunts of both sexes" (151) who gossiped about it during
his childhood. Charles's inheritance of the story gets compared to his
inheritance of a shelf of books in his uncle's home,

> not the books which his grandfather had chosen or heired in his turn from his
> father, but the ones which his grandmother had chosen and bought on the
> semi-yearly trips to Memphis . . . through which moved with the formal ges-
> tures of shades the men and women who were to christian-name a whole gen-
> eration: the Clarissas and Judiths and Marguerites, the St Elmos and Rolands
> and Lothairs: women who were always ladies and men who were always brave,
> moving in a sort of immortal moonlight without anguish and with no pain from
> birth without foulment to death without carrion, so that you too could weep
> with them without having to suffer or grieve, exult with them without having
> to conquer or triumph. (149)

These are women's stories—and they are false, sentimental, unrealistic,
and somewhat ridiculous, the structural equivalent of Chandler's silly
British mysteries. Moreover, Faulkner makes clear that this story is pure
slick-paper melodrama. Here is how the narrator introduces the cast
of characters: "the wealthy widow (millionairess, the county stipulated
it), the softly fading still softly pretty woman in the late thirties, and the
two spoiled children a year apart somewhere under twenty-one, and the
Argentine army captain house-guest, the four of them like the stock characters in the slick magazine serial, even to the foreign fortune-hunter"
(148). The story goes back to Mrs. Harriss's adolescence (when she was
Melisandre Backus), however, so the community has been watching it

unfold for more than twenty years "as the subscribers read and wait and watch for the serial's next installment" (149).[49]

The most intriguing part of the Harriss story—"a legend to or within or behind the actual or original or initial legend"(150–51)—is about a secret betrothal that predated Melisandre's marriage to the bootlegging outlander, Harriss, who turned the family into globetrotting sophisticates and built a gaudy mansion in place of the modest ancestral home ("like the Southern mansion in the moving pictures, only about five times as big and ten times as Southern" [162]).[50] The narrator explains that

> it was something about a previous involvement, prior to the marriage: an engagement, a betrothal in form in fact, with (so the legend said) the father's formal consent, then broken, ruptured, voided—something—before the man she did marry ever appeared on the scene;—a betrothal in form according to the legend, yet so nebulous that even twenty years after, with twenty years of front gallery gossip for what his uncle called the Yoknapatawpha County spinster aunts of both sexes to have cast that romantic mantle over the shoulders of every male under sixty who had ever taken a drink or bought a bale of cotton from her father, the other party to it had not only no name but no face too. (151)

Clearly, the terms here echo Raymond Chandler's. There are "serious" books that men pass down to their sons and grandsons as libraries, chess games that uncles teach to nephews, and "serious" literary endeavors in ancient languages. These are masculine, old-fashioned, and adamantly noncommercial. Then there is the emergent feminized world of mass culture—slick-paper magazines and movies—that is destroying the old-fashioned, patriarchal social hierarchies of yesteryear. Outlanders bring the fake southern mansions, inspired by the movies. The gossip passed around by spinster aunts of both sexes is little better than the crappy serial stories in slick-paper magazines with their melodrama, false sentiment, and romance.

Faulkner collapses this too-neat binary, however. It turns out that there is something to the gossip. Stevens himself is the long-lost lover, and he not only prevents Max from murdering Gualdres but neatly disposes of all the loose ends/people and marries the wayward Melisandre himself, successfully bringing her back into the fold, married once again not to an outlander but to one of "us."

This ending complicates Chandler's neat mapping of the cultural field into residual/masculine/serious narratives and emergent/feminine/silly mass-cultural narratives. The purely masculine world of the classics, chess, and strategy and the purely feminine world of romance and melodrama are made interdependent. Because of his chess-like strategizing,

Gavin/Gawain Stevens, the knight-errant, captures the queen and the castle from Gualdres, the formidably masculine opponent. Moreover, they are able to avert the attempted murder of Gualdres by Max only because Charles went to the movies and happened to stumble across a (very chatty) man who had just sold a notoriously wild, unbroken horse to Max. Thus enlightened, thanks to his degraded, effeminate taste for moving pictures, Charles runs home to his uncle and bursts into the study uninvited to interrupt Stevens's purely masculine translation work. They then drive a fast car out to the Harriss place just in time to prevent the crime. Max had replaced the docile mare Gualdres kept in an isolated stable to ride in the dark of night with the wild horse. Stevens makes a wager with Gualdres and saves his life. He then marries Gualdres off to the Harriss daughter (Gualdres enlists in the US military shortly thereafter), sends Max off to war, and finishes by sweeping Melisandre off her feet—twenty years late.

At the center of the story, then, is a (hidden) love triangle. Stevens and Gualdres are both after Melisandre, who owns some fine land and is still—oddly—that plain, innocent girl of twenty years ago, curiously untouched by modernity and all of her international travels. Although Gualdres is a fine specimen of manhood—"He looked hard . . . the hardness of metal, of fine steel or bronze" (173)—garrulous, intellectual Stevens outwits him and wins the girl. The better man turns out to be not Yoknapatawpha County's Philip Marlowe or Sam Spade but its Lord Peter Wimsey or Philo Vance. Moreover, unlike the tough loners of hard-boiled detective stories, Stevens ends the story as an uncle, a husband, and a stepfather.[51]

Having collapsed the masculine/feminine, art/mass culture binary, Faulkner deconstructs another of Chandler's distinctions. Although Gualdres is clearly the outsider in this story, he has been made over rather successfully into an insider (although an ambivalent one) by the close. Although Melisandre is a local girl, the visitors to the Harriss place all come to see Gualdres, who hosts all kinds of sporting entertainments that draw crowds of single working men (174).[52] Moreover, a great equestrian, he explores every corner of the county where a horse can go and thus comes to know the land better than many of the natives. Not only does he marry the Harriss daughter, but he joins the US military in the immediate aftermath of the Japanese attack on Pearl Harbor. Although his English remains heavily accented and he probably required an interpreter to do it, he marries an American wife, renounces his Argentine citizenship, and becomes a soldier and citizen of his adopted country (254–55). Later, he tells Charles to give his uncle a message: "Perhaps you are satisfied now" (255), an indication that the bet he lost (that he must marry the Harriss daughter) has put him on the path to a life he might not have otherwise chosen.[53]

There is an additional meditation on narrative modes at the close. Charles actually gets two different versions of the story about why his uncle did not marry Melisandre when they were young, leaving her to marry the bootlegging outlander, Harriss, instead. In the first version, which Stevens tells Charles as they are driving as fast as they can to the Harriss place to save Gualdres's life, Stevens is writing two letters from Heidelberg—one in English to his secretly betrothed, Melisandre, and one in German to his Russian lover in Paris. He puts the letters in the wrong envelopes, and Melisandre—now wise to his two-timing ways—drops him and marries Harriss shortly thereafter.

Later, when Charles is home from war in his uniform, a different story emerges. He confronts his uncle:

> "Those letters. Two letters. Two wrong envelopes."
> His uncle looked at him. "You don't like coincidence?"
> "I love it," he said. "It's one of the most important things in life. Like maidenhead. Only, like maidenhead, you only use it once. I'm going to save mine a while yet." (255)

Charles thinks that this story—like the virginal love celebrated in slick-paper magazine stories Chandler complained about—is just a little too easy.

"His uncle looked at him, quizzical, fantastical, grave. 'All right,' his uncle said. 'Try this . . .'" (255). And in place of the wildly unrealistic, coincidental romance story, he offers a version out of Conrad (256). When Melisandre—already married—came to Paris, Stevens met with her and asked why she had not waited for him. "'You didn't want me,' she said. 'I wasn't smart enough for you'" (257). "Will that one do?" Stevens asks. "Yes," Charles answers. "That's better. I might even buy that one" (257). Charles wisely points out that Stevens and Melisandre are now married, some twenty years later—what changed? The intervening years, Stevens argues, "made me older. . . . I have improved" (258). These are the closing words of the story.

The hard-boiled model is an immature model—manly athletic exploits and mistresses are fine for a young man, but "Knight's Gambit" suggests that there is a better model of masculinity, a better model for Chandler's "man of honor." Christopher Breu describes the hard-boiled hero as "a figure of almost ontological isolation," characterized by the "willful refusal of the ties of community and domesticity."[54] Conversely,

Stevens's model of manhood is familial, intimately enmeshed in his community, and ultimately romantically and intellectually superior to the competing model embodied by Gualdres.

However, Faulkner unmoors even this certainty. Note that Stevens's "masculine" story (the Conrad version) holds the same ontological status as his "feminine" story (the sentimental novel version of switched letters). The Conrad story is not presented as truth but simply as another story that Charles might find more agreeable. Charles concedes that he likes this story better, but only allows that he *might* believe it, not that it is true. More specifically, he says, "I might even *buy* that one" (257; italics added). Whichever kind of story a narrator tells, that person *sells* a particular version of events. Conrad or popular romance, there is no residual (masculine) realm outside of commerce and consumer culture. Chandler's (and sometimes Faulkner's) protestations aside, "Knight's Gambit" deconstructs the art/commerce, masculine/feminine binary that has structured much discussion of modernist narrative.[55] Whether we narrate our lives through Hollywood films, slick-paper magazines, and sentimental novel plots or through chess, Conrad, and the classics, we are still narrating our lives—living through the (commercial) stories our culture makes available to us. The best we can do, Faulkner seems to suggest, is to pick which stories to live by deliberately.

Numerous critics have singled out "Knight's Gambit" as distinct from the rest of the unrevised magazine fiction in the collection. "Why does 'Knight's Gambit' succeed where the rest of *Knight's Gambit* fails?" asks Michael Wainwright.[56] Michael Grimwood argues that *Knight's Gambit* is a "self-parodic text" because the title story "not only attempts to redeem the first five; it also comments on them, rejects them, and moves beyond them."[57] What Grimwood sees in the collection is "the revision of formulaic magazine fiction into serious literature," a pattern many scholars see in Faulkner's republished and revised magazine fiction.[58] Conversely, I am arguing here that Faulkner lays out the binary between the masculine/serious art and the feminine/silly mass culture (an opposition he explicitly embraces in his letters and in public statements), only to deconstruct the distinctions between them. Commercial or literary, what authors do is to write stories and sell them, even if the literary ones have a smaller audience and offer lower rates of financial return. "Knight's Gambit" takes issue with Chandler's mapping of the literary field, demonstrating that modern literature of whatever kind is intimately enmeshed—for better and for worse—with the consumer marketplace.

NOTES

1. See Erin A. Smith, *Hard-Boiled: Working-Class Readers and Pulp Magazines* (Philadelphia: Temple University Press, 2000), 81.

2. For a history of genre fiction as what Robert Escarpit calls "semi-programmed issue," see Erin A. Smith, "Genre Reading," in *Encyclopedia of Recreation and Leisure in America*, ed. Gary S. Cross (New York: Scribner's, 2004), 1:391–95.

3. Joseph Blotner, ed., *Selected Letters of William Faulkner* (New York: Random House, 1977), 217–18.

4. John Faulkner, *My Brother Bill*, quoted in Michael Grimwood, *Heart in Conflict: Faulkner's Struggles with Vocation* (Athens: University of Georgia Press, 1987), 187.

5. W. H. Auden, "The Guilty Vicarage: Notes on the Detective Story, by an Addict," *Harper's* (May 1948): 406–12.

6. See John G. Cawelti, *Adventure, Mystery, and Romance: Formula Stories as Art and Popular Culture* (Chicago: University of Chicago Press, 1977), 105.

7. This literary terrain is mapped in much greater detail in chapter 1 of Smith, *Hard-Boiled*. See also Leslie Fiedler, "Pop Goes the Faulkner: In Quest of *Sanctuary*," in *Faulkner and Popular Culture: Faulkner and Yoknapatawpha, 1988*, ed. Doreen Fowler and Ann J. Abadie (Jackson: University Press of Mississippi, 1990), 86–88 on the ways *Sanctuary* gets positioned within the hard-boiled school versus the middlebrow whodunit.

8. See Smith, *Hard-Boiled*, 19–20.

9. Walter Wenska, "'There's a Man with a Gun over There': Faulkner's Hijackings of Masculine Popular Culture," *Faulkner Journal* 15 (Fall 1999–2000): 42, 43, 55.

10. Smith, *Hard-Boiled*, 19, 21–26, 33.

11. Quoted in ibid., 27–28.

12. Ibid.

13. Ibid., 30.

14. Ibid., 32.

15. Ibid.

16. The essay is reprinted in Raymond Chandler, *The Simple Art of Murder* (New York: Vintage, 1988): 1–18. Subsequent page references are cited parenthetically in the text. There is a more extended discussion of this essay in Smith, *Hard-Boiled*, 36–42.

17. Blotner, ed., *Selected Letters*, 43.

18. Ibid., 128. On Faulkner's money problems and his commercial work, see Lawrence H. Schwartz, *Creating Faulkner's Reputation: The Politics of Modern Literary Criticism* (Knoxville: University of Tennessee Press, 1988), 38–72. On his 1929 effort to write commercial fiction, see William Faulkner, introduction to *Sanctuary* (1931; repr., New York: Random House, 1977), vi, and Joseph Blotner, *Faulkner: A Biography* (New York: Vintage, 1991), 234. See also Joseph Blotner, "Faulkner and Popular Culture," in *Faulkner and Popular Culture: Faulkner and Yoknapatawpha, 1988*, ed. Doreen Fowler and Ann J. Abadie (Jackson: University Press of Mississippi, 1990), 13; Fiedler, "Pop Goes the Faulkner," 76; Anne Goodwyn Jones, "'The Kotex Age': Women, Popular Culture, and *The Wild Palms*," in *Faulkner and Popular Culture: Faulkner and Yoknapatawpha, 1988*, ed. Doreen Fowler and Ann J. Abadie (Jackson: University Press of Mississippi, 1990), 144–45.

19. James B. Meriwether, "Faulkner's Correspondence with the *Saturday Evening Post*," *Mississippi Quarterly* 30, no. 3 (Summer 1977): 461; Susan V. Donaldson, "Dismantling the *Saturday Evening Post* Reader: *The Unvanquished* and Changing 'Horizons of Expectation,'" in *Faulkner and Popular Culture: Faulkner and*

Yoknapatawpha, 1988, ed. Doreen Fowler and Ann J. Abadie (Jackson: University Press of Mississippi, 1990), 183–84.

20. For a discussion of Faulkner's engagement with the *Saturday Evening Post*, see Donaldson, "Dismantling the *Saturday Evening Post* Reader," 180–82, and Meriwether, "Faulkner's Correspondence," 461–64.

21. Fiedler, "Pop Goes the Faulkner," 75–76.

22. Donaldson, "Dismantling the *Saturday Evening Post* Reader," 182.

23. Quoted in Grimwood, *Heart in Conflict,* 190.

24. Blotner, ed., *Selected Letters,* 121.

25. On Faulkner's engagement with these popular forms, see David M. Earle, "Yoknapatawpha Pulp, or What Faulkner *Really* Read at the P.O.," in *Fifty Years after Faulkner: Faulkner and Yoknapatawpha, 2012,* ed. Jay Watson and Ann J. Abadie (Jackson: University Press of Mississippi, 2016), 31–45.

26. Suzanne Bray, "Studying the Masters: Influences from Classic Detective Fiction on Faulkner's *Knight's Gambit,*" in *Faulkner at Fifty: Tutors and Tyros,* ed. Marie Lienard-Yeterian and Gerald Preher (Cambridge: Cambridge Scholars, 2014), 104; Blotner, "Faulkner and Popular Culture," 18; Fiedler, "Pop Goes the Faulkner," 85; Mark Gidley, "Elements of the Detective Story in William Faulkner's Fiction," *Journal of Popular Culture* 7 (1973): 97–98; Hans Skei, "Faulkner's *Knight's Gambit*: Detection and Ingenuity," *Notes on Mississippi Writers* 13, no. 2 (1981): 79–81; Blotner, ed., *Selected Letters,* 169–70; Grimwood, *Heart in Conflict,* 196.

27. Blotner, "Faulkner and Popular Culture," 11.

28. Fiedler, "Pop Goes the Faulkner," 86. See also Wenska, "'There's a Man with a Gun over There,'" 44.

29. Fiedler, "Pop Goes the Faulkner," 85–86; Wenska, "'There's a Man with a Gun over There,'" 44–48.

30. Jay Watson, *Forensic Fictions: The Lawyer Figure in Faulkner* (Athens: University of Georgia Press, 1993), 54.

31. Many critics make the connection between Chandler's Philip Marlowe and Faulkner's Gavin Stevens as chess-playing knights-errant. See, for example, Michael Wainwright, *Faulkner's Gambit: Chess and Literature* (New York: Palgrave Macmillan, 2011), 65–70; William Van O'Connor, *The Tangled Fire of William Faulkner* (Minneapolis: University of Minnesota Press, 1954), 135–36; Lorie Watkins Fulton, "Justice as He Saw It: Gavin Stevens in *Knight's Gambit,*" *Faulkner Journal* 19, no. 2 (2004): 25–48; John T. Irwin, "*Knight's Gambit*: Poe, Faulkner, and the Tradition of the Detective Story," *Arizona Quarterly* 46, no. 4 (1990): 95–116; and Nicole Kenley, "The Southern Hard(ly) boiled: *Knight's Gambit, The Big Sleep,* and Faulkner's Construction of the Popular Masculine Subject," *Mississippi Quarterly* 65, no. 3 (Summer 2012): 339–65.

32. Blotner, ed., *Selected Letters,* 280. See also ibid., 274–75, for the plans for the collected stories.

33. On the publication history of the stories in *Knight's Gambit,* see Thomas L. McHaney, ed., *William Faulkner Manuscripts 18: "Knight's Gambit": Typescripts and Miscellaneous Typescript Pages* (New York: Garland, 1987), vii–xiv. See also Grimwood, *Heart in Conflict,* 190–95.

34. See Blotner, ed., *Selected Letters,* 278.

35. On this redemptive agrarianism and expulsion of "outsiders," see Jerome Klinkowitz, "The Thematic Unity of *Knight's Gambit,*" *Critique: Studies in Contemporary Fiction* 11, no. 2 (1969): 81–100; Grimwood, *Heart in Conflict,* 188, 200–13; Watson, *Forensic Fictions,* 88–91, 140; and Skei, "Faulkner's *Knight's Gambit,*" 82–83, 86–90.

36. See Watson, *Forensic Fictions*, chapter 4. See also William C. Doster, "The Several Faces of Gavin Stevens," *Mississippi Quarterly* 11, no. 4 (Fall 1958): 192.

37. Doster, "Several Faces of Gavin Stevens," 195.

38. William Faulkner, *Knight's Gambit* (1949; repr., New York: Vintage International, 2011), 17. Subsequent page references are cited parenthetically in the text.

39. On critical complaints about Faulkner's failure to respect the "rules" of the detective fiction genre and the "oddness" of his detective stories, see Watson, *Forensic Fictions*, 141–42, and Gidley, "Elements of the Detective Story," 104, 106–7, 109, 110–11.

40. I am disagreeing here with Nicole Kenley, who argues that Faulkner chose to write detective fiction because it was a "masculine" genre in the 1930s and 1940s. I am arguing here that the *kind* of detective stories Faulkner wrote were "effeminate" and actually undermined his manly writing credentials.

41. See, for example, Irwin, "*Knight's Gambit*"; Frances Blazer O'Brien, "Faulkner and Wright, Alias S. S. Van Dine," *Mississippi Quarterly* 14, no. 2 (Spring 1961): 101–7; Gidley, "Elements of the Detective Story"; and Bray, "Studying the Masters." The best discussion of Uncle Abner is in Grimwood, *Heart in Conflict*, 195–200.

42. Blotner, ed., *Selected Letters*, 95–96.

43. See Meriwether, "Faulkner's Correspondence," 474.

44. Blotner, ed., *Selected Letters*, 216.

45. Quoted in Susan V. Donaldson, "Faulkner and Masculinity," *Faulkner Journal* 15 (1999–2000): 7. Donaldson argues that Faulkner performed many (sometimes conflicting) masculine personae, including "financially besieged patriarch" and "solitary artist wary and disdainful of bourgeois respectability" (3). Although he performs the gendered posturing here (and elsewhere), I am about to argue that he explicitly deconstructs the distinction between manly art and feminine mass culture in "Knight's Gambit."

46. Many scholars make these connections. See Irwin, "*Knight's Gambit*," 106–7; Fulton, "Justice as He Saw It," 41–44, 46; Kenley, "Southern Hard(ly)boiled," 354; and Wainwright, *Faulkner's Gambit*, 70.

47. Raymond Chandler, *The Big Sleep* (1939; repr., New York: Vintage, 1992), 3–4.

48. Ibid., 154, 156.

49. Faulkner repeats this language later in the text: the community "watched it as you watch the unfolding story in the magazine installments" (*Knight's Gambit*, 155). Many critics have discussed the commentary in the story about mass culture. For example, in *Heart in Conflict*, Grimwood reads this story as Faulkner's struggle with his vocation, trying to make peace with being a self-consciously literary writer who nonetheless had to write significant numbers of commercial magazine stories about which he felt ashamed or ambivalent (chapter 5). Edmond Volpe argues that the story is self-consciously about the play of reality and fiction/fantasy. See Edmond L. Volpe, "Faulkner's 'Knight's Gambit': Sentimentality and the Creative Imagination," *Modern Fiction Studies* 24 (1978): 232–39.

50. On the story's first page, the home is described as "something a little smaller than a Before-the-War Hollywood set" (*Knight's Gambit*, 141).

51. Kenley argues that Stevens is modeled on the hard-boiled private eye but updated/ revised for the southern context—the hard(ly) boiled detective. I am arguing here that Stevens is explicitly modeled on genteel detectives of classic detective stories and that Faulkner is undermining these gendered distinctions in this story.

52. Wainwright offers a homoerotic reading of the text in which both Max and Gualdres are coded as homosexual (chapter 5).

53. Grimwood sees no ambivalence in Gualdres's makeover into an insider, merely a critique of the redemptive agrarian logic that characterizes the other stories (*Knight's Gambit*, 210). Fulton, conversely, sees a kind of ruthless self-serving imposition of his own

desires by Stevens on the hapless members of the Harriss clan, Gualdres included. This problematic "justice" Stevens metes out resonates with his actions in *Requiem for a Nun*.

54. Christopher Breu, *Hard-Boiled Masculinities* (Minneapolis: University of Minnesota Press, 2005), 126.

55. Although I have made this argument in the context of genealogies of detective stories (pulp and slick), it is nonetheless deeply influenced by Andreas Huyssen, "Mass Culture as Woman: Modernism's Other," in his *After the Great Divide: Modernism, Mass Culture, Postmodernism* (Bloomington: Indiana University Press, 1986), 44–62. Because pulp writers defined themselves (from below) against feminized mass-market magazines and high modernism defined itself (from above) against that same feminized mass culture, there is a great deal of overlap in the gendering and policing of boundaries.

56. Wainwright, *Faulkner's Gambit*, 24. See also Bray, "Studying the Masters," 114.

57. Grimwood, *Heart in Conflict*, 188, 195.

58. Ibid., 194. Numerous scholars suggest that Faulkner's revisions and additions to his republished magazine fiction transmute his commercial fiction into great art by critiquing the very formulas through which he had to write for money. See, for example, Donaldson, "Dismantling the *Saturday Evening Post* Reader."

Packaging Faulkner as a Cold War Modernist

GREG BARNHISEL

In 1946, upon learning that he had been one of the runners-up in the annual Ellery Queen mystery-writing contest (losing to Manly Wade Wellman), William Faulkner complained to his agent, Harold Ober, that "in France, I am the father of a literary movement. In Europe I am considered the best modern American and among the first of all writers. In America, I eke out a hack's motion picture wages by winning second prize in a manufactured mystery story contest."[1] But as many scholars have pointed out, 1946 marked the change of tide in Faulkner's status and reputation in the United States, so that by the time of his death he was as eminent at home as he was abroad. What happened? Did readers just wake up? Partly. But in his 1988 book, *Creating Faulkner's Reputation*, Lawrence Schwartz shows how cultural institutions—universities, intellectual journals, foundations, editors like Malcolm Cowley, publishers like Vintage and Random House, and even fictional corporate persons like "Ellery Queen"—catalyzed the dramatic improvement in Faulkner's literary reputation in the 1940s and 1950s more than anything intrinsic to Faulkner's work itself, which few readers now or then would argue was at its apex after the war.[2] I would add to Schwartz's catalogue the US government: the State Department's books program featured Faulkner's works, he actively participated in United States Information Agency goodwill tours and documentary films, and these activities not only contributed to the remaking of Faulkner's domestic reputation and the expansion of his popularity and readership abroad but were also a key, if largely unknown, episode in the broader reframing of experimental modernism as an expression and defense of the free societies of the West.

I'm not the first one to make an argument about how or why avant-garde modernism became seen as a kind of liberal humanism in the early Cold War period. A spate of 1970s art historians first suggested that the rise of abstract expressionist painting might have been a result of the movement's formalism and contentlessness, and they unearthed evidence that covert agencies such as the CIA had underwritten the movement. In 1983 Serge Guilbaut spun this into a very persuasive book with an irresistible title—*How New York Stole the Idea of Modern Art*. Then, in the 1990s, British historian and filmmaker Frances Stonor Saunders pasted together some of her own original research with the quarter-century-old revelations that the CIA had helped create the Congress for Cultural Freedom (CCF) and the National Student Association to remind us that in the 1950s, culture wasn't innocent of politics. And recently, a few younger writers have published exposés of the CIA connections to beloved literary institutions like the *Paris Review* and the Iowa Writers Program.[3]

I find this cycle of pearl-clutching—you mean culture and literature were used as *propaganda*?—a little disingenuous. Yes, covert agencies in the 1940s and 1950s in the United States, Great Britain, the Soviet Union, East Germany, and other nations used culture. They used everything; they threw a lot of spaghetti at the wall to see what stuck, and in the end they spent a lot less effort and money on literary magazines and art exhibitions than on insurgent movements and double-agent dirty tricks and overthrowing governments in Iran, Guatemala, Hungary, and so on. This doesn't mean that scholars of literature and culture shouldn't critically examine the products. It's important to remember, though, that just because art and literature are crucial to *us*, we shouldn't assume that they were also at the top of the state's priority list. We shouldn't overplay ourselves.

More interesting to me is just what modernism became, given where it came from. What I call "Cold War modernism" isn't an artistic movement or a cohort of writers and artists like the Beats or the romantics. Rather, it was a wide-ranging "extreme makeover" that we tend to forget ever happened. Today, when we just accept that Picasso, Stravinsky, Martha Graham, James Joyce, Ezra Pound, and Jackson Pollock are geniuses, it's hard to imagine a time when the modernist movement itself, across the arts, was seen as crazy and ugly at best and dangerous and subversive at worst. In the 1940s, to the American public James Joyce was an Irish sex maniac, Ezra Pound a fascist traitor, T. S. Eliot inexplicably un-American, Jackson Pollock a fraud, Picasso a Communist dirty old man, and Virginia Woolf a suicidal depressive. And Faulkner? He was the guy with the corncob and the other books you couldn't understand—or even *find* anymore.

Modernism was so dangerous, in fact, that Congress had to deal with it. Conservative groups like the American Artists Professional League testified that even though the Soviet Union officially rejected it, modernist art was in fact Communist to its very bones. Armed with this

information, in 1947 Congress demanded—and got—the scuttling of
Advancing American Art, a touring exhibition of modernist paintings
organized by the Department of State. "There is no art at all in connection with the modernists in my opinion," pronounced President Truman
when he heard about the show and the backlash.[4]

But by the end of the decade, American cultural diplomacy had
embraced modernism. Shows of paintings and prints went on tour,
music and dance featured artists and works that fell squarely in the
modernist camp, and Voice of America (or VOA, the official overseas
radio network of the United States, broadcast in local languages) invited
Marianne Moore, Wallace Stevens, William Carlos Williams, and even
Faulkner on the air to talk about their hometowns. (Faulkner declined
the opportunity.[5]) The modernist paintings showcased in the American
exhibition at the 1958 Brussels World's Fair hung on the walls of a modernist building created for the fair by architect Edward Durell Stone,
who had also designed the Museum of Modern Art on Fifty-Third Street
in New York City. And while the 1959 American National Exposition in
Moscow is justly famous as the site of Nixon and Khrushchev's Kitchen
Debate, largely forgotten is the controversy over the inclusion of modernist painters like Ben Shahn, William Zorach, Yasuo Kuniyoshi, and
Jack Levine, whose *Welcome Home* is a Berlin Dada-esque lampoon of
military-capitalist complacency. And that was a painting that President
Eisenhower—who could be seen obliquely as the subject of its satire—
defended against conservative attacks.

How did this happen? This isn't the place to get into the weeds of
modernist theory, but basically critics and editors and academics and
various other members of the cultural elite in the 1940s and 1950s emptied modernist art of its social and political freight by arguing that artworks should be judged entirely aesthetically, as works of form and style.
(The well-known New Critical approach was only one branch of this
larger evolution.) They then refilled these works with a different kind of
meaning: now, instead of being revolutionary, antibourgeois statements,
these artworks were proof of the vitality and fertility of a society based
on freedom and individualism. Only a society that puts preeminent value
on the free, autonomous individual could produce art this daring, this
new, this accomplished. This act of rhetorical redefinition is what I call
Cold War modernism.

I call it that because this process both served and was motivated by
Cold War interests. Communism, of course, minimizes the importance
of the individual, and Soviet art criticism stressed the need for artworks
to be primarily vessels for an unambiguous revolutionary message. In
fact, in 1934 the Soviet Union had enshrined this philosophy of art as

an actual state and Communist Party policy, calling it socialist realism. So the cultural Cold War's battle lines became pretty clear: on the one side, experimental modernism whose daring techniques showed what innovative things can happen when a free society lets self-determined individual geniuses express themselves without constraints; on the other, so-called *tendentious* (Trotsky's term) art whose purpose was to advance the program of the revolution to create an ideal society.

In what I'm calling the Cold War modernist program (although it was in no way centrally coordinated or directed), the US government, as well as private groups like the Ford Foundation, used modernism to appeal to a key Cold War audience: leftist intellectuals in Western Europe. They mistrusted the United States because they saw Americans as a bunch of militaristic yahoos, but they also feared the Soviet Union because of the increasingly persuasive reports about what life was like under Stalinism. Many of these leftists, in fact, were former Communists who had broken with their national parties in the 1930s. What I'd like to describe here is Faulkner's role in all this: both how Faulkner's participation affected the trajectory and success of the Cold War modernist program and how the Cold War modernist program altered Faulkner's public reputation in the 1950s.

Faulkner was an ideal Cold War modernist because he was well respected by foreign readers and intellectuals—even leftists. In fact, his literary reputation in the 1940s abroad was better than his reputation in the United States. Here, although he had appeared on the cover of *Time* in 1939, most readers knew him as the kind of writer who'd take second place in an Ellery Queen contest or as a Hollywood contract trashmeister hack whose novel *Sanctuary* had been adapted into a film (*The Story of Temple Drake*) that helped spur the imposition of the Hays Code. European and Latin American audiences had much more admiration for him.

But we shouldn't forget that for many of those who *were* fans of modernism, it was precisely those qualities they liked. As Mark Greif points out in *The Age of the Crisis of Man* (2015), the French in particular liked Faulkner *because* he wrote trashy southern Gothics.[6] For them, Faulkner's work for Hollywood wasn't a regrettable episode in the life of a once-promising writer. Rather, his servitude to the studio system and the formulaic yet subtly individual scripts he turned out were further proof of his genius, of his Americanness. His work—both what he produced and *how* he labored—undermined America's glad-handing boosterism and Puritanical morality in the same way that film noir, another French intellectual enthusiasm, does.

It wasn't this gutter Faulkner who became the face of Cold War modernism, though. Starting with the publication of *The Portable*

Faulkner in 1946 and accelerating with the Nobel speech in 1950, William Faulkner became the tribune of the endurance and nobility of man. More importantly for this argument, Faulkner and his work, through his own presence in the public and through evolving critical interpretation of his writings, came to represent the importance and the centrality of the free, individual consciousness.

Although Faulkner rarely made the equation explicit, his idea of the human was in direct opposition to that of the Communists. At the time, there was a lot of anxious discussion around regarding the nature of man. Existentialism was having its moment. As Greif observes, prestige American publishers were turning out books like Jean-Paul Sartre's *Existentialism and Humanism* (1946), Reinhold Niebuhr's *Nature and Destiny of Man* (1943), Lewis Mumford's *Condition of Man* (1944), Hannah Arendt's *Human Condition* (1958), and Herbert Marcuse's *One-Dimensional Man* (1964). The United States Information Agency (USIA), the public diplomacy agency created by President Eisenhower in 1953, sent *The Family of Man*, the Edward Steichen photo exhibition, around the world—including to the American pavilion at the Brussels World's Fair in 1958 and the Moscow Exposition in 1959.

Faulkner's Nobel address slid smoothly into this discourse and in so doing became the key that turned the lock of Cold War modernism. In 1950 American readers knew Faulkner, but the Nobel address reframed him and brought him to a much wider audience. It was reprinted in 1951 in the prestigious *New York Herald Tribune* "Books" supplement and the very middlebrow *Saturday Review of Literature*. (It bears mentioning here that this same *Saturday Review* had only a year and a half before attacked Pound, and modernism in general, during the Bollingen Prize controversy.) The Nobel address helped smooth off Faulkner's rough edges for the American public while inserting him into the transatlantic intellectual discourse about the crisis of man. But it also worked brilliantly as thesis for Cold War modernism.

Faulkner's speech echoed the anxieties about the crisis of man and emphasized the role of creative expression in the "human spirit." "Our tragedy today," Faulkner said, "is a general and universal physical fear so long sustained by now that we can even bear it. There are no longer problems of the spirit. There is only the question: When will I be blown up?"[7] In the face of this fear, though, stands humanity's ability—indeed, compulsion—to create. Unlike Samuel Beckett, who was bunkered in his Paris flat, writing his own great meditations on the nature of man at precisely this time, Faulkner's vision of humanity's need to express is not a "puny inexhaustible voice, still talking"; rather, the creative voice will "help man endure by lifting his heart, by reminding him of the courage and honor and hope and pride and compassion and pity and sacrifice which have been the glory of his past."[8] Apart from the dark warnings about nuclear destruction, Faulkner's insistence that "the problems of the human heart in conflict with itself . . . alone can make good writing because only that is worth writing about" implicitly emphasizes the fundamental value of the individual, in contrast with Communism's denigration of the individual in the face of the needs of society, or the Party, or the State. Faulkner's speech is a powerful endorsement of the values and the interdependence of individualism, creativity, and freedom.

The speech punctuated and accelerated a redefinition of Faulkner's work that was already well in progress. Greif points out that "following the *Portable*, other critics picked out for themselves aspects of Faulkner's books that were . . . recognizably great . . . for their *humanism* and tradition, rather than their nihilism and fragmentation."[9] Critics such as Robert Penn Warren now exalted Faulkner as a "postwar moralist and symbol of solitary literary genius."[10] And—unlike other modernist writers such as Pound, who resisted his publisher's attempts to transform him into a humanist, or Eliot, who had given up on middle-class individualism—Faulkner could take part in this "rereading," as Greif calls it.

American officials didn't immediately do much with Faulkner's speech, although we can credit one of the founders of American cultural diplomacy, Mississippian Muna Lee, with persuading Faulkner to go to Stockholm to give the speech in the first place.[11] The propaganda message that the Truman administration emitted, through Voice of America radio in particular, was crude and confrontational compared to the much more measured tone of the public information campaigns under Eisenhower, and after 1953 cultural diplomats came to use Faulkner's speech differently, focusing on the role of individual creative expression. "The free society values the individual as an end in himself . . . [and] attempts to create and maintain an environment in which every individual has the opportunity to realize his creative powers," stated NSC-68, the 1950 document outlining a comprehensive military, political, economic, and cultural Cold War strategy, and it urged the United States to "demonstrate the superiority of the idea of freedom by its constructive application."[12] The individual becomes key here, and foregrounding how Western societies privilege the individual over the collective now came to permeate our propaganda messages.

The USIA heavily publicized Faulkner's Nobel address through VOA, press releases, and magazine articles. Most importantly, though, Faulkner became an active cultural ambassador, making several trips on behalf of the US government during the 1950s and early 1960s. On those visits, he almost always recited the Nobel address to public audiences.

His first trip was to Brazil in 1954 to attend a writers' conference (and soothe Brazilian anger over the US denial of a visa to leftist writer José Lins do Rego). He then took an extensive trip initially to Japan for a seminar in Nagano with Japanese teachers of American literature and then went to the Philippines, Europe, and Iceland before traveling home.

Following his visit, Faulkner wrote a short piece titled "To the Youth of Japan," in which he praised their nation and people and extolled their democracy (comparing it favorably to the development of the US South, similarly devastated after a terrible war); USIA printed it as a bilingual pamphlet in August 1955 for distribution in Japan.[13] Another essay he wrote during his visit, "Impressions of Japan," became the script for a USIA-produced 16mm film of the same title, which historian Nicholas J. Cull describes as "a particular hit."[14] (It's unclear how and where this film was distributed and exhibited; probably at consulates and USIA reading rooms, I suspect.) Over images of Faulkner's travels through Japan, a narrator reads Faulkner's own impressions in a kind of portentous, faux-Eastern, philosophizing manner, verging uncomfortably at times on an Orientalist idea of "simplicity" typified in the grace and beauty of Japanese culture—geishas, tea, archery, rice paddies, watercolor painting—in this "place of beauty, worked wisely by such kind people." Asked by students what truth is, Faulkner (through the narrator) tells them that man needs to stand on his own feet, "believing in his own toughness and endurance, realizing that man's hope is in man's freedom, not given as a gift but as a right and a responsibility to be earned."[15] State saw Faulkner's Japanese tour as an unqualified success; a foreign service dispatch stated that "in all of his discussions, he unflinchingly answered questions on his works, his style, his philosophy, and American life in general. On two occasions . . . he hit hard against Communism, Socialism, and any form of radicalism in general, defending Democracy as the best system yet devised by man for all its faults."[16] (The dispatch also noted that a woman had written to Tennessee congressman Clifford Davis complaining that Faulkner was an unfit representative for America as he had criticized southern racism in his appearances in Japan.)

In future trips, Faulkner continued to link "freedom" and creativity. In Greece in 1957, upon receiving the Silver Award of the Athens Academy, Faulkner said, "I accept this medal not alone as an American nor as a writer but as one chosen by the Greek Academy to represent the principle that men shall be free."[17] He could also stay on message regarding anti-Communism. Asked by an Icelandic audience about the problems resulting from American troops in a small country, Faulkner responded, "Is it not better to have American forces here in the name of freedom, than a Russian one in the name of aggression and violence, as in the Baltic states?"[18] In 1958 the State Department invited Faulkner to join a group of American writers on a goodwill visit to the Soviet Union, but he declined, saying that it would be a "betrayal" of Dostoevsky, Tolstoy, Chekhov, and Gogol to offer even the "outward appearance of condoning the condition which the present Russian government has established."[19]

After his first trip, a State Department official said frankly that "William Faulkner is a great aid in furthering the objectives—and the inmost meaning—of our program."[20] That didn't change, nor did Faulkner modulate his message even when he wasn't on the clock for the USIA. In 1959 Faulkner addressed the National Conference of the US National Commission for UNESCO in Denver—again connecting with the Brazilian writers and intellectuals with whom he enjoyed such great mutual respect, and concluded by saying

> Mr. Khrushchev says that Communism, the police state, will bury the free ones. He is a smart gentleman, he knows that this is nonsense since freedom, man's dim concept of and belief in the human spirit is the cause of all his troubles in his own country. But if he means that Communism will bury capitalism, he is correct. That funeral will occur about ten minutes after the police bury gambling. Because simple man, the human race, will bury both of them. That will be when we have expended the last grain, dram, and iota of our natural resources. But man himself will not be in that grave. The last sound on the worthless earth will be two human beings trying to launch a homemade spaceship and already quarreling about where they are going next.[21]

I don't know whether that quote is optimistic or the bleakest thing I've ever heard. Greif points out that although Faulkner was happy to "go along" with the uplifting humanist message he was expected to repeat on his USIA tours, in his own work—in *A Fable* in particular—Faulkner seems to have changed his mind entirely, to have rewritten his Nobel speech. "I dont fear man," the general says at the end of that novel.

> "I do better: I respect and admire him. . . . Because man and his folly—"
> "Will endure," the corporal said.
> "They will do more," the old general said proudly. "They will prevail."[22]

Catherine Gunther Kodat also points out that *A Fable* is hardly triumphalist, that it is profoundly disturbed by the "capitalist mass culture" that American hegemony augurs.[23] Nobody in 1955 seems to have noticed, though. *A Fable* may have won the Pulitzer, but it was the Yoknapatawpha Faulkner who was really being honored.

The State Department and, later, the USIA also made sure that Faulkner's works—not just the speech—were available to foreign audiences. From the time of World War II, the US government operated libraries and reading rooms abroad, and European outposts stocked healthy collections of Faulkner. In addition, the USIA undertook to publish anthologies of American literature, in English and in translation, for foreign readers. Hemingway's "The Snows of Kilimanjaro," Fitzgerald's "Babylon Revisited," and Faulkner's "A Rose for Emily" were widely reprinted in USIA-produced anthologies, particularly in Asian languages.

Faulkner also had a story in a 1954 anthology of American fiction published by Franklin Books, the ostensibly private but actually government-run publishing company that operated primarily in the Middle East. But the Faulkner represented in the books program is quite different than the Faulkner of the goodwill tours and the radio features: he is often presented not as an experimentalist or humanist but as a southern realist or regionalist.[24] An example of this would be the publicity packet that Washington circulated to the public affairs officers in Brazil before Faulkner's first trip abroad. Rather than contextualizing Faulkner within experimental literature, these materials included nonfiction books about the Yazoo River country and Mississippi. Knowing that the Brazilian public would be focused on the issue of race, the Department also sent over a transcript of Ralph Ellison, Irving Howe, and Lyman Bryson discussing "The Bear" on Voice of America. "A particularly important item," the instructions specified, "since Ellison, speaking as a Mississippian [sic] and as a negro novelist, tells why he considers 'The Bear' 'a central story in Faulkner's whole work.'"[25]

"The Bear," in fact, merited its own feature on VOA Radio, which aired it sometime around October 9, 1956. The narrator recounts the plot and the killing of Old Ben but entirely leaves out the remarkable fourth section, which delves deeply into Ike McCaslin's psychology, depicts his realization that his family history is marked by incest and miscegenation, and shows how he arrived at his conclusion that slavery had poisoned the land. This omission is probably explicable, even setting aside the obvious political reasons VOA wouldn't want to focus on slavery, rape, and incest; after all, the story was often published without this challenging central section. Instead, the announcer reiterates the party line on Faulkner's essential message: he "has evinced a deep faith in mankind. He seems to say that man—despite his constant battle against *all sorts of wildernesses*—will endure. And that word 'endure' is a favorite of Mr. Faulkner's" (italics added).[26]

Another script a year earlier, reporting on the Pulitzer for *A Fable*, also sought to set readers straight about Faulkner: some have "found him preoccupied with violence, sex, and defeat. These readers have failed to discover his earthy humor, his concern for justice and truth, his deep if not always conventional religious sense."[27] And on his sixtieth birthday, a feature on Faulkner (inevitably) rebroadcast the Nobel speech in its entirety and compared Faulkner to Melville, Balzac, and Dostoyevsky.[28] I suspect it is not coincidental that the three writers mentioned in comparison were the author of the American novel most respected by European audiences; the greatest French realist, creator of a fully fleshed parallel fictional society; and the great pre-Soviet Russian protomodernist. As much as he was covered by VOA, though, Faulkner wasn't all that eager to appear on the radio network; in addition to opting not to talk about Oxford, Mississippi, Faulkner also declined USIA director Streibert's invitation to take part in a VOA symposium on "The Frontiers of Knowledge and Humanity's Hope for the Future."[29]

Faulkner also appeared in the ostensibly private cultural-diplomatic endeavors that helped to shape Cold War modernism, although he was not deeply involved in any of them. The most important of these was the Congress for Cultural Freedom (CCF), the Paris-based intellectual organization that flourished during the 1950s and is best-known for the explosive 1967 revelations of the CIA's controlling hand in its creation and (to a lesser degree) direction. The CCF, headed by Russian émigré composer Nicolas Nabokov and Swiss writer Denis de Rougemont, organized conferences and published journals across Europe and Asia. *Encounter*, its English-language magazine edited (initially) by Stephen Spender and Irving Kristol, is the most famous and influential CCF publication, combining highbrow literary content with cultural and political journalism. Faulkner's travel/history/fiction essay "Mississippi," originally published in *Holiday* magazine in the United States in April 1954, was reprinted in issue 13 of *Encounter* in October 1954. Faulkner spoke more directly to the CCF's concerns when given the podium at the CCF-sponsored Masterpieces of the Twentieth Century arts festival in Paris in the summer of 1952. "In the intelligence of the French members here, and in the muscle of Americans, may rest the salvation of Europe," he told the assembled notables.[30] (I think he was trying to play to each nation's self-image, but this just doesn't work. Clearly he had yet to perfect the delivery of his message.)

Perspectives USA, a Ford Foundation–funded (and thus private) cultural-diplomatic quarterly, founded and edited by James Laughlin of New Directions Books, preceded and in many ways paralleled *Encounter* but was ultimately far less successful. *Perspectives'* stated mission was to give European audiences a taste of the best of American writing and culture that they had missed over the last decade or so. Laughlin's

board of directors is a fascinating snapshot of the intertwined worlds of
literature, publishing, business, and the national security state: Laughlin,
the scion of a Pittsburgh steel fortune; Alfred A. Knopf, Laughlin's mentor as a publisher; H. J. Heinz of the food products company, who was
a childhood mate of Laughlin's; and William Casey, a businessman who
had served in the Office of Strategic Services' London office, which was
an incubator for the CIA. (Norman Holmes Pearson and James Angleton
were just two of the other Yale CIA men who came from that post.) The
poet Hayden Carruth was the managing editor before he had a nervous breakdown, and Jacqueline Matisse—Henri's granddaughter—was
Laughlin's secretary.

But *Perspectives* was pretty dull. It relied almost exclusively on
reprints from magazines like the *New Yorker* and the *Atlantic*, along
with some overviews and appreciations of painters like Arthur Dove and
writers from the New Directions stable such as William Carlos Williams
and Ezra Pound. Like Laughlin's repackaging of Ezra Pound in the postwar period, though, *Perspectives* was an impeccable document of the
aestheticization phase of Cold War modernism in that it drained all of
the revolution out of modernism. *Perspectives* didn't last long; after two
years, Ford conducted a study that concluded the magazine had little
effect in Europe, and the foundation stopped funding it. A terminal grant
allowed it to publish a total of sixteen issues. Yet Faulkner's Nobel address
served as the inaugural statement for the pilot issue submitted with the
Ford proposal in early 1952 and afterward led off the actual first issue.
Its pages present modernism as a style or set of techniques common to
literature, painting, architecture, even consumer products. The nihilism
and antinomianism that so many associated with modernism is nowhere
on display, nor do we see the revivifying potential of modernist literature
that the young Laughlin had earnestly cited sixteen years before as his
very motivation for going into publishing.[31] In *Perspectives*, modernism
is not (yet) a humanism. In fact, just about the only meditation on the
nature of man in the journal's entire run is Faulkner's Nobel address.

Laughlin, though, wanted more Faulkner in the journal, but he was
only able to obtain "Notes on a Horsethief," an excerpt from *A Fable*. He
wrote Saxe Commins twice—in 1953 and 1954—soliciting Faulkner to
write something original, a story or a journalistic piece, for *Perspectives*,
but the answer both times was no.[32]

So much for the supply side. How about the demand? The question I
want to answer, one that I've only just begun to explore fully, is whether
this worked. In one large sense, Cold War modernism worked, because
by the end of the 1950s the loyalties of Western European leftist intellectuals, in play at the end of the 1940s, were almost entirely pro-Western.

Did this happen because of Cold War modernism? Probably a little, but the Soviet Union's invasions of Hungary in 1956 and the throttling of the Polish uprising in the same year, not to mention the official admission of Stalin's crimes in Khrushchev's secret speech that year, did much more. Although we've learned a lot about how Cold War modernism worked in France, Italy, and West Germany, I think we need to wait for more cultural history to come out of the former Eastern bloc nations to tell what effect this art had on intellectuals behind the Iron Curtain.

The other question, then, is how did the Cold War modernist project affect Faulkner? As I've tried to establish, Cold War modernism took advantage of Faulkner's greatly improved literary status in the late 1940s and then supercharged that with the Nobel address to enshrine him as a kind of paragon of artistic humanism. But is that how audiences abroad perceived him? One branch of book history is concerned with recovering reception: how readers understand books and authors and movements, what they feel about them, how they assign importance and meaning to them. And book history, generally, has seen this kind of audience analysis as a really difficult thing, particularly when dealing with audiences using languages other than English, French, Dutch, or German (which have the most vibrant scholarly establishments in book history). So trying to recover how foreign readers, with their own literary histories and cultures that often have little to with the Anglo-American tradition, "understood" Faulkner sixty years ago is a daunting charge. Add to that the fact that in Eastern bloc nations one's response to an American author was a very freighted matter, and it's enough to make one want to pass this off to a graduate student for a dissertation project.

The questions that rise for me, then, are "Was Faulkner really becoming more popular among foreign readers, particularly in Europe, in the 1950s? And if so, was this a result of his cultural-diplomatic activities or his reframing as a Cold War humanist?" And because I don't have access to those languages and archives and scholarly traditions, I have chosen to begin with something I do know how to deal with: editions and contracts.

By far the most in-demand work of Faulkner's in the 1950s among foreign audiences was *Requiem for a Nun*—the dramatic version. The Danes wanted to put it on the radio in 1951. Several German-language theatrical companies and dramatic publishers tried to elbow each other out of the way for the first performance. The Piccolo Teatro della Città di Milano, inspired by the useful maxim that "it's better to beg forgiveness than to ask permission," told Harold Ober that they'd already printed up and circulated announcements that they would be staging *Requiem*, so they really hoped that they could obtain permission to do so.[33] (When they finally received permission, in 1954, the contract specified that 70 percent of the box office take would go to Faulkner, in addition to a 200,000 lire—$320 then, at least $2,500 now—advance.)

Because there were so many requests to stage *Requiem*, Ober contracted with the London dramatic agency Hughes, Massie and Co. to handle them in the summer of 1954. The next six years saw productions in Germany, Denmark, Italy, London, Holland, Greece, Spain, Mexico, and Brazil. Albert Camus was granted permission to adapt *Requiem*, and his version appeared first in Paris and then went to the Venice Festival. Interestingly, staging the show appears to have been a priority for US diplomats, at least in some nations. William Hart, the public affairs officer at the US consulate in Barcelona, Spain, wrote Ober personally in 1956 to urge him to approve the rights for a Spanish *Requiem*, and the USIA sought unsuccessfully to produce a radio version of the play for broadcast in 1959.[34] The show even opened behind the Iron Curtain: in Belgrade in 1959 and in Warsaw in 1960. (Due to currency inconvertibility, Faulkner didn't see the proceeds from those shows; the money stayed in country, available for his use if he ever visited.)

But what about his books? The 1982 and 2000 Faulkner and Yoknapatawpha Conferences dealt with Faulkner in translation extensively, and the conference proceedings have been very helpful in coming up with an answer to whether more people were reading Faulkner abroad. Deborah Cohn traces Faulkner's increasing presence and influence in Spanish American literature and grants that while some of this influence may have been due to the Cold War imperatives I've just been describing, "his fiction offered themes, images, and paradigms that resonated with Spanish American authors," such as an identification with the agrarian and post-plantation society that Faulkner creates and an "empathy with the history of the white South," especially the stigma of defeat by the Norteamericanos.[35] Before 1947 only five Faulkner titles had been published in Latin America—*Sanctuary*, *As I Lay Dying*, *The Wild Palms*, *Light in August*, and *These Thirteen*—but after 1947 basically all of Faulkner's current and older books appeared. Interestingly, given the number of readers in Latin America, the vast majority of editions came out from Buenos Aires publishers; not until 1953, with *Soldiers' Pay*, did a publisher outside Buenos Aires produce a Faulkner translation.

In Japan, interest in Faulkner picked up after the Nobel Prize and his 1955 visit to Nagano. Kenzaburo Ohashi points out that the novelist struck a chord among postwar Japanese writers for similar reasons to those that helped him appeal to Latin Americans: they were also "confronted with the disorder and confusion of the world" after their defeat by the United States.[36]

The shift in attitudes toward Faulkner behind the Iron Curtain is particularly interesting. Sergei Chakovsky explains that Soviet critics of the 1920s and 1930s regarded Faulkner as a decadent modernist, and in a 1947 public lecture in Moscow, the critic Maurice Mendelsohn called Faulkner's work "degenerate . . . a celebration of monstrosity and sexual perversion."[37] The prevailing opinion in the USSR changed in the 1950s, when critics like Elena Romanova contextualized him as an antiwar writer and as a "storyteller"—much better, to the socialist realist, than being a modernist.[38] And publication of Faulkner also picked up: his stories appeared in Soviet literary journals and were reprinted (possibly pirated) in two anthologies published by the Foreign Languages Publishing House that also included critical essays on his work.[39]

While we often think of the Eastern bloc as monolithic, examining things on a more granular level proves that not to be true. Book publishing is an example. The USIA undertook a number of projects to translate and publish American works behind the Iron Curtain, with very different levels of success in different nations. East Germany saw essentially no USIA book-publishing activity; whether this is because books meant for a West German audience found their way there and didn't have to be produced expressly for them or because East Germany was particularly closed, I can't answer right now. Nor did USIA or the State Department undertake book publishing in Bulgaria, Romania, and Hungary to any notable extent. There was a little going on in Czechoslovakia (including a 1958 edition of *The Unvanquished* and a 1957 compilation of ten of Faulkner's stories), but particularly notable is just how active and open the publishing scene was in two other Communist nations: Poland and Yugoslavia. There seems to have even been competition among firms! Several Warsaw publishers produced editions of Faulkner in the 1950s, and in still-unified Yugoslavia, publishers in the various regional capitals (Novy Sad and Belgrade in Serbia and Zagreb in Croatia) offered Faulkner translations—sometimes in the Cyrillic and sometimes in the Roman alphabet.

So an examination of the books program does suggest the answer to one of my questions—whether Cold War modernism worked. If the aim was to cultivate respect for American cultural achievements among a population that had been dismissive of what one French intellectual termed "so-called American culture," then we'd have to say mission accomplished. After the books program had had a decade to really get going, one USIA program officer gleefully noted, in the early 1960s, "the eagerness with which foreign readers seize on the books of William Faulkner and Ernest Hemingway—does anyone now remember that once an English critic asked, 'Who reads an American book?'"[40] And

Faulkner—Faulkner the modernist, Faulkner the prophet of human endurance, Faulkner the liberal humanist, Faulkner the regional colorist, Faulkner the anti-Communist—was absolutely central to the success of this books program and to the Cold War modernist project in general.

In fact, the US government and its collaborators in the foundation world had a tough time letting go of their literary favorites, or perhaps they continued to believe in the power of Faulkner as an ambassador of American culture and Western values long after his death and long after there was any pressing need to advocate for either in the Cold War. As I was putting this essay together, I noticed that the 1982 Faulkner and Yoknapatawpha Conference, titled International Perspectives, was supported by grants from two old stalwarts of the Cold War: the Ford Foundation and the United States International Communication Agency (one of the guises of the United States Information Agency). It seems that Cold War modernism held on a lot longer than it probably even needed to.

NOTES

1. William Faulkner to Harold Ober, January 5, 1946, folder 1, box 1, Harold Ober Files, Albert and Shirley Small Special Collections Library, University of Virginia Library, Charlottesville.

2. Lawrence H. Schwartz, *Creating Faulkner's Reputation: The Politics of Modern Literary Criticism* (Knoxville: University of Tennessee Press, 1988).

3. See Max Kozloff, "American Painting during the Cold War," *Artforum* 11, no. 9 (May 1973): 43–54; Eva Cockroft, "Abstract Expressionism, Weapon of the Cold War," *Artforum* 15, no. 10 (June 1974): 39–41; David Shapiro and Cecile Shapiro, "Abstract Expressionism: The Politics of Apolitical Painting," *Prospects* 3 (1977): 175–214; Serge Guilbaut, *How New York Stole the Idea of Modern Art* (Chicago: University of Chicago Press, 1983); Frances Stonor Saunders, *The Cultural Cold War: The CIA and the World of Arts and Letters* (New York: New Press, 1999); Eric Bennett, "How Iowa Flattened Literature," *Chronicle Review*, February 10, 2014, http://chronicle.com/article/How-Iowa-Flattened-Literature/144531/; Joel Whitney, "The *Paris Review*, the Cold War, and the CIA," *Salon*, May 27, 2012, http://www.salon.com/2012/05/27/exclusive_the_paris_review_the_cold_war_and_the_cia/.

4. Harry Truman to William Benton, April 2, 1947, RG 306, USIA Historical Collection, "Advancing American Art" folder, box 127, United States National Archives, Archives II facility, College Park, MD.

5. USIA director Theodore Streibert to William Faulkner, March 8, 1955, box 2, Harold Ober Files, Albert and Shirley Small Special Collections Library, University of Virginia Library, Charlottesville.

6. Mark Greif, *The Age of the Crisis of Man: Thought and Fiction in America, 1933–1973* (Princeton, NJ: Princeton University Press, 2015).

7. William Faulkner, "Banquet Speech," December 10, 1950, Nobelprize.org, http://www.nobelprize.org/nobel_prizes/literature/laureates/1949/faulkner-speech.html (accessed January 12, 2016).

8. Ibid.

9. Greif, *Age of the Crisis of Man*, 118.

10. Schwartz, *Creating Faulkner's Reputation*, 29.

11. Muna Lee wrote *The Cultural Approach: Another Way in International Relations* (Chapel Hill: University of North Carolina Press, 1947), which became a foundational text for cultural diplomats.

12. "A Report to the National Security Council by the Executive Secretariat on United States Objectives and Programs for National Security," April 14, 1950, https://www.trumanlibrary.org/whistlestop/study_collections/coldwar/documents/pdf/10-1.pdf (accessed January 12, 2016).

13. William Faulkner, *To the Youth of Japan* (Tokyo: United States Information Service, August 1955).

14. Nicholas J. Cull, *The Cold War and the United States Information Agency* (New York: Cambridge University Press, 2008), 115.

15. *Impressions of Japan* (Washington, DC: United States Information Service, 1955), 16mm film.

16. Foreign Service Dispatch on Faulkner's Japan trip, September 22, 1955, folder 14, box 144, Department of State Bureau of Educational and Cultural Affairs Archive, Special Collections Library, University of Arkansas, Fayetteville.

17. Report on Faulkner's trip to Greece, folder 14, box 144, Department of State Bureau of Educational and Cultural Affairs Archive, Special Collections Library, University of Arkansas, Fayetteville.

18. Foreign Service Dispatch, October 25, 1955, folder 14, box 144, Department of State Bureau of Educational and Cultural Affairs Archive, Special Collections Library, University of Arkansas, Fayetteville.

19. William Faulkner to Frederick A. Colwell, May 31, 1958, folder 18, box 144, Department of State Bureau of Educational and Cultural Affairs Archive, Special Collections Library, University of Arkansas, Fayetteville.

20. Philip Raine, memo, June 22, 1954, folder 13, box 144, Department of State Bureau of Educational and Cultural Affairs Archive, Special Collections Library, University of Arkansas, Fayetteville.

21. William Faulkner, "From Yoknapatawpha to UNESCO: The Dream," *Saturday Review of Literature*, November 14, 1959, 21.

22. William Faulkner, *A Fable*, rev. ed. (1954; repr., New York: Vintage International, 2011), 390.

23. Catherine Gunther Kodat, "Writing *A Fable* for America," in *Faulkner in America: Faulkner and Yoknapatawpha, 1998*, ed. Joseph R. Urgo and Ann J. Abadie (Jackson: University Press of Mississippi, 2001), 85.

24. Publicity materials, folder 13, box 144, Department of State Bureau of Educational and Cultural Affairs Archive, Special Collections Library, University of Arkansas, Fayetteville.

25. Publicity materials for transcript of radio discussion between Irving Howe, Ralph Ellison, and Lyman Bryson, folder 13, box 144, Department of State Bureau of Educational and Cultural Affairs Archive, Special Collections Library, University of Arkansas, Fayetteville. Ralph Ellison was, of course, not a Mississippian but a native Oklahoman; he did attend college at Tuskegee, but that school is in Alabama.

26. Ed Gordon, "'The Bear': A Faulkner Theme," VOA broadcast script, October 9, 1956, Library of Congress Microforms Collection, Washington, DC.

27. Harry Sylvester, "William Faulkner," VOA broadcast script, May 10, 1955, Library of Congress Microforms Collection, Washington, DC.

28. Don Agger, "Faulkner at Sixty," VOA broadcast script, September 19, 1957, Library of Congress Microforms Collection, Washington, DC.

29. Theodore Streibert to William Faulkner, January 17, 1956, box 2, Harold Ober Files, Albert and Shirley Small Special Collections Library, University of Virginia Library, Charlottesville. This weekly symposium, which aired in thirty-nine languages over VOA in 1956, featured some eminent intellectuals, including Karl Jung and Bertrand Russell.

30. Quoted in Giles Scott-Smith, "The 'Masterpieces of the Twentieth Century' Festival and Congress for Cultural Freedom: Origins and Consolidation 1947–1952," *Intelligence and National Security* 15, no. 1 (May 2000): 121–43.

31. James Laughlin, "Preface," *New Directions in Prose and Poetry* 1 (1936): vii–ix.

32. James Laughlin to Saxe Commins, October 27, 1953, September 30, 1954, Random House files, Albert and Shirley Small Special Collections Library, University of Virginia Library, Charlottesville.

33. Piccolo Teatro di Milano to Harold Ober, November 4, 1952, folder 1, box 1, Harold Ober Files, Albert and Shirley Small Special Collections Library, University of Virginia Library, Charlottesville.

34. William Hart to Harold Ober, February 2, 1956, box 2, Harold Ober Files, Albert and Shirley Small Special Collections Library, University of Virginia Library, Charlottesville; USIA Broadcast Service to Robert Haas, January 15, 1959, box 2, Harold Ober Files, Albert and Shirley Small Special Collections Library, University of Virginia Library, Charlottesville.

35. Deborah Cohn, "Faulkner and Spanish America," in *Faulkner in the Twenty-First Century: Faulkner and Yoknapatawpha, 2000,* ed. Robert W. Hamblin and Ann J. Abadie (Jackson: University Press of Mississippi, 2003), 54.

36. Kenzaburo Ohashi, "Faulkner and Japanese Novelists," in *Faulkner: International Perspectives: Faulkner and Yoknapatawpha, 1982,* ed. Doreen Fowler and Ann J. Abadie (Jackson: University Press of Mississippi, 1984), 262.

37. Maurice Mendelsohn quoted in Sergei Chakovsky, "Faulkner in Soviet Literary Criticism," in *Faulkner: International Perspectives: Faulkner and Yoknapatawpha, 1982,* ed. Doreen Fowler and Ann J. Abadie (Jackson: University Press of Mississippi, 1984), 215.

38. Elena Romanova quoted in M. Thomas Inge, "Teaching Faulkner in the Soviet Union," in *Faulkner: International Perspectives: Faulkner and Yoknapatawpha, 1982,* ed. Doreen Fowler and Ann J. Abadie (Jackson: University Press of Mississippi, 1984), 177.

39. M. Thomas Inge, "A Chronology of Faulkner Translations into Russian," in *Faulkner: International Perspectives: Faulkner and Yoknapatawpha, 1982,* ed. Doreen Fowler and Ann J. Abadie (Jackson: University Press of Mississippi, 1984), 337.

40. Mary Stewart French, "The Arts and the Educational Exchange Program," folder 18, box 47, Department of State Bureau of Educational and Cultural Affairs Archive, Special Collections Library, University of Arkansas, Fayetteville.

Middlebrow Patriotism, Neighborly Reading

Yung-Hsing Wu

William Faulkner cut quite the figure of war. The belatedness of the 1949 Nobel Prize for Literature—awarded for that year but presented in December 1950—positioned his Nobel in the wake of war, just a few years following the hiatus the foundation put in place from 1940 to 1943, a period when no prizes were awarded.[1] Meanwhile, in his Nobel Prize presentation speech, Gustaf Hellstrom offered a portrait of an author steeped in war, calling "war and violence" the formative background for Faulkner's most important novels as well as for his own personal history.[2] If Faulkner the regionalist could simultaneously mourn the passing of a South and believe in the necessity of its downfall, it was because, Hellstrom explained, he "knows intimately and feels intensely" its history by writing the life of Yoknapatawpha.[3] That intensity, he went on to say, linked the author's motivations for joining up (as a trainee pilot with the RAF in Canada during World War I) to the fictions he wrote, in particular to a fictional "alter ego" whose belief was that war, because it exacts the greatest of human costs, should not be wasted.[4] From the city hall stage in Stockholm, a scant year after the Soviet Union had exploded its first atomic bomb, this rhetorical move sought to stitch literature to life. Suturing Faulkner's personal history to his literary production, the prize placed war at the heart of Faulkner's capacity for literary greatness and constituted that greatness as a service to the world.

Remarks like these about war and writing might seem obvious, given the timing of things. Yet it's worth noting that Hellstrom's comments feature no contemporary reference to global conflict, hewing strictly to Faulkner's biography and subject matter and thereby confining war to a signifying past. Hellstrom's presentation speech in this way continues a pattern, begun in 1940, that brackets World War II: from the four-year hiatus during which the Nobel removed itself from the global stage to a postwar period in which no mention of the war makes an appearance in either the presentation or acceptance speeches. Indeed, this absence remained for ten years until Faulkner in his acceptance speech identified the atomic question—"when will I be blown up?"—only to charge it with occluding the "problems of the spirit" that define the impetus for writing.[5] If the award was vocational in nature, "not made to me as a man, but to my work," the perceived inevitability of nuclear war had practically done away with vocation as a motivating principle.[6] Contrary to Hellstrom's notion, a personal experience of war had not fueled a sense of authorial responsibility in Faulkner, who argued rather that writers ought to see *past* war in order to tap "the old verities and truths of the heart" and "create out of the materials of the human heart something which did not exist before."[7] At least as far as writing was concerned, the human truth took priority over war. Acknowledging the global turn heightened by World War II and its aftermath, Faulkner also bypassed it for the broader terms of a humanism for which writing would serve as "one of the props, the pillars to help him [man] endure and prevail."[8]

Fast-forward six years to 1956, the year the Eisenhower administration launched the People-to-People program, a new effort to position Americanness relative to the rest of the world. By the time Eisenhower asked Faulkner to chair the program's Writers' Committee, the author had already become a Cold War figure, his Nobel status having assured his emergence as an American cultural ambassador on United States Information Agency–sponsored (USIA) stints to Brazil, Japan, Manila, Italy, Germany, and Iceland. The human, as Faulkner had articulated it in his acceptance speech—a universal value—was now claimed as also American; this Cold War Faulkner was enjoined, in other words, to speak a lofty message that was also framed as homegrown. Compared to this strain of cultural diplomacy, the People-to-People program, also a USIA venture, was distinctive for its less highbrow claim that "friendship between peoples" could serve national interests.[9] Its rhetoric of "friendly" politics would, however, find in Faulkner and the Writers' Committee—made up of authors of mixed-brow receptions—both a compelling and troubling instrument. On the one hand, the existence of the committee placed writing, and in particular literature, alongside media and industry as "fields of activity" upon which the broader effort needed to draw. With Faulkner as its head and other equally noted writers participating, the committee afforded the program the cachet attached to his (and others') authorship. Yet the People-to-People impulse toward contact around the globe, or what Harilaos Stecopoulos has called a "middlebrow internationalism," also rendered authorship through a sensibility that embraced identification for its political potential. This emphasis prompted the writers of the committee, many of whom were skeptical of either Eisenhower in particular or any hint of state imperative in general, to assert that vocation, the work of literature and reading, had always superseded the program's political deployment. Their faith articulated the view that literature could not only advance a politics but exist in advance of it.[10]

From the outset the People-to-People initiative sought to distinguish its aims in terms of scale and what might be called order. The invitation Faulkner and other committee heads received in the summer of 1956 suggested, for one, that peace simply demanded *more*; as Eisenhower's letter put it, "There will never be enough diplomats and information officers at work in the world to get the job done without help from the rest of us."[11] Why the work of the state is insufficient is a matter of numbers, to be sure, but beyond that the letter also indexed the extent to which the discourse of the US-Soviet conflict, the "great struggle being waged between two opposing ways of life," was so rigid that it approached the fundamental.[12] When Eisenhower called for "the active support of thousands of independent private groups and institutions and of millions of individual Americans acting through person-to-person communication in foreign lands," he spoke in terms of scale—the magnitude of conflict demands a similar magnitude of response—but also of the difference in approach he ascribed to the People-to-People impulse.[13] For while he described something like reciprocal escalation, that escalation lay not with government contacts and networks but with the most ordinary and daily of acts: communication. In that same month, a commencement speech at Baylor University was the occasion for the president to add a note of voluntarism to the mix; saying that "people are what count," Eisenhower encouraged graduating seniors to understand that if "every international problem is in reality a human one," then only contact between peoples would work to resolve broader conflicts.[14] By September the stage was set for the People-to-People conference with members of the forty-odd committees in attendance. There again is the frank admission of the US-Soviet conflict, of the fact of belief and ideology, of the efforts on each side to promote its view while disdaining the other's. There, too, the gesture to pronounce peace unquestionable so as to justify the participation of all—specifically, by means of the "thousands of methods by which people can gradually learn a little bit more of each other."[15] The logic drafted people *and* interactions, here cross-cultural encounters that would exact incremental force. Bodies and the beliefs for which they stood remained the reference point in this Cold War vision, and the stakes were no less high than they had been during wartime. But the front line had shifted by involving, at least rhetorically, the participation of sympathy and a "do it yourself diplomacy."[16]

It seems to me that the People-to-People rhetoric engaged peace by broaching the prospect of identification, of what the document

announcing the conference called "friendly contact and communication" and "neighborly association."[17] Its urgency had become a staple for
the Eisenhower administration as it entered its second term; thus the
president concluded his 1958 State of the Union address by saying that
his "last call for action" was "a message from the people of the United
States to all other peoples, especially those of the Soviet Union."[18] A
year later, former USIA director Arthur Larson put things explicitly
when he named *identification* the "one word" necessary to "a people-
to-people understanding between our own people and the people of
countries now estranged from us."[19] Larson, like Eisenhower, rendered
identification a horizontal relation, one in which sympathy could yield
the equivalence that peace required. It's for *that* reason—the fact that
identification constituted a horizon of feeling—that the work of writing came to occupy a special place. For by the time the Writers' Committee came on board, separate committees constituted around books
and magazines were already part of the People-to-People effort: print,
like media and business, had industry and volunteer representation.[20]
The October People-to-People newsletter mentioned, for instance, the
organization of book collection drives, fact-finding missions to ascertain
reading habits and preferences abroad (Magazines Committee), private
donations of American Bookshelf libraries, and letter-writing campaigns
taken up by community and veteran groups. The city of Chicago, meanwhile, had set a goal of one hundred thousand books for its collection
drive, leading the way for similar drives planned in Pittsburgh, Cincin-
nati, Indianapolis, Dallas, and Fort Worth. Noting efforts like these, the
newsletter featured their varying range, as if to underscore Eisenhower's
emphasis on nationwide involvement: thus, the news that students of a
small Pennsylvania college had collected 1,300 volumes appeared alongside reports from the more ambitious, big-city book drives. Yet there was
little discourse about which books and magazines made up the collections and donations or how the selections proceeded across participating
cities and civic groups. Only two items hint that such thinking might give
organizers some pause: one mentions that "how to get better books" is
the "No. 1 problem of book collection drives," while a second remarks
that the Book Committee's "first step" is to produce its own circular "to
tell what kind of books do most good overseas."

Print was on this account a matter of acquisition and distribution;
matters of taste, reading, and literary identification remained in the
margins. As a member of this print community, the Writers' Committee
brought the cachet of literary personae and excellence, and implicitly
the issue of cultural taste, to the program's otherwise singular focus
on "American" qualities. This is Eisenhower's point when he urged

Faulkner to bring other "leading authors" to the task of "creating understanding abroad."[21] To a national audience, Faulkner possessed name
and network, thanks to his recent stints playing cultural ambassador,
but he also held sway over an audience of fellow "leading authors," a
number of whom admitted in correspondence that their willingness to
participate hinged on their respect for Faulkner.[22] Everything was very
*high*brow here, directed simultaneously to those fellow writers as well as
to the European Left, which at the time viewed the quality of American
cultural production with skeptical eyes. Describing the writers' task of
"creating understanding abroad," of closing ideological gaps by imagin-
ing people in their capacity of readers, however, Eisenhower touched on
the work of identification, the rhetoric of which was empathetic in tone.
To put it another way, patriotism remained the grounding cause, justified
in idealized terms, but the demands it placed on the Writers' Committee
involved a *prior* creation of a very familiar "understanding abroad," one
through which readers could assume the lives and experiences of characters, one that moved from reader to reader. In this way, the program's
investment in identification—as a literary as well as political dynamic—
suggests that its participation in Cold War modernism brought to that
highbrow project a more middlebrow face.

If the People-to-People vision of peace equated "understanding
abroad" with identification, it echoed a refrain in the contemporary
discourse on middlebrow culture, particularly as it described reading
practices. Reading, for one, appeared in Russell Lynes's infamous chart
delineating brow distinctions in culture, from the material (clothes, fur-
niture, "useful objects") to food (drinks, salads), causes, and leisure and
arts (entertainment, games, sculpture and records, reading).[23] For Lynes,
"reading" lay mostly in identifying the "solid nonfiction, the better novels, [the] quality magazines," and the "book club selections" and "mass
circulation magazines" that appeared on middlebrow bookshelves.[24] The
glimpses of the reader whose belief in taste leads him to the current best
sellers "out of 'curiosity' rather than interest" (upper middlebrow), or
the inveterate self-improver who "ardently believes that he knows what
he likes" (lower middlebrow) begin, however, to describe the middlebrow through reading *practices*, and to do so in the language of belief.
Even with his tongue in cheek, Lynes tapped (in 1949) what Dwight
Macdonald would later, and rather more seriously, characterize as a
delusion that middlebrow culture had created. A "compromise" effected
when the choice between high and low culture—between "reading Tolstoy or a detective story"—generates among readers strain and confusion, the middlebrow was for Macdonald a patch, a "cultural figleaf"
that dissimulates.[25] Readers were dupes of what Macdonald called

Midcult, unknowing in much the same fashion as those novelists whom
he suspected "would be honestly indignant at this description of their
activities."[26] Both Lynes and Macdonald, then, despite their significantly
different positions, found an underlying affect in sincerity: middlebrow
culture promotes a feeling of belief. Thus, when Macdonald fingered
the Book-of-the-Month Club (BOMC) for "supplying its members with
reading matter of which the best that can be said is that it could be
worse," his aesthetic evaluation of the club's selections originated from
his view that the club "is able to pass itself off as *the real thing*."[27]

Henry Seidel Canby would, of course, have disputed this assessment,
but so would he have concurred that the BOMC—for which he served
as editor-in-chief from 1926 through 1954—engaged belief, specifically,
the reader's belief as an effect of the writer's words. As Janice Radway
has argued, the value Canby placed on this relation remained steady
in his time with the club, drawing much of its force from an ambivalence about literary modernism. Thus whatever appreciation Canby had
for modernist formal innovation, Radway notes, he did not relinquish
the view that "what was needed [in literature] . . . was greater sympathy . . . a capacity to connect with others in the service of some larger
good."[28] Indeed, this line of thinking led Canby to write of Faulkner
that his unflinching hatred of "his Mississippi and his Memphis and all
their works" was "neither passionate nor the result of thwarting, but
calm, reasoned, and complete."[29] This dislike of Faulkner's coolness
reveals Canby's preference for the absorption produced by the more
intense relation of identification. That Canby charged Faulkner—and
by extension, modernism—with a lack of passion is thus telling, for it
underscores just how mixed the Writers' Committee was in its member-
ship and how fraught the friction between the political identifications
that the People-to-People program sought and those that the writers
believed literature produced would eventually become. In the year that
Faulkner was involved in the Writers' Committee, no writer associated
with literary modernism appeared on the BOMC list of selections, yet
Edna Ferber, John Steinbeck, and Thornton Wilder, each of whom had
seen at least one novel featured by the club, were invited members of
the Writers' Committee.[30] Indeed, the company of writers making up the
committee was eclectic in professional terms, featuring academics and
critics (Jacques Barzun, Malcolm Cowley, Allen Tate, Lionel Trilling),
novelists (Saul Bellow, Pearl Buck, Truman Capote, Anita Loos, Mary
McCarthy, Robert Penn Warren, William Styron, John Dos Passos, Gore
Vidal), and poets (John Berryman, Elizabeth Bishop, Louise Bogan,
Robert Lowell, Archibald MacLeish, Marianne Moore), constituting a
diversity that its mixing of brows made all the more significant. For this

mix only illuminated the near unanimity with which the writers, when faced with what they had to offer the program, articulated vocation as their response.

Literary and political identification may ultimately be asymptotic. Still, if there's no way to determine the extent to which the Eisenhower administration believed that "understanding" might transcend ideological differences, or even the extent to which the administration believed in its own call for "understanding," then how to register "understanding" if not only cynically? I want to emphasize that the interrelation between these forms of identification did define the People-to-People initiative and that its impact was forceful enough to prompt the Writers' Committee to make its own claims about writing in the world. Whatever the People-to-People program was able to accomplish, its suggestion that identification provided the means by which the literary and the political could be fruitfully yoked elicited strong response from the writers invited to be its representatives. A form of reception, these responses constitute another assessment of what the People-to-People program would be able to accomplish. For when they grumbled that writers should precisely not be involved in a venture of this ilk, or declared, with some self-righteousness, that literature, the exemplary medium for understanding, was best suited to the initiative's goals, the members of the Writers' Committee returned also to identification, in this instance to assert identifications of their own making, and those by which they felt they had been made.

The work began with an initial round of correspondence, with Faulkner and cochairman Harvey Breit [31] asking fifty-odd writers for their view of the program: "Will you send to me in a sentence, or a paragraph, or a page . . . your private idea of what might further this project?"[32] As an offering, Faulkner included his own notion to "anesthetize, for one year, American vocal chords" and "abolish, for one year, American passports."[33] Whether or not the tenor of this first prompt proves Faulkner was weary of playing cultural ambassador, leery of cultural warfare more broadly, or unenthusiastic about Eisenhower, it's hard to miss the double salvo against expression and travel, against voice and body. This rendering of Americanness—too noisy, too brash, too touristy, too *present*—may have signaled less Faulkner's outright rejection of the initiative than his unmasking of the logic by which writers were recruited as bodies, but it's significant how it ended up framing the terms of the responses that his fellow writers sent in. For these responses, from the initial replies that formed the basis for the questionnaire Faulkner and Harvey Breit constructed to the commentary they received on the questionnaire, were statements about literary presence in the world, statements that, as Faulkner and Breit collated them, offer a glimpse into an almost uniform sense of vocation that the writers deployed against the initiative.[34]

The responses to the questionnaire bear material witness to this priority. Made up of a series of individual items (approximately thirty, themselves suggestions and responses taken from the first round of correspondence Faulkner received from his colleagues), the questionnaire asked each respondent to mark his or her preferences on a sliding scale.[35] These ratings reveal that there was widespread agreement on only a few of the items—two suggestions, involving the "free and untempered exchange of books" and communication effected through travel and lectures, received the most support in the form of ticks, checks, and the occasional remark, "yes," "of course," "obviously."[36] Even the items that received support, however, also prompted the kind of commentary that reflects writerly suspicion about a program with its origins in the government. Several wrote on their questionnaires that any effort featuring book exchange needed to come to terms with selection criteria, not to mention the process by which such criteria would be developed and by whom. Penned on the questionnaires, on the margins, or even over the questionnaire items themselves, these remarks become more extended analyses, particularly as they speak to one another on the issue of the public work of writing and as they are developed in letters some of the writers returned with their questionnaires. When Edna Ferber insisted that government involvement was "appalling" because writers should not be "organized for the purpose of directing their writing" but needed to remain "free" and undirected, she articulated a belief implicit in William Styron's statement that "writers should stay at home, unorganized, and work."[37] Indeed, where her suspicion specified the case against government, Styron's claim registered the more fundamental objection to institutionality. Like E. B. White, who wrote that he was "not sure" he wanted to join an organization because he felt "healthier and friendlier when in an non-organized, or disorganized condition," Styron pitted writerly identification against the organized life, going so far as to couch the former in domestic terms.[38] The line-drawing is distinctive because it's so emphatic: the attempt to organize writers is illegitimate, so the argument goes, because writing is opposed to organization.

Perhaps even more emphatic than the gesture to define writing against the programmatic was the critique that accused government work of an act of misrepresentation. Eisenhower was asking writers to "go on missions for the promotion of American ideology," wrote Robert Lowell; in making this request, as Lowell's language suggests, the president was exceeding his authority.[39] A more pointed anger drove Saul Bellow, who was convinced that the work of the Writers' Committee could only be symbolic, as the Eisenhower administration had already confirmed the existence of a hierarchy that positioned (and preferred) "business and war at the top," science "in the middle," and literature ("we") "at the bottom."[40] Bellow's response was to replace that verticality with a different geometry, one through which he could assert that literature *need* not "toy" with such matters *because* they are ideological. This line of thinking was just as stark, and possibly fundamental, for John Berryman, who responded to a proposal to bring individuals from abroad to live in and observe the United States by asking, "What in the name of God do *writers* have to do with . . . importing repres's [sic] of the people who don't like us into America, to see how we live, etc.?"[41] Berryman drew a sharp contrast between writers and foreign representatives, emphasizing that for him, the distinction between the literary and the political is as necessary as it is unbridgeable. From this point of view the work of "a congressman or labor leader," even as it involves representation of a constituency, has no relevance for writing. The implication remains that literature pursues representation in terms that the People-to-People program can neither register nor understand.[42] In this context, it's telling that in his description of the scenario facing the Writers' Committee— "when, flatteringly enough, the great and busy of the political world turn to [writers] for help, whether ritually or sincerely"—Gore Vidal opted for a figure that refers both to page and affect: "perfectly blank."[43]

It's worth noting, I think, that in these two types of comment—the oppositional and the analytical—no single writer argued for an apolitical stance. Several found Eisenhower tiresome, and a number made their preference for Adlai Stevenson plain. Most expressed dismay over the outcome of the Hungarian uprising during the fall of 1956 and decried the brutal Soviet response, even if they did not align themselves with the intensified Cold War rhetoric that emerged in the wake of those events. But perhaps more importantly for the argument I'm making here, most claimed for literature a political and ethical agency that mattered as much as, if not more than, the Writers' Committee and its political charge, which felt like a constraint on writerly autonomy. When (so-called) patriotism was felt to intervene on vocation, vocation was to be reaffirmed; when the People-to-People program came calling on writers to do good work for the good of country, the writers responded, interestingly, by arguing that that work was theirs to begin with. Thus, when Jacques Barzun reported being "both entertained and caught by" the idea of "representing the US abroad," his response derived from his belief that writing is best equipped "to show the country in the round."[44] Like Malcolm Cowley, Barzun was sure that organizing American writers to "give a true picture of this country to other people" had merit but found the nature of the directive at once "simple" and "large and hopeless."[45] (Cowley suggested as alternatives paraliterary institutions: the National Institute, the American Academy, the PEN Club.[46]) Meanwhile, Archibald MacLeish took this line of thinking a step further, claiming that writers were already doing what Eisenhower asked and, interestingly, that "every American writer worth sending the letter to believes he IS giving a true picture."[47] Here the priority accorded vocation corresponded, significantly, with what I've been describing as the priority that the People-to-People effort broadly accorded identification. This correspondence may be a function of coincidence, but I'd like to suggest that it also results from an affinity. In these statements of vocation, then, resided the faith that more than anything else, honesty in writing, and not sloganeering, would guarantee reading—and more than that, the kind of reading performed "not with curiosity alone: with belief, with feeling."

Practically speaking, though, the Writers' Committee under Faulkner's guidance in the People-to-People program did not last long, and in describing its arc, I find it striking that the bumps it encountered should have been the regular occasion for discourse about identification. Hailed by presidential invitation as citizens, the members of the committee, both individually and as a group, negotiated their sense of Americanness in relation to their sense of themselves as writers. This interrelation was a matter of proportion, and in the nine months during which the group corresponded, the writers' responses took an increasingly vocational turn that I want to mark for its strategic and, I believe, sincere impulse. Eventually, after questionnaires and follow-up letters stopped trickling in, Faulkner and Breit did call a meeting, and a number of writers—including Bellow, Ferber, Donald Hall, Robert Hillyer, Elmer Rice, John Steinbeck, and William Carlos Williams—met on November 29, 1956, at Breit's New York City home to try to hash out some concrete proposals.[48] A rather scattered transcript, taken by Jean Ennis, captures the writers' own measure of some of these proposals: they were either a bit soft (increased distribution of books and arts, lecture circuits for writers, subsidies for writerly travel) or unlikely (revision of the McCarran Act, freeing Ezra Pound), however justified. Nonetheless, the eventual summary report, drafted by Faulkner, Hall, and Steinbeck, drew on the discussion in putting forward the committee's suggestions to increase distribution of American culture, to lessen difficulties for Hungarians wanting to travel to the United States, and to encourage more travel from abroad to the States, particularly in the form of prolonged stays that would allow visitors "to live a normal American life."[49] Though none of these proposals asserted what had been so prevalent in the committee's internal discussions and correspondence—the emphasis on what writers do, the work of representation particular to writing, is strangely absent—those views may have reemerged during the trip Faulkner and Breit took in February 1957 to present the report before other committee chairmen and Charles Wilson. As Joseph Blotner and Catherine Gunther Kodat have detailed, Faulkner's seeming change of heart in the hours before the presentation confounded Breit and set the tone for their eventual departure from the gathering before their time to present came. (Blotner reports Faulkner declaring that no exchanges or travel abroad programs were actually necessary because "writers all over the world understand one another."[50]) This departure constituted the end of Faulkner's work with the People-to-People program (Jean Ennis took over by midyear of 1957), and by one measure, it suggests the author's weariness with the effort itself, with cultural ambassadorship, with the difficulty of authorial self-representation. In the context, though, of what I have been arguing, it matters that Faulkner's last words, an echo of the language of identification through which the People-to-People program had articulated its political goals, were also an echo of the vocational discourse in which writers imagined one another as their own fellow readers. In that way, the middlebrow offered a glimpse well worth catching: a glimpse of the work of identification, so pervasive in the assumptions about the relations between culture and people as to be irresistible.

NOTES

1. The Nobel Prize committee did not award a prize in 1949 after judging that none of the year's nominations met the prize criteria. The foundation's statutes allowed the prize to be reserved for a year; thus, Faulkner was officially awarded the 1949 Nobel Prize at the 1950 award ceremony.

2. Gustaf Hellstrom, "Award Ceremony Speech," December 10, 1950, http://www.nobelprize.org/nobel_prizes/literature/laureates/1949/press.html (accessed February 16, 2016).

3. Ibid.

4. Ibid.

5. William Faulkner, "Banquet Speech," December 10, 1950, http://www.nobelprize.org/nobel_prizes/literature/laureates/1949/faulkner-speech.html (accessed February 16, 2016).

6. Ibid. The history of this vocational claim is worth noting. As Greg Barnhisel observes, Faulkner was not keen to make the trip to Sweden to accept the prize, and it took the combined efforts of the Nobel committee, the US government, and personal correspondence to change his mind. Faulkner uses the phrase "the award was made, not to me, but to my works" in a letter explaining his reluctance to attend the prize ceremony. See Greg Barnhisel, *Cold War Modernists: Art, Literature, and American Cultural Diplomacy* (New York: Columbia University Press, 2015), 126.

7. Faulkner, "Banquet speech."

8. Ibid.

9. "White House Conference on a Program for People-to-People Partnership" (1956), in *Faulkner: A Comprehensive Guide to the Brodsky Collection*, vol. 5, *Manuscripts and Documents*, ed. Louis Daniel Brodsky and Robert Hamblin (Jackson: University Press of Mississippi, 1988), 340.

10. Harilaos Stecopoulos, "William Faulkner and the Problem of Cold War Modernism," in *Faulkner's Geographies: Faulkner and Yoknapatawpha, 2011*, ed. Jay Watson and Ann Abadie (Jackson: University Press of Mississippi, 2015), 145.

11. Press release regarding June 12 White House Conference on People-to-People Partnership, May 31, 1956, Dwight D. Eisenhower Records as President, Official File, Box 764 OF325, People-to-People Program (2): National Archive Identification #12649394, https://www.eisenhower.archives.gov/research/online_documents/people _to_people/BinderV.pdf (accessed February 5, 2016).

12. Ibid.

13. Ibid.

14. Dwight D. Eisenhower, "Address and Remarks at the Baylor University Commencement Ceremonies, Waco, Texas" (May 25, 1956), in *The American Presidency Project*, ed. John Woolley and Gerhard Peters, http://www.presidency.ucsb.edu /ws/?pid=10499 (accessed February 16, 2016).

15. "Remarks at the People-to-People Conference" (September 11, 1956), in *The American Presidency Project*, ed. John Woolley and Gerhard Peters, http://www.presidency .ucsb.edu/ws/?pid=10599 (accessed February 16, 2016).

16. Edward P. F. Eagan, People-to-People Sports Committee Progress Report, 9, Jacqueline Cochran Papers, General Files Series, box 98, People-to-People Program 1958 (2): NAID #16436544, https://www.eisenhower.archives.gov/research/online_documents /people_to_people/BinderE.pdf (accessed February 6, 2016).

17. "White House Conference on a Program for People-to-People Partnership," 340.

18. Dwight D. Eisenhower, "Annual Message to the Congress on the State of the Union" (January 9, 1958), in *The American Presidency Project*, John Woolley and Gerhard Peters, http://www.presidency.ucsb.edu/ws/index.php?pid=11162 (accessed February 16, 2016). In an opinion piece, the editor of *US News and World Report* went a step farther, remarking that the president's address was "an appeal above the heads of government to the people of the Soviet Union." See David Lawrence, "People to People," *US News and World Report*, January 17, 1958, 120.

19. See Arthur Larson, *What Are We For* (New York: Harper & Row, 1959), 168.

20. *People to People News* 1, no. 2 (October 1956): 2, Dwight D. Eisenhower Records as President, Official File, box 765 OF325, People-to-People Program (11); National Archives Identification # 16436585, http://www.eisenhower.archives.gov/research/online _documents/people_to_people/BinderRR.pdf (accessed February 16, 2016). George Brett (Macmillan) headed up the Books Committee, while Paul C. Smith (Crowell-Collier Publishing) led the Magazines Committee.

21. Quoted in Joseph Blotner, "William Faulkner, Committee Chairman," in *Themes and Directions in American Literature: Essays in Honor of Leon Howard*, ed. Ray B. Browne and Donald Pizer (Lafayette, IN: Purdue University Press, 1969), 202.

22. Ibid., 206.

23. Russell Lynes, "Highbrow, Lowbrow, Middlebrow," *Wilson Quarterly* 1, no. 1 (August 1976): 154–55. This reprint, as the editor of the *Wilson Quarterly* remarks, is "a slightly condensed version" of the article Lynes originally published in *Harper's* in 1949.

24. Ibid., 153, 156.

25. Dwight Macdonald, "Masscult and Midcult," in *Against the American Grain* (New York: Da Capo Books, 1962), 34.

26. Ibid., 37.

27. Ibid., 39, 38.

28. Janice Radway, *A Feeling for Books: The Book-of-the-Month Club, Literary Taste, and Middle-Class Desire* (Chapel Hill: University of North Carolina Press, 1999), 293.

29. Henry Seidel Canby quoted in Radway, *Feeling for Books*, 293.

30. It is worth noting that the BOMC featured Eisenhower's *Crusade in Europe* as one of its 1948 selections. See http://www.ocf.berkeley.edu/~immer/books1940s.

31. Harvey Breit was then assistant editor of the *New York Times Book Review* and author of the In and Out of Books column. Breit had even interviewed Faulkner for the column in 1955.

32. See Joseph Blotner, ed., *Selected Letters of William Faulkner* (New York: Random House, 1977), 404.

33. Ibid. Where Stecopoulos argues that the letter's absurdity positions the avant-garde as the sole means by which writers can respond to the state (149), I suggest here that their statements of vocation do much the same work.

34. Breit made Faulkner's involvement in the program the subject of his In and Out of Books column of October 14, 1956. As Blotner notes, in it Breit described the objections raised (by writers) that writers ought not mix in politics, as well as Faulkner's response that "a writer doesn't have any obligation to belong, or to stay belonged" (quoted in Blotner, "William Faulkner, Committee Chairman," 209).

35. A large (but perhaps not comprehensive) set of these questionnaires, along with a bulk of correspondence from members of the Writers' Committee, is part of the William Faulkner Collection, Albert and Shirley Small Special Collections Library, University of Virginia, Charlottesville. From these materials, it is not clear how Faulkner and Breit decided what comments or suggestions would appear on the questionnaire.

36. I make this assertion based on the writers' responses to the questionnaires available at the William Faulkner Collection, Albert and Shirley Small Special Collections Library, University of Virginia, Charlottesville.

37. Edna Ferber to William Faulkner, October 2, 1956, William Faulkner Collection, Albert and Shirley Small Special Collections Library, University of Virginia, Charlottesville; William Styron to William Faulkner, October 15, 1956, William Faulkner Collection.

38. E. B. White to William Faulkner and Harvey Breit, October 5, 1956, William Faulkner Collection, Albert and Shirley Small Special Collections Library, University of Virginia, Charlottesville. White goes on to conclude the letter noting that disorganization is the "proper condition of writers in America."

39. Robert Lowell to William Faulkner, September 25, 1956, William Faulkner Collection, Albert and Shirley Small Special Collections Library, University of Virginia, Charlottesville.

40. Bellow wrote this comment on the questionnaire he returned, n.d., William Faulkner Collection, Albert and Shirley Small Special Collections Library, University of Virginia, Charlottesville.

41. Berryman to William Faulkner, November 26, 1956, William Faulkner Collection, Albert and Shirley Small Special Collections Library, University of Virginia, Charlottesville.

42. Ibid.

43. Gore Vidal to William Faulkner, n.d., William Faulkner Collection, Albert and Shirley Small Special Collections Library, University of Virginia, Charlottesville.

44. Jacques Barzun to William Faulkner and Harvey Breit, October 5, 1956, William Faulkner Collection, Albert and Shirley Small Special Collections Library, University of Virginia, Charlottesville.

45. Ibid.

46. Malcolm Cowley to William Faulkner, September 27, 1956, William Faulkner Collection, Albert and Shirley Small Special Collections Library, University of Virginia, Charlottesville.

47. Archibald MacLeish to William Faulkner and Harvey Breit, October 7, 1956, William Faulkner Collection, Albert and Shirley Small Special Collections Library, University of Virginia, Charlottesville.

48. Blotner, "William Faulkner, Committee Chairman," 212–14.

49. William Faulkner, Donald Hall, and John Steinbeck, "Summary Report of the Writers' Committee of the People-to-People Program, December 1956," in *Faulkner: A Comprehensive Guide to the Brodsky Collection*, vol. 5, *Manuscripts and Documents*, ed. Louis Daniel Brodsky and Robert Hamblin (Jackson: University Press of Mississippi, 1988), 354.

50. Blotner, "William Faulkner, Committee Chairman," 220–22. See also Catherine Gunther Kodat, "Unsteady State: Faulkner and the Cold War," in *William Faulkner in Context*, ed. John T. Matthews (New York: Cambridge University Press, 2015), 156–68.

Programmed for Seduction: Faulkner's Fiction and Men's Magazines of the 1950s

KRISTI ROWAN HUMPHREYS

On the heels of *Playboy*'s inception in 1953, the men's magazines *The Dude: The Magazine Devoted to Pleasure* (1956) and *The Gent: An Approach to Relaxation* (1957) began bimonthly publication, appealing to the 1950s male. Beyond being merely "skin magazines," these publications provided a space for modernist fiction, including that of William Faulkner. In 1957 both magazines reprinted short stories by Faulkner: *The Dude*'s March 1957 issue presented "Carcassonne" and *The Gent*'s June 1957 issue included "Divorce in Naples"—two stories that are not just any old Faulkner stories when considering issues of masculine identity. "Carcassonne" is clearly preoccupied with the link between art and the erotic, although that erotic element is not overtly heterosexual, and "Divorce in Naples" presents one of the most explicitly queer male couplings in all of Faulkner's oeuvre. Magazine editors made the curious decision to reprint these stories, ripe with overtones of sexual ambivalence,[1] alongside more explicitly heterosexual erotic spreads. This essay contends that the motives behind these choices are twofold. First, these decisions can be viewed as responses to a male postwar desire for homosocial bonding as men sought to contest the domestication of masculinity even while operating within it. Second, they indicate the possibility that the heterosexual male was not the sole target audience.[2]

Following World War II, the 1950s witnessed what historians have considered a crisis of masculinity as men returned from the war and attempted to adjust to a rather disorienting new realm of women, children, and mass consumption,[3] while at the same time navigating issues of post-traumatic stress, suburbanization, domestic consumerism, the transition to a white-collar corporate economy, and Cold War fear.[4] In his work *Men in the Middle: Searching for Masculinity in the 1950s*, historian James Gilbert calls this decade unusual for its "relentless

189

and self-conscious preoccupation with masculinity, in part because the period followed wartime self-confidence based upon the sacrifice and heroism of ordinary men."[5] Historians developed a term for this intense uncertainty regarding masculine identity: male panic, which emerges at times "when men self-consciously rebel against real or imagined 'feminization' developing within the workplace, public spheres, and/or domestic relationships."[6]

As many women returned to the home in the 1950s after wartime work, they functioned as the chief purchasers for their families in a time when the country was regarding the consumption of household goods as an American duty. By the standards of Nixon's kitchen debate in the 1950s, the prevalence of suburban homes, complete with modern appliances, was in fact proof of the strength of the nation. Consequently, advertisers, television programming, magazines—popular culture in general—targeted women and encouraged consumer-based conformity. Eventually, as Gilbert claims, "A vast and widely read critical literature emerged around social and cultural conformity, the censure of suburban life, and the condemnation of mass culture. A fundamental element of each critique revealed fears of masculine decline."[7] Simply put, postwar society regarded conformity, suburban life, and mass culture as feminizing forces, and one method for combating these forces involved a renewed focus on male individualism and a return to traditional masculine vigor.[8]

The desire to construct new "real masculinities" was directly related to the prevalence of men's magazines in the 1950s, as they functioned as texts of masculinity. In his book *All Man! Hemingway, 1950s Men's Magazines, and the Masculine Persona* (2009), historian David M. Earle reveals that "between about 1952 and 1961, hundreds of new men's magazines were published,"[9] and they were constructed to seduce and create desire. This desire was not just to buy the issue, but to emulate and perhaps become the types of masculine individual found within its covers—to live vicariously through the content. With their elements of sex, adventure, travel, war, literature, and art, these magazines "offered some kind of antidote to the mass-marketed conformity of life and culture as portrayed in popular magazines such as the *Saturday Evening Post*."[10] These magazines promoted a cure for the domestication of masculinity that involved men learning—or relearning—to dominate. Consequently, the magazines, according to Earle, produced "fantasies of masculinity, tall sexist tales to bolster men's adequacy in the quickly shifting time after the war and before the cultural upheaval of the 1960s."[11] They also stood in contrast to white domestic television of the 1950s, where viewers watched bumbling fathers like Ozzie Nelson learn the same weekly lessons over and over.

Around 1956, Gilbert tells us, "Writer and critic Auguste Comte Spectorsky surveyed the world of letters . . . and despaired at his discovery—or better—at what he could *not* find, which was a thriving, masculine high culture."[12] As the new managing editor at *Playboy*, Spectorsky sought to go beyond merely bringing sophisticated cultural and artistic tastes to the magazine. His mission was a bit more ambitious, as he aimed to "remasculinize high culture."[13]

Near the same time, and with the same purposes in mind, *The Dude* and *The Gent* began bimonthly publication, and these magazines provided a space for modernist fiction and poetry. According to Earle, it was quite common to reprint modernist writers in these types of magazine. He writes, "Of course, 1950s men's magazines relied on the aura of respectability that republishing modernist authors gave them. But more than this, the fiction of these authors was often concerned with either travel and adventure or sexuality."[14] Like *Playboy*, these magazines constructed and sold a type of masculinity that was sophisticated, culturally savvy, and of good taste, and the recipe for this brand of manliness involved a solid familiarity with literary modernism. Furthermore, Earle specifically observes that the "masculine tone of these modern writers . . . created a fantasy lifestyle of the modern artist."[15] Modernist periodicals were marketed in a way that suggested intellectual elitism, unlike popular literature, which was commonly identified as effeminate. In fact, a lifestyle of travel was frequently romanticized in this literature because it underscored the advantages of creating distance from the domestic sphere and a feminized world. From this perspective, modernism was promoted as being strong and masculine—"all that effeminate popular fiction was not."[16]

Faulkner was certainly a part of the modernist literature—the highbrow, elitist content—found alongside the lowbrow in men's magazines of the 1950s. The characters and themes in Faulkner's fiction integrate with the adjacent content and work together toward the magazine's ultimate goal of seduction. An analysis of these integrations—of Faulkner's reprinted short stories and their neighboring content—within both 1957 issues of *The Dude* and *The Gent*, certainly reveals Faulkner's fiction to be programmed for seduction. Moreover, the choice to reprint these particular short stories indicates something significant about the specific mode of seduction. If magazines sought to select content that would promote a robust, dominating, sophisticated, and heterosexual version of masculinity, these stories are not obvious choices. Why would magazine editors choose to place stories seasoned with overtones of sexual ambivalence amidst explicitly heterosexual erotic spreads? The queer energies of Faulkner's stories work within the spaces of the overtly erotic spreads

in the same way the postwar male, divided between familial responsibilities and allegiances to peer groups, worked within postwar definitions of
masculinity. Faulkner once said about "Carcassonne" that he "was still
writing about a young man in conflict with his environment,"[17] and as
men returned home from the war in the 1950s to a confusing new world
of domesticity and mass consumption, in many ways Faulkner's words
evoke the terms of postwar masculinity as well.

Furthermore, the decision to include these stories indicates the possibility that the heterosexual male was not the sole target audience of
1950s men's magazines. In his work *Homosexuality in Cold War America: Resistance and the Crisis of Masculinity* (1997), Robert J. Corber
describes the midcentury pressure felt by men who did not choose the
suburban-home lifestyle to "distinguish themselves from gay men" or
from a socially constructed gay male persona.[18] In discussing the emergence of a gay macho style in the 1940s and 1950s, Corber suggests
that "in adopting a theatrically masculine appearance, gay men identified
themselves with an oppositional form of masculinity."[19] The decision to
reprint the sexually ambivalent Faulkner stories, ripe with queer energies, may have been an attempt to appeal to the postwar homosexual
male cultivating oppositional forms of masculinity during a time of
intense homophobia.

Both stories were first published in 1931 in the short story collection *These 13*. Faulkner held the short story form in high esteem,
and scholar Hans H. Skei claims this is evident in the ways "in which
he tried to superimpose a design or a structure upon the otherwise
disparate short stories" in his collections.[20] *These 13* has three sections: the first includes World War I stories, while the second section
is about Yoknapatawpha; "Carcassonne" and "Divorce in Naples" are
found in the third section, which reveals themes of sexuality and tales
of American experiences abroad—adventures away from Yoknapatawpha. The stories were reprinted in *Collected Stories* in 1950 and in
The Dude and *The Gent* in 1957. The repackaging of Faulkner's stories
in a Cold War environment is part of a larger reframing of Faulkner
that shifts the perception of Faulkner from the "corn-cob man,"[21] to,
as Lawrence H. Schwartz describes, "an emblem of the freedom of
the individual under capitalism" and "a chronicler of the plight of man
in the modern world."[22] During a time when the nation's overriding
ethos was the moral superiority of America, Faulkner's position as a
leading literary voice is understandable, and considering his attention
to human effort and endurance, especially among the outcast, it is not
so surprising that postwar men's magazines would choose to reprint
Faulkner stories.

The June 1957 issue of *The Gent* features a verbatim reprint of "Divorce in Naples,"[23] a story about a group of merchant sailors out for a night on the town in Naples—the narrator devotes special attention to the homoerotic relationship between George, the mess man, and Carl, the mess boy. George decides that Carl, an eighteen-year-old male, should lose his virginity to a woman on this night, so the men go to a dive to drink. When George goes to the restroom, he returns to find that Carl has left with an Italian female prostitute.[24] Carl returns to the ship a few days after his adventure, but the men ignore each other while still in port. As the ship leaves Naples and heads out to sea, the men reconcile and are seen dancing, "in decorous embrace," to the music of a Victrola.[25] Faulkner's story—one involving sailors, prostitutes, sexuality, and loss of innocence—is preceded by a four-page pictorial essay of the Parisian Sphinx Night Club's star seminude attraction, Yvette Le Mazou. The spread is titled "Mademoiselle Le Mazou: From Mannequin to Moliere," and states, "Beyond this tough little world of night-clubs, with their audiences of moneyed, pleasure-hungry tourists, lies the real Pigalle: a vortex of intrigue, ambition, violence—and for a lucky few—success."[26] The next page describes Yvette, who is, in a way, depicted as having undergone the same loss of innocence as Carl in Faulkner's story, and who is wiser for it: "Nineteen-year-old Yvette Le Mazou, the star dance attraction at the Sphinx night club, has been lucky so far. She's clever and ambitious enough to avoid the Pigalle pitfalls of dope, liquor, and (need we say more?). A ballet student in her youth, she now dreams of a theatrical career, studies Moliere . . . and the modern French dramatists. . . . Yvette works hard, plays hard, and dreams a lot about the future."[27] Through Yvette one reads about the result of industrious approaches to business and pleasure—the result is success. In a postwar era that defines masculinity by success, these aspects of Yvette would likely appeal. Yvette's function, however, goes beyond symbolizing success and heterosexual fantasy. Erin A. Smith observes of hard-boiled fiction that the genre "is often structured by love triangles in which the love of two men for each other is mediated through the body of a woman."[28] I argue Yvette performs a similar function here. The love of George and Carl for each other is mediated not only by the female prostitute in Faulkner's story, but also by Yvette's preceding spread, meaning that readers enter Faulkner's world of sailors and prostitution through a former ballet dancer turned stripper who reads Molière. At the same time, Faulkner's prose serves to activate Yvette and bring her to life. From this perspective, Faulkner's words, to quote Candace Waid, "speak with animal vigor casting shadows of life"[29] onto Yvette, and they work together to seduce the reader and inspire the masculine imagination.

Yvette herself is an integration of high and low art as a nightclub dancer who appreciates and enjoys French literature. Yvette's placement flavors the ways in which Faulkner's story is read, as one cannot help but think of her when dives and prostitution, albeit in Italy instead of France, are mentioned in "Divorce in Naples." The integration of highbrow and lowbrow is so strong that it becomes difficult to ascertain when Yvette's story ends and Faulkner's begins. As Gilbert claims, just as these magazines "sold the idea that it was necessary to be familiar with literary modernism if you were to be culturally savvy," those "who read these authors were arbiters of good taste."[30] Yvette is all of these things, too, integrating her with "Divorce in Naples" in a way that both fosters heterosexual masculinity and sells it.

Faulkner's story is followed by a two-page pictorial essay of a woman in a black negligee frolicking in the sea with a male mannequin. Titled "Rehearsal in the Sand: Solo for the Modern Dancer," the spread includes the following text:

> This budding young miss in the black negligee has not been sleeping *en plein air* (out-of-doors, that is). She is taking a shore-side romp to limber up for practice class. Although most of her performances are solo, who in the audience can criticize her lack of form for trying to combine studio work with a little boning up in the ancient, magical art: Catching The Man? Everything's fine—so far. She's got the knowhow. She's doing her best but: a dummy's a dummy and there's a limit to patience, even the patience of an accomplished artiste.[31]

Just as these spreads shape the way Faulkner's modernist story is read, its presence between them integrates to program these females as objects of highbrow desire. "Divorce in Naples" works to connect male readers, many of them World War II veterans, to their desires for brotherhood and homosocial bonding as it portrays men living a lifestyle of travel, adventure, and separation from a domestic or feminized world. And in the end, the men in the story choose each other. This accentuation of brotherhood, in a way, is supported by Yvette and the modern dancer as they create a desire in the reader to be a part of their worlds, but not at the cost of masculinity. These ladies have masculine tastes, as defined by postwar pop culture. They have affinities for high art, hard work, hard play, and success—and they are no-nonsense girls: all traits signified as masculine in 1950s popular culture. In this way, they do not, as women, threaten but rather support masculinity. In other words, they are not the types of women that the typical suburban male breadwinner, whether heterosexual or closeted homosexual, sought for a wife—a role that in the 1950s involved feminine traits of domesticity, passivity, and mass consumption. By focusing on the masculine qualities of Yvette and the modern dancer, the magazines depict the women as nonthreatening to masculinity and male bonding.

Whereas these cursory elements of placement and structure reveal links between Faulkner's characters and the adjacent spreads, the crux of "Divorce in Naples" involves the homoerotic relationship between George and Carl, which might initially appear to be at odds with the magazine's ultimate goals. Even though the story does not identify the relationship explicitly as homosexual, George and Carl appear to be more than friends, as they spend their evenings in their undershirts embracing and dancing, and their shipmates refer to Carl as George's wife and to their relationship as a marriage. At the same time, there are elements of sexual ambivalence and confusion in the story as well, because George seeks the companionship of female prostitutes for Carl, and Carl later discusses wanting to give these women gifts. Considering that homo-eroticism is a defining aspect of the story, the mere inclusion of "Divorce in Naples" in a men's magazine of the 1950s begs further investigation and potentially underscores deeper issues of postwar masculinity. In his book *Guys Like Us* (2004), historian Michael Davidson points out that "while same-sex relationships had been reinforced during the war, when servicemen or factory workers returned to civilian life, those links survived."[32] The 1950s male was pressed to follow, as Corber puts it, a "model of masculinity that stressed domesticity and cooperation"[33] while simultaneously feeling the pull of male homosocial desire promoted during the war. It is not surprising, then, that the sexual ambivalence and confusion underpinning "Divorce in Naples" might appeal to postwar males who, in historian Suzanne Clark's words, had been plunged "into a confusion about identities that literature as well as mass culture struggled to address."[34]

The issue of belonging is also significant here. Clark finds that in the 1950s, "the problem of belonging no longer seemed a problem of the community, but rather a problem for the individual, to be thought about through isolated figures."[35] This explains, in part, the joiner ethos of masculine culture in the 1950s, which celebrated male clubs and organizations as convenient and appropriate opportunities for bonding and belonging.[36] Cold War fears directed males to be cautious of how they bonded, as "one of the ways in which the national security state discouraged forms of male homosocial bonding that conflicted with the Fordist organization of production and consumption was by homosexualizing them."[37] Postwar masculinity meant feeling a level of anxiety about relationships that had brought comfort both during and following the war. These themes have a strong presence in "Divorce in Naples." Even though George and Carl's version of homosocial bonding is homosexual-ized by their shipmates, the story's placement in a 1950s men's magazine means the two men can be viewed through a postwar lens as isolated masculine figures. Through this lens, a heterosexual male reader might conclude that it is not the homosocial bonding but the men's inability to belong that leads to their being homosexualized by others.

The March 1957 issue of *The Dude* featured a precise reprint of Faulkner's story "Carcassonne"—the tale of an unnamed protagonist who lives in a rat-infested attic over a cantina and dreams about being a poet as he fantasizes about the heroic actions of medieval crusaders.[38] Preceding this story is a pictorial essay titled "Intrigue," depicting two lovers on a beach, claiming the following:

> It was hot that day. Devilishly hot. I had gone down to the beach. I wanted to be alone. The hell I wanted to be alone! I was bored. Perhaps, I thought, something will happen. Something . . . intriguing. I saw something stir in the distance. Then come closer. And closer. Then I recognized her. Drat! It was my wife. My unintriguing wife. Then something happened. Suddenly, I wasn't quite so bored anymore. In fact—I was a little intrigued. She was really intriguing as hell, I decided. I looked down at her loveliness . . . and kissed her loveliness . . . and touched her loveliness . . . and I wanted her loveliness, and it was mine forever.[39]

Then, following "Carcassonne," we find "From Garret to Runway," a spread revealing one of Paris's most colorful Bohemian traditions, alleg-edly "shown here for the first time."[40] The text continues:

> Each year the male citizenry of the 14th *arrondissement* (district) of Paris gather in public conclave for a special treat: selecting the ideal artist's model. Twelve to fifteen contestants are nominated by the neighborhood's painters and sculptors. The *atelier* lovelies parade before the discerning eyes of the crowd, and the judges, with due consideration for audience reaction, pick the winner. Poise, grace, and artistically perfect dimensions are what the judges look for. . . . Strictly, you might say, a case of art for art's sake.[41]

David M. Earle describes the dual function of highbrow art and authors alongside sexual spreads. He claims one use was pragmatic, "giving such magazines cultural capital to fight censorship."[42] Faulkner would have contributed significantly to this cultural capital. As Greg Barnhisel tells us, through his involvement with US state-sponsored book programs, Faulkner did more for 1950s cultural diplomacy than any other modern-ist author.[43] Additionally, Earle claims that modernist works in sexualized contexts also "recapture the innate risqué nature they held at their original publication, lost in their usual sanctioned surroundings of academic anthologies or editions."[44] The "From Garret to Runway" spread provides an example of how midcentury men's magazines sexualized modernism, as that final "art for art's sake" refers to naked women's bodies. In this way, magazines such as *The Dude* sold the highbrow by maintaining connections between transgressive sexuality and modernism.

In *A Critical Companion to William Faulkner* (2008), A. Nicholas Fargnoli, Michael Golay, and Robert W. Hamblin provide insight into "Carcassonne," claiming that although Faulkner apparently never visited the actual town of Carcassonne in France, "the city came to represent for him . . . a symbol of the creative imagination. Once asked to comment on the source of southern literature, Faulkner said, 'I myself am inclined to think it was because of the bareness of the Southerner's life, that he had to resort to his own imagination, to create his own Carcassonne.'"[45] This point is related to Faulkner's own Yoknapatawpha, which Hamblin elsewhere contends represents a fusion of real and imaginary.[46]

We see these same ideas depicted in the content adjacent to "Carcassonne" in *The Dude*. In the first pictorial essay, we find the subject matter of a man's dreams and fantasies, merging with "Carcassonne," where the protagonist regards his bed "as a pair of spectacles through which he nightly perused the fabric of dreams."[47] "Intrigue" fuses the real (the man's wife) with the imaginary (an erotic, spontaneous seduction on a beach) as it presents a man, just as "Carcassonne" does, who must resort to his own imagination to engage in masculine stories of heroism—to construct his own masculinity. And just as modernist literature is credited with teaching readers to read in a new way,[48] the "Intrigue" spread invites the reader to fantasize in new ways about spouses and marriage as it redefines desire as an unexpected, erotic encounter with one's wife—not in the typical feminized private sphere of the home, but in the masculinized public sphere of the beach. Faulkner's story activates and empowers the masculine imagination to engage retrospectively with the "Intrigue" pictorial essay.

Read in a more linear fashion, the "Intrigue" spread prepares the reader to recognize Faulkner's empathy for the "other." Jaime Harker notes that "Faulkner had a special affinity for other outsiders in his community, especially sexual outsiders," and that "sexual and gender outlaws are heroes" in his fiction.[49] The "Intrigue" spread presents literal outsiders—figures on an isolated, abandoned beach stretching for miles. Even though the relationship appears heterosexual in nature, they embody sexual deviance in their public display of eroticism as they lie together in seductive embrace on the sand. These aspects of the "Intrigue" spread function to underscore the outlaw qualities of the couple and, consequently, connect it to the outsider qualities of the struggling poet in "Carcassonne." Like the young poet, the male character of "Intrigue" oscillates between despair and hopefulness—moving from "Drat! It was my wife" to "She was really intriguing"—and experiences a similar sustained epiphany: wives can be seductive and surprising. The outsider poet in "Carcassonne" also wavers between hope and despair as he grapples with issues of life, death, and artistic vision in his isolated, rat-infested attic space.

Furthermore, in the second pictorial essay, "From Garret to Runway," we find the joining of the garret space to the protagonist's attic space in "Carcassonne," seducing the reader to move seamlessly from one attic to another. And the event of the runway display is located in France, also connecting it to the title "Carcassonne." In a way, "From Garret to Runway" focuses on the real, while the preceding spread, "Intrigue," focuses on the imaginary, allowing Faulkner's fiction to exist in the middle, performing an integration of real and imaginary—the ultimate seduction. The 1950s men's magazine, while still integrating highbrow and lowbrow content to define masculinity, is using Faulkner's story to underscore the power and importance of the imagination, of dreaming as a means to escape reality, while the postwar male searches for ways to adapt to a new feminized, suburban, and domesticated world.

The binary of real versus imaginary, so integral to "Carcassonne," introduces further binaries fundamental both to the story and postwar masculinity. Faulkner's tale, for example, explicitly distinguishes the protagonist from his "skeleton," and Skei adds that "the poet-dreamer" of the story "thinks of the Norman steed, cut in half and still galloping, perhaps unaware of the parallel to his own divided self."[50] "Carcassonne" thus underscores the divided nature of the self, a problem that would have resonated with postwar males, heterosexual and homosexual. As mentioned earlier, the postwar heterosexual male was split between familial responsibilities and allegiances to peer groups—between a desire to maintain same-sex relationships fostered during the war and a need to fulfill a suburban-breadwinner ideal, devoted exclusively to home and family. The homosexual male was additionally split between realities and personas, the revealed and the concealed.

Even beyond these splits, the postwar male experienced a different fissure, as returning home from war led many to conclude that the familiar often felt strange, while the strange had become familiar. David Minter has addressed these binaries: "In 'Carcassonne,'" he writes, "this going back and forth is not only between heaven and earth, imagination and reality, art and life, nor merely between grand gestures for empty dreams and deeds done. It is also between Faulkner's own divided response to the evocations of the far and the strange and the presence of the near and familiar."[51] Minter indicates a division within Faulkner that was experienced by both the protagonist in the story and later by many postwar males as well. On a related note, "Carcassonne"'s emphasis on the independent existence of the protagonist's skeleton may be a way of evoking the proverbial "skeleton in the closet" (a phrase that had entered English usage by Faulkner's time). If so, this "closeted" figure might have struck a chord with midcentury homosexual readers, calling to mind the veil of secrecy under which many were forced to live during a time of intense homophobia in America. In the same vein, both "Carcassonne" and "Divorce in Naples" dwell in the darkness, in what occurs at night, whether it be the dreams and fantasies of the former tale or the sexual encounters of the latter. These aspects of the stories not only connect the fictional characters to the nightlife-driven content of "From Mannequin to Moliere" and "From Garret to Runway" but also parallel the concealed qualities of postwar male identity and existence.

As I conclude, even though it does not constitute a substantial part of my argument, I would be remiss if I did not mention the characters of Mrs. Widdrington in "Carcassonne" and the manipulative female prostitute in "Divorce in Naples." Philip Wylie's famous text *A Generation of Vipers*, first published in 1942 and re-released widely in 1955, coined the term *momism*. In describing the book, Davidson finds that Wylie blamed "the loss of (male) authority on overly protective, domineering mothers, whose productive functions had been diminished by industrialization and whose primary activities now involved consumption and the repression of her family. . . . Most insidiously, her overly protective nature damaged national will, weakening the resolve of soldiers, making them vulnerable to brainwashing and causing the early termination of the Korean War."[52] The popularity of Wylie's work might point toward additional connections between the reprinting of the Faulkner stories and postwar male identities. In "Carcassonne," Mrs. Widdrington is depicted as an unreasonable, possessive, and domineering woman who "owned the garret and the roofing paper, owned the darkness too."[53] "She'd make a poet of you too, if you did not work anywhere. She believed that, if a reason for breathing were not acceptable to her, it was no reason."[54] She even "owned the rats too."[55] And in "Divorce in Naples," George finds Carl's prostitute to be forceful and manipulative, claiming, "She was the one made him done it."[56] If postwar America subscribed to an image of woman that was overbearing, a force threatening to seize male authority, and of mass culture conformity as feminizing and debasing, male readers may have understood Faulkner's female characters—characters that

200 KRISTI ROWAN HUMPHREYS

embody the same domineering qualities identified as threats by Wylie in 1955—in this context.

Ultimately, Faulkner's reprinted short stories are programmed to seduce, but the seduction goes beyond merely integrating modernist fiction with lowbrow erotic content to redefine and sell a version of masculinity that is strong, sophisticated, enlightened, and intellectually elite. Determining just who is being seduced, how, and to what end, however, is not such a simple task, especially during a time when masculinity was on trial. Sure, *The Dude* and *The Gent* used Faulkner's fiction in an attempt to redefine masculinity as a fusion of high and low art, real and imaginary, and in turn, as Spectorsky claimed of his aims for *Playboy*, to "remasculinize high culture," but even beyond that, the reprinting of these stories alongside erotic spreads complicates issues of postwar identity and 1950s readership, bringing to the fore compelling issues of homosocial bonding, homosexuality, and divided, often fluid, male identities.

NOTES

1. Edmond L. Volpe discusses general ambivalence in "Divorce in Naples" in "A Tale of Ambivalences: Faulkner's 'Divorce in Naples,'" *Studies in Short Fiction* 28, no. 1 (Spring 1991): 41.

2. Eve Kosofsky Sedgwick provides helpful discussions of "homosocial bonding" in *Between Men: English Literature and Male Homosocial Desire* (New York: Columbia University Press, 1985).

3. James Gilbert, *Men in the Middle: Searching for Masculinity in the 1950s* (Chicago: University of Chicago Press, 2005), 12.

4. David M. Earle, *All Man! Hemingway, 1950s Men's Magazines, and the Masculine Persona* (Kent, OH: Kent State University Press, 2009), 6–7.

5. Gilbert, *Men in the Middle*, 2.

6. Ibid.

7. Ibid., 4.

8. Ibid.

9. Earle, *All Man!*, 2.

10. Ibid., 5.

11. Ibid.

12. Gilbert, *Men in the Middle*, 13.

13. Gilbert discusses Spectorsky and *Playboy* further on page 13 of *Men in the Middle*.

14. Earle, *All Man!*, 112.

15. Ibid., 12.

16. Ibid., 111.

17. Quoted in Hans H. Skei, *Reading Faulkner's Best Short Stories* (Columbia: University of South Carolina Press, 1999), 80.

18. Robert J. Corber, *Homosexuality in Cold War America: Resistance and the Crisis of Masculinity* (Durham, NC: Duke University Press, 1997), 145.

19. Ibid., 145.

20. Skei, *Reading Faulkner's Best Short Stories*, 6.

21. Lawrence H. Schwartz, *Creating Faulkner's Reputation: The Politics of Modern Literary Criticism* (Knoxville: University of Tennessee Press, 1988), 58.

22. Ibid., 4.

23. I compared the reprinted version in *The Gent* (6–11, 65–66) to the original version in William Faulkner, *These 13* (New York: Jonathan Cape & Harrison Smith, 1931), 330–51.

24. A fine summary of this story can be found in *A William Faulkner Encyclopedia*, ed. Robert W. Hamblin and Charles A. Peek (Westport, CT: Greenwood, 1999), 59–60.

25. William Faulkner, "Divorce in Naples," in *Collected Stories of William Faulkner* (1950; repr., New York: Vintage International, 1995), 892.

26. "Mademoiselle Le Mazou: From Mannequin to Moliere," *The Gent: An Approach to Relaxation*, June 1957, 2.

27. Ibid., 4.

28. Erin A. Smith, *Hard-Boiled: Working-Class Readers and Pulp Magazines* (Philadelphia: Temple University Press, 2000), 188.

29. Candace Waid discussed this in her keynote presentation "Beyond Words: Faulkner Defining and Defying Print through Pictures" at the Faulkner and Yoknapatawpha Conference titled Faulkner and Print Culture, July 19, 2015.

30. Gilbert, *Men in the Middle*, 12.

31. "Rehearsal in the Sand: Solo for the Modern Dancer," *The Gent: An Approach to Relaxation* 1, no. 5 (June 1957), 12.

32. Michael Davidson, *Guys Like Us: Citing Masculinity in Cold War Poetics* (Chicago: University of Chicago Press, 2004), 17.

33. Corber, *Homosexuality in Cold War America*, 5.

34. Suzanne Clark, *Cold Warriors: Manliness on Trial in the Rhetoric of the West* (Carbondale: Southern Illinois University Press, 2000), 1.

35. Ibid., 66.

36. See Davidson, *Guys Like Us*, 17.

37. Corber, *Homosexuality in Cold War America*, 11.

38. I compared the reprinted version in *The Dude* (6–7, 59) to the original version in Faulkner, *These 13*, 352–58.

39. "Intrigue," *The Dude: The Magazine Devoted to Pleasure* 1, no. 4 (March 1957), 2–5.

40. "From Garret to Runway," *The Dude: The Magazine Devoted to Pleasure* 1, no. 4 (March 1957), 12.

41. Ibid., 12–13.

42. David M. Earle, *Re-Covering Modernism: Pulps, Paperbacks, and the Prejudice of Form* (Burlington, VT: Ashgate, 2009), 2.

43. Greg Barnhisel, *Cold War Modernists: Art, Literature, and American Cultural Diplomacy* (New York: Columbia University Press, 2015), 124.

44. Earle, *Re-Covering Modernism*, 2–3.

45. A. Nicholas Fargnoli, Michael Golay, and Robert W. Hamblin, *Critical Companion to William Faulkner: A Literary Reference to His Life and Work* (New York: InfoBase Publishing, 2008), 67.

46. Quoted in Fargnoli, Golay, and Hamblin, *Critical Companion to William Faulkner*, 67.

47. William Faulkner, "Carcassonne," *Collected Stories of William Faulkner* (1950; repr., New York: Vintage International, 1995), 896.

48. See Earle, *All Man!*, 111.

49. Jaimie Harker, "Queer Faulkner: Whores, Queers, and the Transgressive South," in *The New Cambridge Companion to William Faulkner*, ed., John T. Matthews (Cambridge: Cambridge University Press, 2015), 109, 117.

50. Skei, *Reading Faulkner's Best Short Stories*, 76.

51. David Minter, "'Carcassonne,' 'Wash,' and the Voices of Faulkner's Fiction," in *Faulkner and the Short Story: Faulkner and Yoknapatawpha, 1990*, ed. Evans Harrington and Ann J. Abadie (Jackson: University Press of Mississippi, 1992), 90–91.

52. Davidson, *Guys Like Us*, 8.

53. Faulkner, "Carcassonne," 897.

54. Ibid.

55. Ibid., 898.

56. Faulkner, "Divorce in Naples," 883.

The Wild Palms, The Mansion, and William Faulkner's Middlebrow Domestic Fiction

JAIME HARKER

Calling Faulkner "middlebrow" is a deliberate provocation—particularly since, for many Faulkner scholars, much of Faulkner's writing, especially his Cold War writing, has not lived up to the modernist highbrow aesthetic standards of his "golden period."[1] For scholars interested in recuperating that Cold War writing, distancing it from the middlebrow has been an axiomatic strategy.[2] *Middlebrow*, from its earliest emergence as a term describing Book-of-the-Month Club readers, has been a pejorative, a slur upon the social climbing and aesthetic inferiority of an implicitly middle-class reading community.[3] That pejorative is also implicitly gendered; the specter of middle-class female consumers—the "Victorian matriarch" in Ann Douglas's formulation[4]—haunts the imaginations of modern writers and critics from the interwar period onward. The vitriol with which generations of highbrow critics have denounced the middlebrow also suggests its potential to destabilize the aesthetic hierarchies and "natural" categories of taste that those critics are so desperate to establish. The middlebrow's potential, as a theoretical crowbar, to uncover the assumptions and instabilities of our aesthetic categories has long fueled my own scholarly work.[5]

Recent middlebrow scholarship has shifted to more descriptive modes of middlebrow reading and writing communities—positing certain periodicals, authors, and reading practices as a distinctive mode of print culture emphasizing affect, identification, and the symbiotic relationship between reader and writer,[6] with sometimes conservative but often surprisingly progressive takes on contemporary American culture. Middlebrow periodicals, presses, genres, reading practices, and modes of authorship are still being mapped and analyzed, both in the interwar and Cold War periods, and that scholarly work will be as illuminating for Faulkner scholarship as investigations of pulp have been for understanding Faulkner's work,[7] especially (but not limited to) novels like *Sanctuary* and *Pylon*.

In our introduction to the *Mississippi Quarterly* special issue on Oprah's summer of Faulkner, Jay Watson and I note the myriad ways in which Faulkner engaged popular literary tropes and publication venues in his own writing career.[8] Today I want to suggest an aspect of middle-brow print culture that has been understudied in Faulkner scholarship: women's magazines. During the interwar period, when Faulkner began his writing career, and through the end of the 1950s, women's magazines had circulations in the millions. Unlike little magazines, which usually had wealthy patrons to float them, women's magazines were subsidized largely by advertisements—glossy, full-page color ads that sought to transform women readers into consumers. They also continued what, in nineteenth-century scholarship, has been called the "cult of true womanhood." Ideologies of domesticity and femininity, often conservative and focused on motherhood and traditional roles, circulated throughout the pages of women's magazines. It was often a contradictory, even schizophrenic model of womanhood; both interwar and Cold War women's magazines contributed to the double bind women found themselves in, particularly regarding sexuality and agency. Within patriarchal disciplinary strictures, however, there were often remarkably frank discussions of women's sexuality within the pages of women's magazines—and more complicated and nuanced discussions than one would expect. These magazines also provided a forum for women to engage in political discourse, with discussions of presidential candidates, contemporary issues, and international affairs.[9] In this article, I analyze women's sexuality and political discourse in Faulkner's own engagements with women's magazines.

There have been a number of excellent studies of women's magazines, and of women's domesticity more generally, in both the interwar period and the Cold War period.[10] Most, however, do not emphasize what a significant reading and writing community women's magazines represented. They paid well for short stories and serialized novels and used fiction as a draw to engage readers with their articles and their advertisements. A number of famous writers regularly placed short stories and articles in women's magazines, including Virginia Woolf, Evelyn Waugh, F. Scott Fitzgerald, and George Bernard Shaw, just to name a few. More broadly, women's magazines supported a whole generation of women writers during the interwar and Cold War periods, most of whom have been forgotten. That is a shame, because women's magazine fiction was often significantly more complicated than the advertisements in the magazines would suggest; indeed, ideologically, this fiction was frequently at cross-purposes with the more conservative, consumerist ethos of mass circulation magazines. While they rarely described sex explicitly, middlebrow domestic writers wrote about sexuality extensively.

William Faulkner was well aware of the market that women's magazines represented. In an oft-quoted letter to his agent in 1936, he pondered writing "trash" for *Cosmopolitan*: "Since last summer I seem to have got out of the habit of writing trash but I will still try to cook up something for Cosmopolitan. Maybe I can get hold of one of the magazines and take a story that they will buy and change locale and names, etc. That's probably hard work too and requires skill, but I seem to be so out of touch with the Kotex Age here that I cant seem to think of anything myself."[11] Faulkner maintains the disdain for a feminized consumer culture that seemed obligatory for so many male modernists of the time. But he also reveals two other relevant facts: one, he was aware of the market of women's magazines and how well they paid, so much so that he was willing to write "trash" to tap into the field; two, he knew how to "take hold" of a magazine and read it to study the market, whether or not he himself subscribed to it or read it in public. Women's magazines were glossy monthlies, and they remained on coffee tables in living rooms and beauty parlors for weeks, potentially reaching many more people than just the subscriber. Faulkner likely would have had easy access to a number of women's magazines through casual socializing; his own wife subscribed to *Harper's Bazaar*, and other women's magazines would have been in private homes in his neighborhood. Finally, Faulkner revealed a willingness to adapt popular tropes and reframe them as his own—a constant throughout his career. He was not nearly as out of touch with the Kotex Age as he pretended.

Faulkner didn't publish in women's magazines in the interwar period (though he did in the Cold War period, which I discuss below). But that wasn't for lack of trying. From 1930 until 1932 (the period for which such a record exists), Faulkner submitted ten stories to the *Woman's Home Companion* (WHC).[12] Though he submitted to a number of middle-class magazines, the *Woman's Home Companion* is the only women's magazine in the interwar period to which he definitely submitted. This is likely because of both the famously high prices the magazine paid (it regularly paid $20,000 for serialized novels) and its reputation as a serious venue for fiction. Edited by the legendary Gertrude Lane, WHC was packed with fiction—usually a serialized novel plus three or four short stories—and articles. It was proud of its role as an arbiter of fictional taste, as its sixtieth anniversary issue cover made clear (see Figure 1). One of the prototypic authors of the *Woman's Home Companion* was popular novelist Dorothy Canfield. Canfield was a well-known novelist and essayist in the interwar period who serialized five novels in WHC from 1924 to 1939; she was also the only woman on the first board of Book-of-the-Month Club judges. Her 1933 novel *Bonfire*, serialized in WHC in 1932, just as Faulkner was actively trying to get published there (and likely studying the market), is a useful example of the women's domestic fiction Faulkner read in WHC and which he would later transform and incorporate into his 1939 novel *The Wild Palms*.[13]

Bonfire received the highest advance ever negotiated from a periodical: WHC paid $30,000 for the novel at the height of the Depression. Even more significant is that the novel, written for a white middle-class women's audience of housewives, is all about sexuality. The novel's plot centers around Lixlee, a working-class femme fatale from the lower-class township Searles Shelf with sexual appeal so raw that even spinsters like Anna Craft are susceptible. Lixlee seduces the nice, middle-class medical doctor in town, Anson Craft (Anna's brother), and after they are caught in bed together (because her former lover breaks in and shoots at them, thus revealing their affair), he marries her. But when he leaves her in the middle of lovemaking to answer a medical emergency, she vows revenge and proceeds to seduce her way through the men in town, thus publicly cuckolding the nice doctor, and she finally runs away with the wealthiest bachelor she can find.

For Lixlee, sex is an overpowering natural impulse, with unforeseen, uncontrollable consequences—not unlike the "bonfires" men are always lighting and thinking they can control but that suddenly get beyond them. Sexuality is only barely contained by society. Indeed, in the lexicon of the novel, sex is the most natural thing in the world. *Bonfire* describes desire in frank terms. If it isn't describing the mechanics of sex (as viewed from a window or on a screen), it is focusing on how desire feels, emotionally and even physically, from the inside. Lixlee is sympathetically depicted—not just a ballbreaker, as Anson maintains, but a woman deeply hurt by the exploitive uses men put her to and finally determined to get what she can out of men, since love failed her so deeply. In the end, what one does with the bonfire of desire is what determines character. For Anson, desire was all about his personal gratification, like having a really expensive car. Lixlee embraces passion until she is betrayed, and then she learns to parlay her sexuality for material things, since men insist on using her that way. The parallels between this novel and the plot of *The Wild Palms* are obvious. Reading Charlotte Rittenmeyer and Harry Wilbourne through the romantic love plots of interwar women's domestic fiction could reframe our understanding of the novel, especially as a bold and original take on sexuality. Compared

Fig. 1. Sixtieth anniversary issue cover of *Woman's Home Companion*

to *Bonfire*, a domestic drama written by an exemplar of middlebrow fiction, *The Wild Palms* seems conventional and conservative.

Like Lixlee, Charlotte is a sexual force. Unlike Lixlee, who generally leaves her sexual partners pining for her but relatively unscathed, Charlotte convinces the virgin Harry to abandon his medical career and become a thief, an adulterer, a pulp writer, an abortionist, and finally a convicted murderer. Charlotte's sexual power unleashes a force that destroys both herself and her naive lover—a view of "female" sexuality seemingly more at home in the Apostle Paul's sermons and pulp novels than in a decadent modernist writer. It is Canfield, supposedly the epitome of conservative middlebrow values, who treats sexuality in a matter-of-fact, cavalier attitude. When the heroine, the spinster Anna Lee, first meets Lixlee, she notes her remarkable sexual draw: "Under her gaze the girl's eyelids, thick and very white, slowly lifted. She raised her dark eyes imploringly. Their impact on Miss Craft was startling, sending her subterranean current suddenly down a steep straight channel to a well-formulated conclusion, 'Why the girl's a man-eater. One of the natural-born sirens. She all but got *me* going!'"[14] That Anna feels Lixlee's sexual appeal causes no sexual panic or identity crisis. After Anson and Lixlee run away together, the town accepts their liaison through the fecund images of spring:

> The grass greened; the brooks ran brimful of noisy water; life centered about the care of capering lambs and baby chicks and tottering calves; . . . finally, incredible miracle of every May, clouds of pink and white bloomed in apple orchards where yesterday the children had been tunneling in snowdrifts. And in hearts that had been dry and matter-of-fact, inner springs melted too and ran brimful; flowers burst into bloom in minds that had been heaped with snow, and—secretly—separately—many of the tall men in overalls, plowing or harrowing or spreading manure, or silently seeding down with old ritual gestures a stony buckwheat field, thought of Anson Craft with more liking than they ever had for him.[15]

Sexuality in *Bonfire* is framed as natural—something to be managed, for men and women, but nothing innately destructive or sinful.

In *The Wild Palms*, sexuality is also depicted as natural but defined by the catastrophic—think natural disaster, not spring foaling. This pathologizing of female sexuality is where the two narratives of *The Wild Palms* come together: the convict's "taking" by the flood is equated with Harry's "taking" by Charlotte's desire, with equally destructive results. Here, too, Canfield is more direct about depicting arousal and sexuality, particularly women's sexuality. Witness this depiction of Lixlee's desire from Anson's perspective:

> In the silence he could hear how her breath came faster as her eyes deepened from laughter to passion, as her face darkened into the grave contained fury that made him feel a god, not a man. The pounding of his pulse spread from his breast to his temples, to his ears, to his finger-tips. Although he was

awaiting her fall, when with a soft exhalation of her breath she dropped with all her warm weight, his heart stopped beating—and then sprang into a clamor of nervous pulsations.[16]

In *The Wild Palms*, the images of arousal are displaced onto the "Old Man" sections in an elaborate metaphor of female desire depicted through the 1927 flood; female desire is a terrifying event beyond the man's control. When he rescues a pregnant woman, the convict is repelled by her physicality, by "the inert and inescapable mass of female meat before him," and "when he looked upon the swelling and unmanageable body before him it seemed to him that it was not the woman at all but rather a separate demanding threatening inert yet living mass of which both he and she were equally victims."[17] That sense of being taken by a (female) life force is made explicit in the convict's subsequent experience fighting against the flood, described by Faulkner in sexual terms:

> He was doomed; they were less than the figments of smoke or of delirium, and he driving his unceasing paddle without destination without even hope now, looking now and then at the woman sitting with her knees drawn up and locked and her entire body one terrific clench while the threads of bloody saliva crept from her teeth-clenched lower lip. . . . He looked back, still driving the paddle, and saw it, curled, crested with its strawlike flotsam of trees and debris and dead beasts. . . . He now contemplated with savage and invulnerable curiosity the further extent to which his now anesthetized nerves could bear, what next could be invented for them to bear, until the wave actually began to rear above his head into its thunderous climax. Then only did he turn his head. His stroke did not falter, it neither slowed nor increased. (175–76)

It should surprise no one that when the convict is jolted onto land and carries the pregnant woman up the Indian mound, he steps upon a snake. A man, a woman, a snake: sexual knowledge casts him out of the garden.

In this morality tale, however, Faulkner seems to invert the roles of Harry and Charlotte, making Harry the innocent ingénue and Charlotte the charming rake who ruins him. The text's emphasis on Charlotte's masculine qualities—that she is a better man than Harry is—only reinforces this impression. Like the ruined heroines of eighteenth-century seduction novels, Harry faces imminent death for transgressing societal norms regarding sexuality, and like those heroines who read trashy novels before their own literal seductions (against their guardians' advice), Harry's fall is enmeshed with print.[18] Harry's engagement with pulp writing serves as a metacommentary on the tragic romantic plot (just as the convict's investment in pulp leads to his incarceration). He would

sit down to the typewriter, entering without effort and without especial regret
the anesthesia of his monotonous inventing. . . . He began to dispense with
lunch altogether . . . writing steadily on, pausing only to sit while his fingers
rested, a cigarette scarring slowly into the edge of the rented table, staring
at but not seeing the two or three current visible lines of his latest primer-
bald moronic fable, his sexual gumdrop. . . . Then the hour would arrive and
with the ink sometimes scarcely dry on the stamped sealed and self-addressed
envelope containing the latest story beginning 'At sixteen I was an unwed
mother' he would leave the apartment. (122–23)

Faulkner is, of course, discussing the fraught role of art, and love, in a
culture that prefers mass-produced fakes; Charlotte and Harry are led
to a tragic end just because of the lack of secure livelihoods in their
transgressive life, despite numerous attempts to find employment. Yet
how is "at twenty-nine I was an abortionist" (which could serve as the
opening line of Harry's life story) any less melodramatic than "at sixteen
I was a teenage mother"? Faulkner seems as in thrall to the conventions
of feminine domestic fiction as the implied readers of Harry's "sexual
gumdrop"—more so, indeed, than Dorothy Canfield. Lixlee believes
only in sex; Charlotte dies in her quixotic quest for love, determined "to
drown in the ocean [rather] than be urped up onto a strip of dead beach
and be dried away by the sun into a little foul smear with no name to it,
just *This Was* for an epitaph" (83).

This sense of the catastrophe of female desire, the necessary melodrama of transgressive sex, sets up the implausibly tragic end of *The
Wild Palms*. In contrast to Faulkner's own multiple and unpunished
infidelities, here he must fictionally punish his adulterous characters for
their improper sexuality: Charlotte is killed by her lover's hand, despite
his medical training and the successful abortion he performs upon his
coworker's wife. In many ways Faulkner's insistence on melodramatic
punishment is even more formulaic and conservative than the women's
domestic fiction that likely inspired it. Lixlee escapes with her latest con-
quest; Charlotte dies painfully and maddeningly, her death a catastrophe
for Harry, not for herself.

It wasn't until 1959, with the publication of *The Mansion*, that
Faulkner created a female heroine who could transgress and triumph.
Linda Snopes Kohl is a woman of independence, a bastard who is willing
to flaunt convention—living with her Jewish lover without being married, going to Spain to fight the fascists in the 1930s, advocating for black
workers and better schools in the segregated educational system, working for the war in factories on the coast. Faulkner is constructing a Popular Front hero well after that era had been denounced as un-American,

somewhat belatedly coming out on the side of nonconformism, free love, and modern womanhood. As so often in Faulkner's writing, multiple male narrators, in various stages of cluelessness, filter our understanding of Linda, but we finally understand her master plan: to orchestrate revenge on Flem Snopes for his shameful treatment of her mother, Eula Snopes, who kills herself rather than be denounced publicly as a whore. Linda doesn't mind being called a whore; when "KOHL COMMUNIST JEW" is written outside Flem Snopes's house, she continues without concern.[19] When she finally succeeds in getting Mink Snopes released from prison—knowing he will immediately kill Flem—she sends him money to help him get away, using Gavin Stevens and V. K. Ratliff as secret agents.

Faulkner makes Linda suffer. He takes from her both her mother and her lover in the war and brings her back deaf (with a "duck voice"), and he makes her activism so misguided and impossible that the African Americans themselves ask her to stop (a truly implausible move in 1958, as civil rights activism contradicted the "go slow" policy Faulkner favors fictionally).[20] But Faulkner also allows Linda to triumph. She has ordered a new convertible when she appeals for Mink's release, and she has it delivered to Flem's house so the whole town can see her drive away in it, a big FU to Jefferson. Linda may be the first and only noncomforming female heroine in Faulkner who isn't punished for her sins and is allowed to ride off into the sunset.

Faulkner was late to the girl-power party, doing in the 1950s what Canfield did in the 1920s and 1930s. But the key transformation may have been the different political context of the Cold War, both in Faulkner's own life and in women's magazines of the Cold War Era. Linda may have been allowed to triumph because of her political commitment rather than her sexual freedom.

Women's magazines had always engaged in politics, and some made progressive politics a primary focus. Dorothy Canfield's preferred magazine, the *Woman's Home Companion*, made a name for itself by coming out in favor of women's suffrage, and it featured a number of political articles in its pages, including features for new voters.[21] Cold War women's magazines continued this trend, though they seemed to be moving away from the text-heavy layout of interwar magazines and becoming more committed to glossy photographs. *Mademoiselle* was also a lucrative place to publish fiction. Fiction editor Margarita Smith published a number of southern authors, including Carson McCullers, Eudora Welty, Flannery O'Connor, William Goyen, and—once—William Faulkner. *Harper's Bazaar* was even more fashion-conscious than *Mademoiselle*, but it still published a number of good writers in the Cold

War era, including Capote and Faulkner. It was during the Cold War that Faulkner committed fully to the Kotex Age; his author's biography in *Mademoiselle* was faced by a bright yellow advertisement for, you guessed it, Kotex (see Figure 2).

In 1954 Faulkner published a short sketch called "Sepulture South: Gaslight" in *Harper's Bazaar*—the women's magazine his wife, Estelle, subscribed to, and which came into his home. The reminiscence about his grandfather's funeral is generally a nostalgic look back, with a tone reminiscent of his later novel *The Reivers*. "Sepulture South" is not explicitly political, except in its opening two paragraphs. After taking a strange swipe at Depression-Era WPA, Faulkner inserts a brief note about African Americans' claiming of the freedom to change jobs once the white employer dies:

> But that was the way Negroes did: left after a death in the family they worked for, as though obeying not a superstition but a rite: the rite of their freedom: not freedom from having to work, that would not occur to anyone for several years yet, not until the W.P.A., but the freedom to move from one job to another, using a death in the family as a moment, the instigation, to move, since only death was important enough to exercise a right as important as freedom.[22]

In the political context of *Brown v. Board of Education*, decided earlier in the year, such a rumination could hardly be innocent, but what Faulkner is claiming here is, as ever, ambivalent at best. Is he surreptitiously endorsing the civil rights movement's bid for freedom and the physical dangers it brought for its activists? Or is he claiming that southern African Americans already had the most profound kind of freedom, one that trumped the less majestic form at issue? He gives no clues here, simply moving on to other memories from the day.

His 1955 engagement with a women's magazine is more substantial and explicitly about the political process. That year, *Mademoiselle* published "By the People," an excerpt from *The Mansion*, the final volume in the Snopes trilogy and the only one of Faulkner's novels excerpted in a women's magazine. This fact has a certain logic. *The Mansion* is one of Faulkner's novels most indebted to the tradition of women's domestic fiction, with an intriguing and independent heroine. Before tracking down "By the People," I had assumed that the excerpt would be about Linda Snopes Kohl. But here's the thing—it isn't. Instead, *Mademoiselle* excerpted a section about Ratliff's ingenious defeat of a racist, protofascist politician, Senator Clarence Snopes. In other words, "By the People" was an excerpt that engaged with pressing political issues of the day, specifically civil rights, rather than with women's roles specifically.

Fig. 2. Page containing Kotex ad in *Mademoiselle*

Which is not to say that the excerpt doesn't consider women's roles within a broader racist and patriarchal context. Much like *Intruder in the Dust*, the excerpt imagines a form of political intervention for outsiders who can't confront entrenched prejudices directly but must find other means to undermine the status quo. Clarence Snopes is a prototypic fascist leader (like the one memorialized in Sinclair Lewis's 1935 classic *It Can't Happen Here*), and his populist racism makes him all but invincible in his race for the US House of Representatives. When Snopes brands a World War II veteran and war hero as a "Negro lover," Gavin Stevens bows his head in despair.

The hero? Bachelor V. K. Ratliff. In the excerpt, Faulkner frames Ratliff as a seller of domestic goods to women in their homes, from sewing machines and organs to radios and televisions. He makes his living, in other words, by appealing to the same female consumerism that sustained women's magazines and by selling many of the same goods. He is aligned with women, observing passively but as a great student of human nature:

Ratliff in the parlor with the anti-macassars and bell-domed wax flower and synthetic sea shells while the doctor's or lawyer's or merchant's or banker's wife tried the machine . . . bland, courteous still, not exactly discoursive now but simply bearing his part of the conversation, since he was indeed a universal: his diction still rather that of Varner's store in Frenchman's Bend than Jefferson, the vehicle of his wit still that of his tieless state, but the wit itself and the wisdom it did not always conceal was that of any man who had watched human folly yet still remained capable of believing in human aspiration.[23]

Ratliff, then, is perfectly framed to wreck the aims of loathsome Clarence Snopes without leaving any fingerprints, as the subordinate, Faulkner implies, must learn to do. Snopes is defeated not by arguments or by direct confrontation or by reason but by surreptitiously brushing the backs of his trousers with switches soaked in the urine of every dog in the county, thus turning the would-be senator into a walking fire hydrant. The humor here is clear: the political message less so. Is Faulkner suggesting that direct confrontation of racist prejudice won't work? That voters aren't smart enough to care about the issues and not good enough to overcome their bigotry? Ratliff's solution is not even a permanent one. In the end, decent people must find some way of thwarting the worst in human nature. It is hardly a rousing sentiment, nor is it a revolutionary transformation of the kind that was just beginning to sweep the South. But it is a remarkably pointed political allegory in one of the top women's magazines of the day.

There is much more to be done to understand the role of women's domestic fiction in Faulkner's work, both directly, in pieces published in women's magazines, and indirectly, in their influence on his plots and characters. Future research into women's magazines and Faulkner's fiction should reveal this understudied element of Faulkner's own fictional vision—the women's domestic fiction that he read, adapted, and transformed.

NOTES

1. For a recent example of this thesis, see Philip Weinstein's *Becoming Faulkner: The Life and Art of William Faulkner* (Oxford: Oxford University Press, 2012).

2. This is epitomized in John T. Matthews, "Many Mansions: Faulkner's Cold War Conflicts," in *Global Faulkner: Faulkner and Yoknapatawpha, 2006*, ed. Annette Trefzer and Ann J. Abadie (Jackson: University Press of Mississippi, 2009), 3–23.

3. See Janice Radway's *A Feeling for Books: The Book-of-the-Month Club, Literary Taste, and Middle-Class Desire* (Chapel Hill: University of North Carolina Press, 1999).

4. Ann Douglas, *Terrible Honesty: Mongrel Manhattan in the 1920s* (New York: Farrar, Straus and Giroux, 1995).

5. See Jaime Harker, *America the Middlebrow: Women's Novels, Progressivism, and Middlebrow Authorship between the Wars* (Amherst: University of Massachusetts Press, 2007); and Jaime Harker, *Middlebrow Queer: Christopher Isherwood in America* (Minneapolis: University of Minnesota Press, 2013).

6. See Harker, *America the Middlebrow*.

7. See David M. Earle, *Re-Covering Modernism: Pulps, Paperbacks, and the Prejudice of Form* (Burlington, VT: Ashgate, 2009).

8. Jay Watson and Jaime Harker, "The Summer of Faulkner: Oprah's Book Club, William Faulkner, and Twenty-First-Century America," *Mississippi Quarterly* 66, no. 3 (Summer 2013): 355–79.

9. For more information, see chapter 2 of Harker, *America the Middlebrow*.

10. See Helen Damon-Moore's *Magazines for the Millions: Gender and Commerce in the "Ladies Home Journal"* (Albany: State University of New York Press, 1994), and Elaine Tyler May's *Homeward Bound: American Families in the Cold War Era* (New York: Basic Books, 2008).

11. Joseph Blotner, ed., *Selected Letters of William Faulkner* (New York: Random House, 1977), 95–96.

12. James B. Meriwether, *The Literary Career of William Faulkner: A Bibliographical Study* (Columbia: University of South Carolina Press, 1961), 180.

13. I use the published title, *The Wild Palms*, rather than Faulkner's original idea (and the title of the Vintage corrected text), *If I Forget Thee, Jerusalem*, because a posthumous "correction" of the title based on authorial intention obfuscates the novel's print culture history. The novel was published as *The Wild Palms* and continued to be reprinted under that title throughout Faulkner's writing career.

14. Dorothy Canfield, *Bonfire* (New York: Harcourt, Brace, 1933), 43.

15. Ibid., 171–72.

16. Ibid., 207–8.

17. William Faulkner, *The Wild Palms* (New York: Random House, 1939), 170, 154. Hereafter cited parenthetically.

18. Shelly Jarenski, "The Voice of the Preceptress: Female Education in and as the Seduction Novel," *Journal of the Midwest Modern Language Association* 37, no. 1 (Spring 2004): 63–64.

19. William Faulkner, *The Mansion* (1959; repr., New York: Vintage, 1983), 253.

20. Ibid., 222.

21. See Harker, *America the Middlebrow*, chapter 2.

22. William Faulkner, "Sepulture South: Gaslight," *Harper's Bazaar*, December 1954, 85.

23. William Faulkner, "By the People," *Mademoiselle*, October 1955, 86.

Contributors

Greg Barnhisel is professor of English at Duquesne University, where he currently chairs the English Department and has also directed the first-year writing program. Professor Barnhisel's books include *James Laughlin, New Directions, and the Remaking of Ezra Pound* (2005), *Pressing the Fight: Print, Propaganda, and the Cold War* (2010), and *Cold War Modernists: Art, Literature, and American Cultural Diplomacy* (2015). His essays have appeared in *Modernism/Modernity*, *English Literary History*, *Book History*, and a number of edited collections on twentieth-century literature.

John N. Duvall is the Margaret Church Distinguished Professor of English and the editor of *MFS: Modern Fiction Studies* at Purdue University. Among his authored books are *Faulkner's Marginal Couple: Invisible, Outlaw, and Unspeakable Communities* (1990), and *Race and White Identity in Southern Fiction: From Faulkner to Morrison* (2008). He has also edited *Faulkner and His Critics* (2010) and (with Ann J. Abadie) *Faulkner and Postmodernism* (2002).

Kristin Fujie is assistant professor of English at Lewis and Clark College. Her essays appear in *William Faulkner in Context* (2015) and *Faulkner's Sexualities* (2010). Her current work focuses on Faulkner's early novels.

Sarah E. Gardner is professor of history and director of Southern Studies at Mercer University. She is the author of *Blood and Irony: Southern White Women's Narratives of the Civil War, 1861–1937* (2004). Her manuscript, "Reviewing the South: Readers, Writers, Critics, and the Idea of an American Region," is at Cambridge University Press.

Jaime Harker is professor of English and the director of the Sarah Isom Center for Women and Gender Studies at the University of Mississippi. She is the author of two monographs, *America the Middlebrow: Women's Novels, Progressivism, and Middlebrow Authorship between the Wars* (2007), and *Middlebrow Queer: Christopher Isherwood in*

America (2013), and the coeditor of *The Oprah Affect: Critical Essays on Oprah's Book Club* (2008), *1960s Gay Pulp Fiction: The Misplaced Heritage* (2013), and *This Book Is an Action: Feminist Print Culture and Activist Aesthetics* (2016). She is on the editorial board of the Literary Texts and the Popular Marketplace series, published by Pickering & Chatto, and is currently finishing a book on southern lesbian feminism and feminist print culture.

Kristi Rowan Humphreys is assistant professor of critical studies and artistic practice and coordinator of the fine arts doctoral program in art at Texas Tech University. Her first monograph, *Housework and Gender in American Television: Coming Clean*, was published in 2016.

Robert Jackson is associate professor of English at the University of Tulsa. He wrote *Seeking the Region in American Literature and Culture: Modernity, Dissidence, Innovation* (2005) and the forthcoming "Fade In, Crossroads: A History of the Southern Cinema."

Mary A. Knighton is professor of literature at Aoyama Gakuin University in Tokyo, Japan. Her essays have appeared in *Faulkner and Twain* (2009), *Mark Twain Studies*, and *US-Japan Women's Journal*.

Jennifer Nolan is an assistant professor of English at North Carolina State University. Her research and publications focus on twentieth-century US print culture and reading practices, with a current interest in and forthcoming publications on literature published in popular magazines during the interwar period by authors such as F. Scott Fitzgerald.

Carl Rollyson is professor of journalism at Baruch College, City University of New York. He is the author of *Uses of the Past in the Novels of William Faulkner* (1984) and biographies of a distinguished series of writers and film artists, including Marilyn Monroe, Sylvia Plath, Lillian Hellman, Norman Mailer, Amy Lowell, Walter Brennan, Rebecca West, Susan Sontag, Dana Andrews, Martha Gellhorn, Michael Foot, and Jill Craigie. His current work in progress is another biography, *This Alarming Paradox: The Life of William Faulkner*.

Tim A. Ryan is associate professor of English at Northern Illinois University. He is the author of *Yoknapatawpha Blues: Faulkner's Fiction and Southern Roots Music* and *Calls and Responses: The American Novel of Slavery since "Gone with the Wind"* (2008).

Jay Satterfield is special collections librarian at Rauner Special Collections Library at Dartmouth College. He is the author of the 2002 study, *"The World's Best Books": Taste, Culture, and the Modern Library* (2002). His essays have appeared in numerous journals and edited collections, including *The History of the Book in the West: 1914–2000* (2010) and *The Oxford Companion to the Book* (2010). His curating work includes nine major exhibitions at Dartmouth College, the University of Chicago, and the University of Iowa.

Erin A. Smith is professor of American studies at the University of Texas at Dallas, where she has taught since 1997. Her publications include *Hard-Boiled: Working-Class Readers and Pulp Magazines* (2000), *What Would Jesus Read? Popular Religious Books and Everyday Life in Twentieth-Century America* (2015), and essays in *American Literary History*, *The Cambridge Companion to Popular Fiction* (2012), *Book History* (2010), *Radical Teacher*, and *Frontiers: A Journal of Women's Studies*.

Jay Watson is Howry Professor of Faulkner Studies at the University of Mississippi and the director of Faulkner and Yoknapatawpha. He is the author of *Forensic Fictions: The Lawyer Figure in Faulkner* (1993) and *Reading for the Body: The Recalcitrant Materiality of Southern Fiction, 1893–1985* (2012), which received Honorable Mention for the 2013 C. Hugh Holman Award sponsored by the Society for the Study of Southern Literature. He is also the editor of *Faulkner and Whiteness* (2011), *Conversations with Larry Brown* (2007), and coeditor of four volumes of the Faulkner and Yoknapatawpha conference proceedings.

Yung-Hsing Wu is associate professor of English at the University of Louisiana at Lafayette. Her work has appeared in *PMLA*, *MFS*, *Profession*, *Children's Literature Association Quarterly*, the *Digital Humanities Quarterly*, and the *Mississippi Quarterly*. She is wrapping up a book project on contemporary reading practices and has just begun a project on feminism and the evolution of close reading.

Index

Page numbers in *italics* refer to illustrations.